Ojibwe, Activist, Priest

Father Philip Bergin Gordon in headdress, 1933. Courtesy of the Wisconsin Historical Society, Image WHi-140674.

Ojibwe, Activist, Priest

The Life of
Father Philip Bergin Gordon,
Tibishkogijik

Tadeusz Lewandowski

THE UNIVERSITY OF WISCONSIN PRESS

The University of Wisconsin Press
728 State Street, Suite 443
Madison, Wisconsin 53706-1428
uwpress.wisc.edu

Gray's Inn House, 127 Clerkenwell Road
London ECIR 5DB, United Kingdom
eurospanbookstore.com

Printed in the United States of America
This book may be available in a digital edition.

Library of Congress Cataloging-in-Publication Data
Names: Lewandowski, Tadeusz, 1973– author.
Title: Ojibwe, activist, priest: the life of Father Philip Bergin Gordon,
Tibishkogijik / Tadeusz Lewandowski.
Description: Madison, Wisconsin: The University of Wisconsin Press, [2019] |
Includes bibliographical references and index.
Identifiers: LCCN 2019014991 | ISBN 9780299325206 (cloth: alk. paper)
Subjects: LCSH: Gordon, Philip B., Rev., 1885–1948. | Catholic Church—
Clergy—Biography. | Priests—Wisconsin—Biography. | Indian activists—
Wisconsin—Biography. | Ojibwa Indians—Wisconsin—Biography. |
LCGFT: Biographies.
Classification: LCC E99.C6 G644 2019 | DDC 282.092 [B]—dc23
LC record available at https://lccn.loc.gov/2019014991

The whole Indian Bureau system of managing Indian business to the detriment of the Indian but for the benefit of a few greedy and voracious whites is the most dramatic autocracy in existence the world over.

—Father Philip Bergin Gordon,
1923 letter to the Superior *Telegram*

Contents

Contents

Acknowledgments

At the University of Wisconsin Press, I would like to thank executive editor Gwen Walker for her extraordinary support throughout the publishing process. Thanks also to acquisitions assistant Anna Muenchrath for her kind help in numerous technical matters and to managing editor Adam Mehring and copyeditor Scott Mueller for their excellent work. I especially thank Mark Thiel of the Marquette University Archives in Wisconsin for his generosity over the many years I have requested materials from him. This book would have been impossible without his aid and advice. Thanks, too, go to Professor Margaret Ann Noodin and Professor Rand Valentine for their help with Anishinaabemowin. As well, I thank Lisa Marine at the Wisconsin Historical Society for her help with acquiring illustrations. I express my gratitude to my mother, Linda Lewandowski, and my wife, Marzena, for their assistance with this biography. Thank you to Arnold Krupat, who commented on an early version of the manuscript. And finally, a very big thanks to Jane Vavala of Hinkle Library at Alfred State College, New York, for her deeply appreciated tracking down of numerous and varied sources.

Author's Note

This biography relies heavily on primary sources such as typeset newspaper reports and letters, both handwritten and typed. Many of these materials contain minor errors in spelling and punctuation. I have corrected these errors to avoid the use of [*sic*] and thereby enhance readability. Idiosyncratic capitalizations of words have, however, been preserved. Words underlined for the purpose of emphasis have been rendered in italics. All emphases appear in the original documents unless otherwise indicated.

Ojibwe,
Activist, Priest

Introduction

When the *New York Times* announced the news of Father Philip Bergin Gordon's death in October 1948, the paper noted that his legacy as "Wisconsin's Fighting Priest" had been cemented by "his campaigns for bettering the conditions of the Indians."[1] "Wisconsin's Fighting Priest" was also an apt moniker for a man whose combativeness frequently put him at odds with every institution he encountered: the Catholic Church, Bureau of Catholic Indian Missions, Bureau of Indian Affairs, Young Men's Christian Association, and Society of American Indians, among others. Gordon indeed exhibited a talent for making enemies— often suffering as a result. Commissioner of Indian Affairs Charles H. Burke described him as "an agitator, Bolshevist and troublemaker," and he bedeviled the Catholic hierarchy so often that he found himself dismissed from posts more than once.[2] What drove these conflicts, however, was a worthy goal anchored in Gordon's own indigenous heritage. As the *Times* obituary stated, his overriding concern was justice for the nation's Native peoples.

Philip Gordon was born to an Ojibwe mother and a father of Ojibwe and French descent in the town of Gordon, Wisconsin, in 1885. His family history had some luster. The town of Gordon had been named after Philip's grandfather, Anton Gordon, the son of an early pioneer in the region. Philip's great-grandmother Owanishan (Young Beaver) was the sister of Hole in the Day the Elder and aunt of Hole in the Day the Younger, both of whom sought to be chief of all the Ojibwe clans during their lifetimes. Philip Gordon himself remains noteworthy for his own reasons. In December 1913, age twenty-eight, Gordon—whose Ojibwe name was Tibishkogijik, meaning Looking into the Sky—became the first indigenous person to be ordained as a Catholic priest within the United States.[3] This distinction began a volatile career as Indian missionary, chaplain, reservation priest, and Native rights activist, which largely ended in Gordon's virtual exile by the Catholic Church to the small parish of Centuria, Wisconsin, in 1924. There, he continued his activism as best he could, dying at age sixty-three. During this thirty-year period, Gordon rubbed shoulders with such figures as Progressive Senator Robert LaFollette, New York governor Alfred Smith, and Vice President Henry Wallace in an effort to alter federal Indian policy for the better.[4]

Philip Gordon well knew the problems facing Native peoples, having seen the struggles of the Ojibwe to maintain their integrity under policies instituted by the Bureau of Indian Affairs (BIA), created in 1824 as part of the Department of the Interior.[5] He witnessed not only the grinding poverty and onerous curtailments of freedom forced upon the Ojibwe but also the rapid dispossession facilitated by the bureau administration. In Gordon's time, Indians had few allies except a handful of Christian organizations such as the Quaker-led Indian Rights Association (IRA), or the Friends of the Indian, founded in 1882. Unfortunately, these groups had one primary goal for the Native population: assimilation. Efforts along these lines had already, in fact, been underway before the group's inception. In December 1869, President Grant announced his "peace policy," intended to replace the inhumane conquest and slaughter that had dominated Indian-white relations in the first half of the nineteenth century. Grant hoped that by creating a Board of Indian Commissioners to oversee the BIA, exploitation and violence could be stemmed. Staffing the board with persons recommended by religious groups, giving the Friends of the Indian control over some reservations, and selecting an indigenous commissioner of Indian Affairs, the Seneca Army officer and attorney Ely Samuel Parker, would likewise ensure humane treatment. Ultimately, with this system in place the values of "civilization" and Christianity would transform Indian peoples for inclusion in white society.[6]

An essential and deeply regrettable part of assimilation policy became educating Indian children in off-reservation boarding schools. In 1879, an

Army officer, Richard Henry Pratt, helped open the first such Indian institute in Carlisle, Pennsylvania. Born in upstate New York and raised in Indiana, Pratt had joined the Union Army as a teenager and begun a military career. In 1875, while guarding Native American prisoners in Marion, Florida, he realized that, despite their different ways, his charges were just as human and capable as he. Forthwith, Pratt developed a program of education meant to inculcate Euro-American culture and ideals within his captives. His passion for the project convinced Secretary of the Interior Carl Schurz to fund the creation of an assimilationist institution in a vacant Pennsylvania Army barracks in Carlisle. At the newly christened Carlisle Indian Industrial School, Pratt instituted a curriculum based on strict military discipline, designed to sever Native children from the traditions of their elders. He and other supporters of this policy hoped that graduates would use education to become productive, Christian citizens civilized through contact with white society.[7] In the interim, reservation life was to be transformed by the Dawes Act, passed in 1887. The act set in motion the allotment of communally held land on reservations to individuals who, the government wished, would take up the plow, adapt to a self-sufficient farming lifestyle, become "competent," and earn citizenship.[8]

Though the authors of such policies had good intentions, the results were regularly disastrous. Native children, separated from their parents and thrown into a cold world of rigid, boarding-school routine, suffered terribly and frequently died prematurely of European diseases, malnutrition, and plain homesickness.[9] The Dawes Act, too, was a grand failure, resulting in the loss of eighty-six million acres (60 percent) of Indian lands and little palpable benefit for indigenous nations. Nor did it lead to citizenship.[10] Meanwhile, desperation, penury, and demoralization afflicted reservation populations under the thumb of a BIA apparatus that precluded traditional lifeways and meaningful development toward modernity. Philip Gordon, though a firm believer in adopting white ways, spent much of his life fighting against the government institution he felt caused more pain to his people than any other: the Bureau of Indian Affairs.

That Gordon detested the BIA so greatly reveals deep irony, for in some ways he was a product of bureau policy dating from the Grant era—

specifically, the placing of religious groups on reservations. Before 1869, Catholic missions, churches, and schools had been established on Indian lands throughout the West, including the northern Great Lakes region.[11] Upon the introduction of Grant's peace policy, the Roman Catholic Church evinced a keen interest in government-supported missionary work among indigenous nations. The BIA initially allowed the Catholic Church an official presence on seven agencies, though they desired more. Two men took up the cause. Augustin Magloire Alexander Blanchet, bishop of Nesqually, Oregon, and his brother, Francis, archbishop of Oregon City, lobbied Archbishop James Roosevelt Bayley of Baltimore to establish the Office of the Catholic Indian Commissioner (OCIC) in 1874. Headed by Civil War veteran General Charles Ewing, the OCIC sought to broaden the church's reach by acquiring other agencies on which to seek potential converts.[12] In 1879, the office's name was changed to the Bureau of Catholic Indian Missions (BCIM).[13] During a brief part of his life, from 1915 to 1917, Philip Gordon worked for the Catholic Bureau as an Indian missionary, traversing reservations in the Midwest trying to attract Indians to the church.

Gordon's own beginnings as a Catholic, however, date from the last decade of the nineteenth century, when as a boy he was baptized by Father Odoric Derenthal, a traveling Franciscan priest based in Bayfield, Wisconsin.[14] The Franciscans had arrived in Bayfield in 1878, establishing a mission for the few Catholic loggers in the area.[15] When in 1882 Washington began allowing missionaries to work freely on Indian lands, the number of Native converts increased greatly. By 1900, there were, reportedly, 101,000 Catholic American Indians in the United States supported by 154 missions and parishes in total, with 68 government-funded Catholic schools in operation.[16] Philip Gordon became the most illustrious graduate of one such school, St. Mary's in Odanah, Wisconsin, on the Bad River Reservation.

Despite the notoriety Gordon enjoyed during his lifetime, he has received scant attention in accounts of the Progressive-era, Native activists involved in the Society of American Indians (SAI).[17] At the time of the SAI's founding, 1911, Progressivism dominated the American political landscape, where reformers, usually white, upper-middle-class Protestants, sought to remedy the nation's social ills following decades of economically polarizing industrial development. Such zeal for social improvements rallied those interested in change under the wide ideological discourse of "uplift." By tending to society's disadvantaged masses—whether through settlement houses, temperance advocacy, Christian charity, government regulation, or the civilizing balm of education—America's advance toward the righteous bounty of liberal democracy would ostensibly be ensured.[18] The Progressive era thus saw the institution of significantly positive reforms, including the extension of suffrage to American women, the direct election rather than appointment of U.S. senators, a graduated income tax, and increased regulation of business.[19] Some American Indians, concerned with the welfare of the indigenous population, became swept up in this fervor for implementing social change through organization. A small group of intellectuals, dubbed "Red Progressives" by Hazel Hertzberg in her seminal study, *The Search for an American Indian Identity*, were the first Natives to organize outside of any white association for the purpose of self-help and "uplift" for their own peoples, an effort that would defend Natives from the many threats they faced.

Given their groundbreaking work, the SAI progressives have been the focus of considerable scholarship.[20] SAI leaders and luminaries such as the Santee Dakota physician and writer Charles Eastman, Seneca museologist Arthur C. Parker, Yavapai physician Carlos Montezuma, Ho-Chunk/ Winnebago Presbyterian minister Henry Roe Cloud, and Yankton Dakota writer and activist Gertrude Bonnin (Zitkala-Ša), have all received scholarly biographical treatments. No one, however, has written on Philip Gordon's role in the Society of American Indians or produced work on his life outside the organization, thus far denying him due recognition.[21]

The fact that Gordon has been so long overlooked is not altogether fair, for rather than being just a supporting player, he was a driving force in the SAI as one of the original radicals who pushed for the abolition of the BIA. His 1916 Indian rights journal, *War-Whoop*, meant to "sound a new battle-cry for the awakened Indian," was also the inspiration for Carlos Montezuma's noted anti-BIA newsletter, *Wassaja*.[22] And in seeking his goals, Gordon always took real action. He worked his way up through the SAI, becoming its final president and, in truth, one of the main catalysts of its demise—having helped destroy any unity that could have been channeled into achievable aims.[23] This last fact is unfortunate, but there is also the remainder of Gordon's life, which he spent agitating vociferously for his own people, the Ojibwe, and other important causes in the struggle for American Indian rights.

Notwithstanding their devotion to the protection of indigenous peoples, the SAI activists have sometimes incurred censure from modern scholars as a result of their assimilationist stances.[24] This is so for several reasons. First, many of the Red Progressives were educated in boarding schools and thus felt that if Indians were to survive, adaptation was necessary. Second, the Red Progressives often made the case that if given equal opportunities, Native peoples could excel in the Euro-American world. And finally, proving that Natives could thrive in white society meant that protections, for instance United States citizenship, could secure the Indian's status and libertate indigenous nations from the government strictures that confined them on reservations. Yet still, none of these integers of a larger equation meant a denial of or disloyalty to Indian heritage. Nor did it mean an uncritical acceptance of white society and its institutions. The SAI activists had assimilationist leanings, but none should discount their sincere efforts to improve the lives of their kinsmen.[25]

As a Catholic priest and missionary, Gordon desired to minister exclusively to Native peoples. He vigorously and consistently sought to convert Indians from what he called "paganism," and never questioned his course of action.[26] For the Indian, Gordon believed that spiritual salvation came in the form of Catholicism, while secular salvation came with assimilation to Euro-American norms. But as he looked into the sky for justice and deliverance, he was always eager to fight for Native rights on earth. In defending his views and beliefs, Gordon could be acerbic, sarcastic, demanding, self-righteous, and brazenly critical. Fortunately, the combativeness undergirding these qualities made him an all-the-more-fierce defender of Native peoples and advocate of liberation from the Bureau of Indian Affairs. Gordon was an assimilationist, but he stood up for his humanitarian beliefs without compromise, confident that once set free from burdensome government wardship Indians could easily excel in white society just as he had. His outspokenness concerning basic human rights and his insistence on fair treatment for indigenous peoples ensured that, even twenty years after his death, Gordon was vividly remembered in Wisconsin by those who survived him.[27]

Recounting Philip Gordon's story has entailed difficulties due to the dearth of primary and secondary source materials relating to his life. His epistolary record—the lifeblood of any biography—dwindles precipitously after 1924. As a result, this succinct biography is necessarily middle-heavy. Yet given its aims, a stress on Gordon's middle period is appropriate. The following pages offer the first scholarly rendering of Gordon's struggle for BIA abolition and assert his prominence within early twentieth-century Native rights activism. By extension, this biography foregrounds "Wisconsin's Fighting Priest" within the rich history of the Red Progressives.

CHAPTER I

The Ojibwe and the Gordon Family

The Ojibwe, also known as the Anishinaabe, Anishinaabeg, Ojibway, Ojibwa, or Chippewa, inhabited the regions north of Lake Huron and northeast of Lake Superior, now Canada, from approximately 1200 AD. Oral tradition, however, states that the Ojibwe in fact returned to the Great Lakes, their first home, after a previous migration. As the self-described first or original human beings, the Ojibwe spoke Anishinaabemowin, part of the larger Algonquin language family that once predominated throughout the northeast of the North American continent to the Rocky Mountains. At the zenith of their influence, the Ojibwe were one of the largest tribes in North America, numbering as many as thirty-five thousand and occupying a string of encampments, or villages, across Canada and the Great Lakes region and farther west. On these lands the Ojibwe built wigwams, fashioned birchbark canoes, and subsisted on fish and game while harvesting wild rice in the autumn and tapping maple sugar in the winter.[1]

Given their large population, the Ojibwe did not operate as one group but lived in what could be called clans, or doodemag. Among these groups were the Mississippi band (who settled in central Minnesota and along the Mississippi River), the Pembina band (North Dakota), the Rocky Boy band (Montana), and the Lake Superior bands (found today in northern Wisconsin). These clans shared spiritual beliefs but did not always have same sociopolitical structure. Generally, however, men assumed leadership roles, with decision-making done in councils sensitive to will of the people. The Ojibwe bands had three kinds of leaders: civic, military, and religious. Religious leadership was most important among these, and religious leaders needed much time to gain status. For political leaders, or chiefs, family succession was often helpful, though respect and standing were usually earned through service to the tribe over many years or gained through oratorical skills. Such chiefs shunned the accumulation of wealth. Those who did accumulate material riches normally then dispersed them among their tribespeople. Military leaders gained their positions by demonstrating bravery and success in battle. Marriage, which had a different meaning than in Euro-American society, could not occur between members of the same band. Polygamy was sometimes practiced. When marriages did not work out women could simply return to their own bands, where kinship held greater sway.

Women played crucial roles in Ojibwe life, and were regularly consulted about tribal decisions before council meetings. Groups of women carried out the essential rice harvests and maple sugar processing, organizing the efforts themselves. This was part of a gendered division of labor that nonetheless respected the idea of equality between the sexes. Women also had an important place in the medicinal sphere, where their knowledge of plants enabled them to work as healers. All religious decisions had to be approved by the head woman in the band. Some women, usually lesbians, could rise to powerful positions as leaders, taking on traditional male roles like hunting and warfare. Some men also functioned within the bands as women, performing their roles. The Ojibwe considered such men spiritually strong.[2]

Ojibwe spiritual beliefs defy easy summary. The creation story tells of Kitchi Manito (the Great Mystery), who fashioned Mother Earth, her Grandmother the Moon, and her Grandfather the Sun. The Earth has Four Sacred Directions, North, South, East, and West, as well as physical and spiritual powers. The Creator placed all things upon Earth, including the first man, created in Kitchi Manito's image. The Original Man traversed the Earth naming her animals, plants, and features. The seasons, he noticed, were a never-ending cycle that encompassed the totality of life. It is from this Original Man that peoples and tribes spring, all of whom are brothers, though divided by language. Ojibwe stories also speak of a spirit named Nanabozho, a link between man and the Earth's spiritual

entities. Nanabozho is a key player in many Ojibwe tales and is credited
with re-creating the Earth after a great flood sent by Kitchi Manito to
purify her of evil and disharmony. His stories often inculcate proper
behavior and values. The Midéwiwin, also known as the Grand Medicine
Society, or Midé Society, featured in Ojibwe spiritual life. This order of
priests conducts annual religious ceremonies, rites of passage, and healing
measures. Fasting and Vision Quests are undertaken to reveal spiritual
knowledge. The Midéwiwin hands down teachings of the interconnected-
ness of all on Mother Earth to successive generations, providing a connection between old and young that stretches throughout time, back to the
origin of the Ojibwe themselves.[3]

In the early seventeenth century, the Ojibwe came into contact with
the French, their expanding fur trade, and Jesuit missionaries.[4] By the
late seventeenth century, environmental and economic changes brought
about by European encroachment and attacks by the Iroquois led many
Ojibwe to move southwest between the Great Lakes and Hudson Bay.
In 1679, at a council with the Dakota Sioux near present-day Duluth,
Minnesota, the Ojibwe negotiated a pact whereby they would act as
mediator between the Dakota and the Europeans in trade matters. The
Dakota, in return, allowed the Ojibwe to move into present-day Wisconsin, where large groups settled at Lac du Flambeau and Lac Courte
Oreilles. The peace lasted many decades, until 1736, when war ensued and
the Ojibwe, armed with French firearms, pushed the Dakota onto the
Great Plains. The Ojibwe also displaced other nations such as the Fox and
Kickapoo as they settled across present-day Michigan, Wisconsin, Minnesota, and eventually North Dakota. Following this period, the Ojibwe
became drawn into several Euro-American conflicts. They participated in
the French and Indian War (1754–63) by fighting against the British, who
upon victory forced the French to cede their eastern lands in Canada. In
the War of 1812, the Ojibwe sided with the British against the Americans.
After the British loss, the Crown continued to pay the Ojibwe annuities
in hopes that they would join another war against the nascent United
States.[5] Washington, meanwhile, made concerted, deceitful, and unsuc-
cessful efforts to remove the more easterly Ojibwe westward to present-
day Minnesota.[6]

As the French fur trade continued to penetrate Ojibwe lands in present-day Michigan, Wisconsin, and Minnesota, it brought Frenchmen who intermarried into the clans. One of them, Jean Baptiste Gaudin, great-grandfather of Philip Gordon, made a life for himself among the Ojibwe in the late eighteenth century. Gaudin, from Quebec Province, had arrived in La Pointe some years earlier.[7] La Pointe (now located in Wisconsin) was a center of the French and British fur trade, which became increasingly dominated by the American Fur Company as the nineteenth century progressed.[8] Gaudin took up work as a voyageur, or hired boatman, transporting goods and passengers throughout the region's trading posts.[9] Though little else is known of Gaudin, he is of note for his marriage into an auspicious Ojibwe family. Sometime around 1810, he wed Owanishan (Young Beaver), sister to a boy who would become one of the Ojibwe's most prominent chiefs, Bagone-giizhing, or Hole in the Day.

Born in La Pointe around 1800, Hole in the Day first made his name as a warrior among his Mississippi band of Ojibwe. After killing a Dakota man at a young age, he earned himself an eagle feather and a place at war councils. Slowly, Hole in the Day built a base of support among his peoples through his bravery and oratorical powers, ever careful not to offend tribal elders. In January of 1812, the marriage between Hole in the Day's sister, Owanishan, and Jean Baptiste Gaudin bore fruit. At Sandy Lake, now Aitkin County in present-day Minnesota, Owanishan gave birth to a son named Antione. Antoine spent his boyhood among the Ojibwe. His formal schooling lasted just three months. When Antoine was twelve, Jean Baptiste and his family moved to Sault Sainte Marie, Michigan. Several years later, the Gaudins returned to La Pointe, where the American Fur Company was newly headquartered.[10] The company's presence reflected Washington's growing interests in the region.

In 1825, the United States called a conference, aiming to consolidate its power over the Great Lakes by opening the British-dominated trade zone to American interests. The Ojibwe had become dependent on trade to sustain their standard of living and hegemony over the Dakota, and they saw the treaty conference as an opportunity to impress the American delegation and secure peaceful exchange in goods such as knives, copper pots, and textiles. The resulting Treaty of Prairie du Chien, which Hole in the Day helped negotiate, drew borders between Ojibwe and Dakota territories but ceded no land or prompted any immediate changes. Nonetheless, the treaty's delineation of borders among not only the Ojibwe and the Dakota but the Winnebago, Sac, Fox, Ioway, Menominee, and other nations in the surrounding areas signaled a major shift in Washington's relations with Native peoples in the region. With new lines drawn on the map, U.S. negotiators could direct coming efforts at land concessions with concentrated pressure and geographical precision. Then in 1827, at a meeting between the Ojibwe and Dakota overseen by the U.S. Army stationed at Fort Snelling (built in 1819 with Dakota permission and situated at the confluence of the Mississippi and Minnesota Rivers), Hole in the Day suffered a spinal injury in an assassination attempt. A group of Dakotas fired upon him and his companions, mortally wounding Hole in the Day's daughter. After taking their revenge in a mass execution, Hole in the Day and his entourage returned home. By 1836, Hole in the Day had established himself at Gull Lake, in the center of present-day Minnesota, maintaining an uneasy peace with the Dakota and aspiring to be the chief of all the Ojibwe. The various bands, however, preferred to retain a decentralized model of council rule by consensus.[11]

During this period Antoine Gaudin, an ardent Catholic, began to make his own mark among the community at La Pointe.[12] There had been a Catholic missionary presence among the Ojibwe since 1830, and policymakers in Washington, even at this early time, hoped that the spread of Christianity could help "civilize" the Ojibwe and lessen threats to American expansion.[13] At times, Ojibwe villages became veritable battlefields between Catholic and Protestant missionaries vying for souls.[14] Antoine, though not consciously, had a part in this mission of Christianization. In 1835, at age twenty-one, he played a major role in the erection of a Catholic Church at La Pointe. Only the strong objections of his mother, Owanishan, deterred Antoine from joining the priesthood.[15] Ojibwe women were expected to take on the religion of their husband when they married Christians, but Owanishan's conversion to Catholicism was evidently not that thoroughgoing.[16] She and her husband Jean Baptiste both died in 1840.[17]

Denied the cloth, Antoine put his energies into commerce. By 1845, he had opened a general store at La Pointe, simultaneously making inroads into the burgeoning lumber industry by transporting felled trees from the mouth of the Bad River to Superior on the *Algonquin*, a boat he co-owned.[18] While there are no details on record of Jean-Batiste Gaudin's or Owanishan's personality traits, several recollections of Antoine Gaudin's personal qualities have survived.[19] Despite his lack of formal schooling, Antoine was a literate autodidact fluent in French, Anishinaabemowin, and English. He also understood Dakota and, inspired by his interest in Catholicism, could read Latin.[20] This last fact aided him in directing his church's choir.[21] Such religiosity informed Antoine's behavior, which was marked by integrity in business and an eschewal of alcohol and tobacco.[22] The former was a rare quality in La Pointe, where the American Fur Company fed its profits with pelts bought from the Ojibwe at absurdly low cost.[23] A famed Métis trader in the company's employ, Michel Cadotte, ensured good relations with the Ojibwe.[24] Surrounded by the rampant fleecing, Antoine retained a sophisticated sense of humor, dependent on wordplay among the various languages he spoke.[25] His wit, success in commerce, and honest character soon won him a bride, Sarah Dingley, also of Ojibwe and French lineage.[26]

Sarah's father, Daniel Dingley, was a Massachusetts Yankee who had gone west to make his fortune in fur trading. Upon arriving in Ojibwe territory, he established a friendship with Chief Chigagons, whose clan lived along the Pokegama Lake near the Namekagon River, a tributary of the St. Croix. The Ojibwe gave Daniel Dingley the name Kitchi Mako-manence, meaning Little Big Knife or Little American. Though Daniel's physical stature must have been unimposing, he did well enough. In the 1820s, he established a trading post by the Yellow River, eventually acquiring 160 acres of land near St. Joseph, present-day Michigan, on which he ran a general store. As far as can be determined, Daniel married an Ojibwe-French woman, Isabelle La Prairie, in the mid-1820s. Isabelle was reported to be tall and striking. Her union with Daniel produced five children, the first two dying prematurely. Sarah was their third child, born between 1827 and 1831. Just six or seven years later, Daniel left for a morning hunt and never returned. His rifle was later found resting on a log. Isabelle returned to La Pointe and remarried. Sarah was left with Ojibwe relatives but rejoined her mother on the island after reaching womanhood. There she met and married Antoine Gaudin in 1843. Sarah was in her early teens. Antoine was thirty-one.[27]

Around the time of Sarah and Antoine's wedding, the Ojibwe were under increasing stress from American expansion. The 1825 Treaty of Prairie du Chien had set the stage for the 1826 Treaty of Fond du Lac, which gave the U.S. government the right to expropriate metals and minerals from Ojibwe lands.[28] Though the Ojibwe accepted the American presence and considered trade vital to their standard of living, they would eventually be overwhelmed.[29] With the beaver population dwindling significantly, economic imperatives influenced tribal decision-making.[30] A little over a decade following Fond du Lac, in 1837, the Ojibwe signed another treaty with the United States that relinquished territory in what would later become Wisconsin and Minnesota. Forty-seven Ojibwe chiefs participated in the negotiations at Fort Snelling, but Hole in the Day played an important role in convincing others to sign. Delegations from Lac Court Oreilles and Lac du Flambeau arrived late, only to find that their lands to the east had been offered for sale. The settlement was highly disadvantageous to Ojibwe, though it did not immediately appear so. None, for instance, were asked to relocate, and they had, in theory, retained the right to hunt, fish, and gather as they pleased. In reality, the Ojibwe had lost much: the title to a large tract of land that was now open to American settlement. The compensation they received, due in annuity payments, could never make up for the white invasion that followed, which brought on a deadly smallpox epidemic.

Many Ojibwe were left disgruntled by the 1837 treaty, fueling resentment for Hole in the Day. Undeterred, he negotiated another treaty in 1842.[31] The Treaty of La Pointe, signed by many of the Ojibwe clans, ceded swaths of northern Wisconsin and Michigan's Upper Peninsula, opening the door wider for white squatters. The Lake Superior Wisconsin bands refused to participate in negotiations until their right to remain was assured.[32] These treaties continued to erode traditional Ojibwe life and territorial hegemony. Between 1840 and 1850, the population of settlers in Wisconsin areas increased threefold, from one hundred thousand to three hundred thousand. One hundred thousand of the new arrivals were foreign-born, coming from Europe, primarily Scandinavia, Germany, and Ireland; the remainder came predominantly from the American Northeast.[33] U.S. Army presence also increased considerably.[34] One can easily imagine the environmental pressures caused by this rapid invasion of whites, who began to hunt, fish, and divide land into homesteads. Buoyed by this population boom, Wisconsin became the thirtieth state in 1848.[35] A year before Wisconsin achieved statehood, Chief Hole in the Day died and was succeeded by his son, Hole in the Day the Younger (nephew of Owanishan, Jean-Batiste Gaudin's wife). Hole in the Day the Younger, like his father, aspired to be the leader of all the Ojibwe clans.[36]

Despite the profound flux occurring in the 1840s, Antoine and Sarah Gaudin were able to make a comfortable living in La Pointe. Both Antoine's general store and lumber transport business thrived and at some point, perhaps in keeping with the expansion of American influence westward, Antoine anglicized his surname to Gordon and his first name to Anton. The Gordons' marriage produced five children in its first seven years, three girls and two boys. The last, William, born in 1850, would later father Philip Gordon. Five years after William's birth, the Gordons relocated to St. Croix, near the mouth of the Snake River, establishing themselves at a trading post maintained by Michel Cadotte. There they traded with Indians until the early 1860s. Anton then sold his stake in the Algonquin lumber transport business and took his family to the town of Amik (Anishinaabemowin for Beaver), in what is now northern St. Croix County, Wisconsin. He purchased a sizable plot of land from speculators based out of the growing city of St. Paul, adjacent to Fort Snelling.[37] Amik was situated on a stagecoach and mail route from St. Paul to Bayfield, a trip that took six days to travel the approximately two hundred miles. The fare was a hefty twenty dollars, one dollar extra for daily meals and boarding.[38] Gordon built a boarding house to accommodate coach passengers, as well as a general store.[39]

Soon after the Gordons established themselves in Amik, white encroachment into Ojibwe territories began to inspire serious resistance. In 1854, the Ojibwe signed the second Treaty of Fond du Lac, resulting in reservation life for most of the clans living in Minnesota.[40] For the Lake Superior bands in Wisconsin, the treaty created the Bad River, Red Cliff, Lac Court Oreilles, and Lac du Flambeau Reservations, each located in the north of the state.[41] The signatories retained hunting, fishing, and gathering rights in the region.[42] Just a year later, in 1855, the U.S. government made another aggressive bid for Ojibwe lands to the west, summoning several leaders, Hole in the Day the Younger among them, for negotiations. The result was the Treaty of Washington, which created the Leech Lake and Milles Lacs Reservations and promised regular material assistance.[43] Though lands had again been given up, Hole in the Day could boast about the coming annuity payments, even if he had begun to alienate many of his own people.[44] With the Native residents now largely confined, Minnesota became a state in 1858. As whites poured in, the Ojibwe became a marginalized minority population whose resources were quickly evaporating.[45] Perhaps worse, they had also come under the thumb of the Bureau of Indian Affairs, which increasingly administered reservation life throughout the United States. In the 1860s, the Office of the Interior asserted control over the Ojibwe in Wisconsin and Minnesota through their agency in Bayfield. Mostly ruinous consequences ensued. The BIA was simply unable to stem growing poverty, disease, and alcoholism boosted by a thriving, illegal whisky trade that operated on dry reservations.[46]

For giving up most of their ancestral lands under the 1855 treaty, Hole in the Day and the Minnesota Ojibwe had been guaranteed annuity payments of $20,000 for twenty years. In 1861, the annuity payment came in late December, having been considerably delayed. Upon its issuance, Hole in the Day immediately noticed the amount was less than promised.[47] Such frustrations were shared by Hole in the Day's westerly neighbors, the Santee Dakota, then living along the Minnesota River. The issue was the same: treaty stipulations and annuity payments had not been honored by Washington, a betrayal that caused hunger, hardship, and recriminations.[48] In August 1862, tensions in the region reached a climax. Dakota warriors attacked white settlers, prompting Hole in the Day to exploit the situation by circulating a rumor that President Lincoln was planning to enlist Ojibwe bands to fight in the American Civil War. Joining the Dakota uprising, he argued, was a better option. The situation was quickly defused by an official delegation to Hole in the Day's camp.[49] Another voice urging caution was Anton Gordon's. He traveled from Amik to convince his cousin not to take up arms. An early historical source on

his family states: "At the time of the Sioux War in Minnesota, in 1862, Mr.
Gordon went on foot over a hundred miles to remonstrate with three of
his cousins who were chiefs of the Chippewa and who were importuned
to join the Sioux in a war of extermination against the Whites. One of
these cousins, Chief Hole in the Day, was very determined, but the influence of Mr. Gordon prevailed, and thus the lives of many white people
were saved."[50] Though Anton Gordon was given credit for convincing
Hole in the Day to avoid conflict, it is doubtful he had much influence
over his cousin, who was consistently open to peaceful negotiations with
whites throughout his life. It is also unlikely that Gordon made the journey solely on foot—canoe and horseback being more realistic.

In October, the U.S. government tacitly admitted fault for the incomplete annuity payment by paying reparations.[51] Yet Hole in the Day had
gambled badly in suggesting the Ojibwe would be drafted by Lincoln.
While Washington continued to treat him as the Ojibwe's primary leader,
the fabricated rumor garnered ire among the Mille Lacs and Leech Lake
Ojibwe. In 1867, Hole in the Day negotiated a treaty that created the
White Earth Reservation in Minnesota, his last major act as chief. Not
long after, in 1868, he was assassinated by a small group of Leech Lake
Ojibwe hired by white men concerned they might be banned from doing
business on White Earth.[52]

Anton and Sarah Gordon were undoubtedly outraged by Hole in the
Day's murder, but their lives did not otherwise suffer. They continued on
in Amik, where they had built a life. (William Gordon, Philip Gordon's
future father, had just turned seventeen.) Anton, known to all as Tony,
was becoming a leading citizen. His trading post, frequented by Indians
and whites alike, handled furs and dietary staples such as tea, salted pork,
and beans.[53] Still a committed Catholic, Anton played an instrumental
role in the construction of the town church in 1874, donating the land and
personally bearing much of the construction costs. In 1883, Anton built
a school for Indians and whites that provided religious instruction on
Sundays. Sarah Gordon was recognized in the area as a skilled midwife.
Throughout the years, Anton filled multiple roles in town administration: postmaster, supervisor, and school treasurer. He became so prominent that when the North Western Railroad began construction through

Amik in 1882, the company named the station Gordon in Anton's honor
after he deeded the land for passage. As time went on, Amik became known
as the town of Gordon, which today sits in Ashland County, Wisconsin.[54]

Considering the status of his father, William Gordon's childhood
entailed certain responsibilities. These did not include school. Like his
father, William only had a month of formal education, yet spoke English,
Anishinaabemowin, and some French. Also like his father, William rejected alcohol and demonstrated considerable wit. His only weakness was
tobacco. While still in his teens (and before the North Western Railroad
was built) William took on duties as a summer mail carrier on the route
to Bayfield. The job required him to wake up at three in the morning for
a thirty-five-mile hike on a forest trail. At a log cabin between Gordon
and Bayfield he would hand off the mail to another carrier. The walk usually took until evening. William would return the following day. Anton
disallowed him from making the trips in the winter, for this was poten-
tially dangerous work. William's fellow carrier once found himself pur-
sued by wolves and was forced to spend the night in a tree to escape them.
He survived, but the mail was irretrievably lost.[55] In 1874, William (then
twenty-four) married Ategekwe (Gambling Woman), or Sarah Mekins, a
full-blooded Ojibwe from the Lac Court Oreilles Reservation, which lay
to the south of Gordon. The marriage would produce fourteen children,
seven girls and seven boys. Three sons would succumb to tuberculosis, as
would one daughter. Philip Gordon was born on March 31, 1885. He was
given the Ojibwe name Tibishkogijik, meaning Looking into the Sky—
quite appropriate for a future priest.[56]

CHAPTER 2

From Boyhood to the Priesthood

When Philip Gordon was born in 1885, he entered an Ojibwe world much changed since the appearance of Europeans on tribal lands. By the 1890s, the inception of reservation life had brought with it the allotment process. This misguided effort by the BIA to make farmers of the Ojibwe was accompanied by attempts to assimilate the younger generation through government and mission schools. White education caused disruption on many levels. The young generally wore American-style clothing and spoke English, while Ojibwe parents disliked how schooling interfered with the traditional family's economic life, which included harvesting wild rice and maple sugar processing. Fear that children would be sent away to boarding school also gripped parents. Older Ojibwe, even if they had some white education, usually preferred their own language. Younger tribe members sometimes reverted to Anishinaabemowin once their English schooling was completed, though in some cases they had to relearn the language after years of English instruction. As a result, in the early 1890s only a small percentage of the older, adult population spoke English.

In tandem with these wrenching changes in daily life, unscrupulous logging practices by white speculators and mixed-bloods on Ojibwe reservations caused numerous problems. Though the BIA supervised logging companies and insisted they use Ojibwe labor, whites exploited the environment beyond sustainability. Authorized to harvest only dead and fallen trees, logging concerns frequently exceeded their mandates by cutting down everything they could and cheating the Ojibwe landowners of the profits.[1] At Leech Lake, dissatisfaction over logging practices even sparked a violent uprising that was put down by the U.S. Army.[2] The logging industry meanwhile helped fuel the liquor trade and consequent alcoholism. Ojibwe reservations were officially dry areas under BIA jurisdiction. White bootleggers paid little mind, servicing customers illegally. Demoralized by these outside forces, many Ojibwe could not cope economically with the various changes thrust upon them. The only remaining choice was dependence on BIA rations.[3]

In giving a greater idea of the scale of loss experienced by the Ojibwe and the psychological costs it brought, numbers help tell the story. Under the many treaties signed by the clans, the United States had gained nineteen million acres in lands and one hundred billion boards of timber— not to mention vast quarries, water sources, countless tons of copper, and most of the game that once thrived on the land. The Ojibwe, in return, had received reservations encompassing just a few thousand acres and annuities totaling a fraction of the wealth seized from their lands.[4] Nationwide, Indians were suffering equally from such usurpation. In 1900, the U.S. census recorded that the Native American population was at an all-time low. Most whites believed (erroneously) that indigenous peoples would soon vanish. Very few mourned the fact.[5]

During the second half of the nineteenth century, Christianization efforts among the Ojibwe increased thanks to the greatly expanded presence of missionaries supported and subsidized, in part, by the U.S. government. Though Methodists and Presbyterians established missions and schools on Ojibwe lands, eventually Catholics came to dominate on-reservation schooling because of greater investments and the establishment of permanent Catholic missions run by Benedictines under the Bureau of Catholic Indian Missions.[6] In 1870, for instance, the BIA claimed that 99 percent of one Ojibwe agency in Minnesota had become converted Catholics.[7] Missionaries were able to gain acceptance among the Ojibwe and other Native American communities because they were seen as separate from other white people, distinguished by their black robes, celibacy, love of ritual, and willingness to speak, study, and translate Indian languages.[8] Such missionaries also had, quite literally, a captive audience.

Those Ojibwe who ostensibly converted in the mid-nineteenth century often had different ideas of what it meant to be a Catholic. While some may have been more or less complete converts, others (likely most) chose to combine Christian ideas and teachings with traditional spiritual beliefs, seeing no contradiction between the two. To them, the concept of Kitchi Manito and the Christian God were, ultimately, the same thing.[9] These tribe members imbued Catholic rituals with their own meanings and continued to believe in the healing power of traditional Ojibwe songs, dances, and medicines, and the meaningfulness of dreams and stories, sacred places, and the natural world. In this way, aspects of Midé Society survived.[10] Ceremonies like All Saints Day were practiced along, or mixed, with Ojibwe customs like the Ghost Feast, which likewise honored those who had passed.[11] Catholic missionaries and the church often tried to impose new ideals, such as their notions of marriage, on the Ojibwe. This meant that women, once married, were to belong to their husbands rather than clans, while their unions were supposed to remain insoluble.[12] Catholic missionaries also looked with disdain upon Ojibwe tribal dances, exposed bodies, and face painting. These church prejudices became government policy. Throughout the nineteenth and early twentieth centuries, the BIA would frequently ban and discourage traditional dances throughout the United States.[13] Philip Gordon, coming from a long line of Catholics, understood this clash of cultures and the subtleties in the way the Ojibwe adapted their beliefs in the face of Catholicism. Throughout his career, he would seek to integrate traditional elements of Ojibwe spiritual beliefs into his own faith.

That said, little is known about Gordon's first twelve years in Gordon, Wisconsin. Sources based on his recollections state that Philip spent much time at his grandfather's trading post, where he played with a relative, Mesabi, or Joe Mesabi, who despite being Philip's uncle was about the same age. Grandfather Anton Gordon and father William remained devoted Catholics, and at some point, Philip was baptized by Father Odoric Derenthal, who ministered to Catholics from the Franciscan mission in Bayfield.[14] Known as Father Odoric, Derenthal was born to a family of farmers in Roesbeck, Prussia, in 1856. He began his preparation for the priesthood at age twelve, joining the order of Franciscans in Westphalia in

1873. After immigrating to America in 1875, Derenthal studied theology
in Illinois before his ordination in 1880. He thereupon commenced mis-
sionary work among the Ojibwe, eventually founding St. Joseph's Indian
Industrial School in Keshena, Wisconsin.[15] Father Odoric and Philip
Gordon would later form a personal and professional relationship when
Philip entered the priesthood.

During his childhood in Gordon, Philip attended a one-room schoolhouse built to replace the one his grandfather had constructed in 1883. The
course of study was three years. There also exists an account—possibly
apocryphal—of young Philip fashioning a priest's robe out of curtains
and forcing his younger cousins to pray for hours on end. In June 1897,
the Gordons briefly relocated to Ategekwe's birthplace on the Lac Court
Oreilles Reservation. They then moved on to the Bad River Reservation,
settling in the administrative center of Odanah. Bad River, like most
Wisconsin lands at the time, was dominated by pine forest and, hence,
the logging industry. Odanah's population of about two thousand was
divided evenly between white loggers and Ojibwe. Still, the move put
Philip in direct contact with Ojibwe traditions—along with the hardships
many Ojibwe experienced on the reservations. The summer of his family's
arrival, Ategekwe aided in the rice harvest. William Gordon became the
agency's chief of police, and later, official interpreter. The family enrolled
as tribal members, qualifying for allotment under the Dawes Act.[16]

In September 1897, Philip began his studies at St. Mary's Mission School
in Odanah, run by the Sisters of Perpetual Adoration of La Crosse. St.
Mary's had opened in 1883, two years after the U.S. government had given
permission for the Franciscans to establish the school. The local community built the two-room schoolhouse, which was staffed by two nuns,
Sisters Catherine and Rose.[17] St. Mary's offered an "industrial" curriculum, including trade instruction for boys and sewing and baking classes
for girls. Students who advanced to higher grades received instruction
in more "literary pursuits," as the Catholic Bureau's flagship publication,
the *Indian Sentinel*, phrased it.[18] By the time Philip became a pupil, St.
Mary's had been granted government sponsorship under the continuation
of Grant's peace policy of Indian assimilation. Pupils could board or, if
they lived nearby, attend during the day. Though the Gordons resided in

Odanah, Philip boarded at the school—perhaps because of the massive size of his family.[19]

Philip took his first communion while at St. Mary's on January 21, 1899; he was also confirmed in Odanah, likely by Father Odoric, who was the school's pastor.[20] Apart from his studies, Philip worked winters at logging camps and sawmills in the capacities of company store shopkeeper and clerk, as well as physical laborer. In later notes on his life, Father Gordon wrote that he kept up the family tradition of being a teetotaler despite contact with the rough company typically found in a sawmill town, where drunken workhands smoked, drank, and danced with impunity. And despite suffering intermittently from poor health as a youth, Philip became a skilled basketball and baseball player. Most importantly, he excelled in his studies, becoming a standout student. At St. Mary's, Philip made such an impression that Sisters Catherine and Rose suggested he attend Wisconsin's State Normal School in Superior, founded in 1893. Normal schools could be likened to colleges today, training high school graduates in pedagogy and curriculum. Studying at the Normal required passing the county examination that certified teacher qualifications. Philip took the exam in 1900, age fifteen. Sisters Catherine and Rose made him promise that whether he passed or not, he would finish the three-year term at St. Mary's. Philip did pass, though many of the older high school students who took the exam failed.[21]

Once Philip gained acceptance to the Normal, the questions of where in Superior he would live and how he would support himself became pertinent. Fortuitously, Father Walter Fardy, who resided just one-half mile from the Normal, offered him room and board.[22] It is also likely that Sisters Catherine and Rose raised money for Philip's studies.[23] Several of Philip's letters have survived from the period he spent studying in Superior. They depict a highly conscientious young man devoted to Catholicism and immersed in his education. On December 3, 1900, Philip wrote to the sisters in Odanah to say he was "getting along finely at the Normal." He dutifully reported that his two-year course consisted of numerous subjects. Arithmetic was his poorest because he had missed the first two weeks of the semester. But with some tutoring, he had already "caught up to the class." Luckily, his other courses were "not very hard."[24] Philip wrote the sisters again in the spring of 1901 with more good news to share. In history and physiology, he was "doing excellent," and after a special twenty-week penmanship course his left-handedness had been "corrected." "I can now write with my right hand equally as good as with my left," he announced proudly to the sisters.[25]

A long letter to Philip Gordon's brother James has also survived from this time, dated May 8, 1901. It discusses how Philip was chosen to give a commencement address on the Wilmot Proviso. In this task, Father Fardy's library had been of "great assistance." The letter counseled James on education and religion in most optimistic terms:

> When I entered the Normal, I did not have to take any examination, but immediately entered into the Freshman class which is very seldom for a student coming from a graded school and all this shows that parochial schools as equally as good as and in my estimation far better for Catholic children to attend than other schools. Whyfore attend a public school when you can learn with a reasonable amount of study the subjects that are taught in all schools, in parochial schools as well as the greatest thing to be learned in life—the true faith. Cynics might suggest that this what seems a most extraordinary jump from a parochial to a Normal school is due of exceptional good talents etc. but I suggest this! That with a reasonable amount of study anybody can easily overcome the difficulties that might arise and I would suggest one more thing, that you acquire a taste for good reading or books where you may learn lessons and gain information.

Philip closed by acknowledging the role Odanah's sisters had played in his achievements. "I owe most of my success to the friendly aid of the Sisters and I shall never cease to thank them for their kindly interest & favors in my behalf," he told James, "Regards to all and may God favor us with success."[26] Unfortunately, these are seemingly the only letters that exist from Gordon's youth. The epistolary record only picks up a full eight years later, making for scarce detail on this formative period.

Following his time in Superior, Philip went on to North Wisconsin Academy (today Northland College), in Ashland, Wisconsin. The academy was a private liberal arts institution founded in 1892, with strong ties to the Congregational Church.[27] How he financed these studies in unclear. Philip spent just a year at the academy, but managed to date two young women, one named Lena, the other Emma Heany. Despite these distractions posed by the opposite sex, Philip was already thinking seriously about entering the priesthood. In 1903, he contacted the Provincial Seminary in St. Francis, Wisconsin, requesting information. Soon after, he got a curt, unenthusiastic response from the admissions officer, who had made inquiries about him. The officer coldly related that Philip had been "well recommended," though "doubts" existed concerning his suitability for the priesthood. (These "doubts," one might conclude, smacked of some racism.) Still, if he truly had "the intention and a strong desire" he could enroll, but the tuition would have to be paid up front. The admissions officer added that the "St. Francis League for indigent students" might offer some help in this regard. Insulted, Philip Gordon looked elsewhere. At the suggestion of an Ojibwe friend and theological student, John Medegan, he continued his education at St. Thomas College in St. Paul, Minnesota.[28]

St. Thomas College, founded in 1885 by the archbishop of St. Paul and Minneapolis John Ireland, was originally an all-male Catholic seminary. In 1894, the institution split into a private liberal arts college and school of divinity. A year before Philip arrived, 1903, St. Thomas created a compulsory military program. It quickly became so prominent that in 1906 the U.S. War Department classified St. Thomas as a military school. Philip enrolled in 1904, meaning that he took part in obligatory military training.[29] He likely worked off campus to pay tuition while living with his parents during the summer months. Though no letters exist from Philip's time at St. Thomas, excerpts from the college's official paper, the *St. Thomas Collegian*, offer a view into his activities on campus. The *Collegian* records that Philip was a formidable athlete and "ideal leader," who played football and basketball in a "very aggressive" style. His left-handedness aided his basketball game, and by the end of his studies he had received more letters in sports than any other student in the college's history. Athletic life was balanced by participation in the Committee of the Temperance Society, captaining Company C in the Military Department, and taking part in student plays. His interpretation of Towel Fairfax in *The Toastmaster* garnered considerable praise for its "smoothly eloquent speech and intellectual ways."[30]

There also exists a copy of Philip Gordon's grade sheet from the 1904–5 academic year, found in the Franciscan Sisters of Perpetual Adoration Archives in La Crosse, Wisconsin. It records that Philip scored 99 percent in Christian Doctrine, 89 percent in Latin, 85 percent in Greek, 87 percent in English, 79 percent in Mathematics, and 90 percent in German. He received 96 percent for conduct and 95 percent for application. He earned his second highest mark, 97 percent, for "Attention to Religious Duties."[31] Thanks to this stellar academic performance, young Gordon attracted the attention of many within the Catholic Church. The Catholic Bureau's *Indian Sentinel* recorded Gordon's achievements at St. Thomas in an article on St. Mary's in Odanah. After distinguishing him as one of the school's most ambitious and able graduates, the *Sentinel* quoted St. Thomas's president, who declared that Gordon was doing "really well" and was among the "most popular" students at the college.[32]

In 1907, the year before his graduation, Gordon's grandfather, Anton, died at age ninety-five. Anton was buried in a cemetery nearby the trading post he had established in the early 1860s.[33] He was in good mental and physical health until the end of his long life, though the final year he suffered from "dropsy," or oedema, a condition in which excess water builds up in the tissues of the body. "I cannot forbear mentioning the remarkable example of Christian fortitude displayed by my grandfather during his last illness," Gordon later wrote. "Taken to his bed . . . for two whole months he tossed in the agonies of the dread dropsy, but always with a cheerful and ready mind. His last few hours were spent in admonishing those gathered at his bed side never to fail in that duty, the reward for which he was about to enter."[34] Whatever tensions Philip Gordon felt regarding his mixed ancestry or racial and cultural identity, by the time of his pioneer grandfather's death one can safely state that he had decided white education and religion were superior not only for him, but for his fellow Ojibwe. As he often said, "Indian traditions must be preserved, but in books." Even so, Gordon considered himself first and foremost—and proudly—a Native person, never in his life even hinting publicly that he had some French ancestry. Gordon graduated from St. Thomas College in 1908. The *Collegian* noted that he received a gold medal for academic excellence, a special award for his mastery of Latin, and "first distinction" in Greek and English. Immediately after earning his diploma, Gordon enrolled in St. Thomas's divinity school, St. Paul Seminary. He was not yet ready to leave St. Paul and the successes he had achieved there.[35]

The year Gordon spent at St. Paul Seminary was one of his happiest. In a letter to Sister Catherine dated March 14, 1909, he apologized for being remiss in contacting her more regularly and described the joy his duties brought:

> We have generally several hours of work always on our hands. Still, I find Seminary life the most agreeable of any that I have ever experienced. Persons who have been through the Seminary keep telling us that we are having the happiest times of our lives and I believe it. Of course, our happiness, I suppose, is not the kind that would appeal to the ordinary fellow-about-town but it appeals to me as being the ideal for its purpose. We have set hours for all our exercises and so arranged, it seems, that what one wants and needs most at any particular time, comes at that time, studies, prayers, recreation, meals and sleep. The discipline is very strict but no one seems to be the worst for it.[36]

Despite his good cheer, Gordon was preoccupied about the status of Catholic Indian schools overseen by the missions and whether they were properly funded. There was good reason. In 1900, Congress had abruptly cut financial aid to religious schools on Indian reservations.[37] Gordon had recently written to Father William H. Ketcham, director of the Bureau of Catholic Indian Missions, attempting to ascertain as much information as possible on the subject. Ketcham had replied by sending a series of pamphlets. Gordon now requested any information Sister Catherine could furnish on Odanah concerning "its history, trials, means of support and prospects." He hoped that once he collected sufficient information, he could assist St. Mary's in any way within his means and power. Gordon's

motivation for ensuring the school's "future prosperity" was his realiza-
tion that the sisters' work with the children in Odanah was "absolutely
necessary" for Catholicism to flourish.[38]

What plans Gordon had to assist Catholic Indian schools are unclear.
His own future prosperity, however, was itself secured by the end of his
first year at seminary. Through the Dawes Act, he was allotted a tract of
land on the Bad River Reservation. His parents, William and Ategekwe,
had since relocated to Clear Lake in Sherburne County, Minnesota, but
Gordon was able to acquire a choice plot of pine-timbered land thanks
to his father's former position as police chief and interpreter. The profits
from any logging were Gordon's, with one minor catch. He was barred
access to the monies without the permission of the agency superintendent, Samuel M. Campbell. Fortunately, Gordon and Campbell, a Civil
War veteran, developed a friendly relationship. Campbell aided in selling
the pine logged on Gordon's allotment for the grand sum of $10,000—
the equivalent of nearly $250,000 today when adjusted for inflation.[39] It
is not known precisely when Gordon received this windfall, but it largely
funded his education. Directly after leaving St. Paul Seminary in 1909,
Gordon sailed for Europe to further his studies.[40]

Unfortunately—as is the case with many of Gordon's early years—little
detail on his European sojourn exists. The *Indian Sentinel* updated readers
on Gordon's studies abroad in 1910 and 1912, asking that readers "pray
earnestly that God may design to make of this young man an instrument
of grace and power for the salvation of the Chippewa people."[41] No other
contemporary sources appear to exit. Nonetheless, later reports state that
Gordon spent one year at the American College in Rome, then two at
the University of Innsbruck, Austria. While on the old continent Gordon
traveled throughout western Europe during summer vacations, becoming fluent in German, French, and Italian, while improving his reading
in Latin and ancient Greek. Summers were spent in the medieval city of
Touraine, France, being tutored in the language. Some of his time was also
spent in the south of Austria's state of Tyrol, in the Alps. There Gordon
recovered from suspected tuberculosis and underwent an operation on
his lymph nodes, which left him with a scar on his neck.[42] The only impressions recorded from these three years can be found in subsequent

newspaper articles containing Gordon's recollections. Rome, reportedly, impressed him greatly. One account noted that he "visited the Forum where the elegant voice of Cicero thrilled the multitude; the Coliseum where innocent Christians were offered to the beasts of prey; St. Peter's Dome where Michelangelo immortalized his genius; the Catacombs where Christianity concealed itself during three long centuries of persecution; and the innumerable edifices of divine worship, each and every one of which is a monument to Christian faith, zeal, and generosity." Gordon himself commented that it would take several lifetimes "to study all the monuments of the Eternal City." Nevertheless, he preferred his time in Innsbruck, where the mild weather was more conducive to study than the "hot climate" of Italy.[43] Gordon returned from Europe in 1912, convinced that the priesthood was the only path for his life. He did some traveling across America, briefly visiting the Carlisle Industrial Indian School in Pennsylvania.[44] Thereafter, he resumed his studies at St. Paul and St. John's University in Collegeville, Minnesota, where he prepared in earnest for his induction into the priesthood.

On Monday morning, December 8, 1913, Philip Bergin Gordon, age twenty-eight, was ordained by Bishop Joseph M. Koudelka in the Sacred Heart Pro-Cathedral in Superior, Wisconsin.[45] Koudelka, born in Austria in 1852, had been appointed bishop of Superior the previous summer. He spoke eight languages, including Anishinaabemowin.[46] The ceremony he officiated gave Gordon the distinction of becoming the first American Indian priest ordained in the United States. (Albert Negahnquet, a Potawatomi, had previously been ordained in Rome for the Diocese of Oklahoma.) The *Indian Sentinel* carried the news of Gordon's ordination but, willfully or not, mistranslated his Ojibwe name, Tibishkogijik, not as Looking into the Sky, but Gift from Heaven.[47] Like the Catholic *Sentinel*, the Wisconsin press took interest. They reported that Gordon was "still close to the primitive Indian in America" despite all his "conscientious study, extensive travel and [work at] the best Catholic seats of learning." Because he still loved "his race and with patriotic and religious devotion," his desire was to labor among the Ojibwe at the Indian missions. Gordon took the occasion of his ordination to draw attention to his major concern: Indian education in the Diocese of Superior, in particular at St. Mary's.

He explained to a reporter that the school was "not self-supporting" and that "the Sisters have about all they can do to keep above water." Though St. Mary's had grown to 350 pupils with 15 Franciscan nuns in the teaching faculty, the school's facilities (6 classrooms and 47 other rooms for boarding and activities) were "in a state of physical decay" without funds for repairs. Even more worrying, the withdrawal of support from Washington meant only two teachers were still paid by the government. Upon their retirement, St. Mary's would be dependent on local donations.[48]

Following his ordination, Gordon spent several weeks at his parents' home preparing for his first mass, to be held in Odanah at St. Mary's Church at the beginning of the New Year. The local news bulletin, the *Star*, heralded the event with much advance fanfare. "Every member of the Chippewa tribe has reasons to be proud of Mr. Gordon's record," the paper proclaimed, "and each and every one will, no doubt, do his share to make his first mass an event long remembered in the annals of the village and the Chippewa tribe."[49] The same page boasted the headline, "Electric Lights Possible." If plans came to fruition, "every dwelling in the village" would be fitted "with electric lights," a mark of progress to be "hailed with joy by our citizens." The *Star* only hoped that the news would not turn out to be "idle talk."[50] This coming wave of modernity had already washed over St. Mary's Church, which had been remodeled and fitted with a sturdy, handsome asbestos roof. Much of the labor had been supplied by the boys at St. Mary's. Referring to this community effort, the *Star* observed how "the whole inspires a feeling of devotion and a vague sense of the Divinity."[51]

With Gordon's first mass set for January 6, 1914, Odanah began preparations. The local general store, Stearns Co., quickly sold out their supply of torches, forcing the torch-less to inquire at St. Mary's, which had a cache of fifty set aside for the occasion. The planned celebration was rich in Catholic pageantry. When Bishop Koudelka arrived at the local train station, he was greeted by the Odanah Band. He then led the "grand parade" on its way to St. Mary's, followed all the way by the excited townsfolk. So many locals attended that the crowd filled the aisles and rear of the church. More spectators stood in the entrance, spilling out of the doors. Despite the general commotion, the crowd hushed when

Gordon, Koudelka, and St. Mary's father Optatus Loeffler entered the doors at 10 a.m., preceded by three local girls. The Odanah *Star* described the quaint scene: "As a symbol of Gordon's union with, or espousal to, the Church of Christ, the newly ordained priest is given a bride of very tender years, clad in spotless white, and wearing a wreath and veil. Upon little Madeline Holliday fell this great honor, and her parents duly appreciate it, and she appeared in due time for the procession a veritable little queen. Her maids . . . Hazel Van Buren and Margaret Paro were also clad in ermine robes. Holding in her tiny hands a beautiful wreath, the symbol of the young priest's espousals to the church and her sacred cause, Madeline and her maids . . . advanced to the communion railing." In the girls' wake, Gordon, Koudelka, and Loeffler made their way up the church's center aisle as the assembled choir sang *Ecce sacerdos magnus* (Behold the High Priest). Gordon followed them by singing *Veni creator* in a "sweet clear voice," the choir accompanying. In his sermon, the young priest, his voice shaking with strong emotion, recalled how as a young boy he had been baptized by Father Odoric Derenthal in the small town of Gordon.[52]

The next day, Odanah saw another major event: the Feast of the Epiphany. Bishop Koudelka again presided over the festivities, showing off his linguistic skills by addressing those assembled in English, Czech, and Polish. He then addressed the Ojibwe in their native tongue, declaring that there was "none more beloved" at St. Thomas College than their kinsman, Father Philip Gordon. A group of twenty area priests also attended, and after the ceremony St. Mary's school provided a "sumptuous banquet" that made reference to Ojibwe traditions—the menus boasting "birch bark designs on easels and the place cards tiny birch canoes." The *Star* predicted that the fine day in Odanah would "go down as the brightest, the most memorable in her annals." But with the celebrations over, Gordon had new duties to consider. Koudelka had assigned him a post as assistant Indian missionary to Father Odoric.[53] The time of youth and travels had ended.

CHAPTER 3

The Society and the Missionary

In 1911, while Philip Gordon was enjoying his extended European sojourn, a major milestone in American Indian activism occurred back home. On Columbus Day (October 12) of that year, a small group of prominent indigenous men and women founded the Society of American Indians in Columbus, Ohio. The meeting was the brainchild of the Yavapai physician Dr. Carlos Montezuma and Professor Fayette Avery McKenzie, a white sociologist at Ohio State University.[1] In Columbus, those gathered formed a Temporary Executive Committee. Soon after, they established an office in Washington, DC, and drew up a constitution.[2] Though Gordon was not present at either assembly, he would become a major player in the SAI and a close friend to Carlos Montezuma, whose life had contained considerable drama.

Born in present-day Arizona in the mid-1860s, as a child Montezuma survived a violent raid by Pima Indians who killed many of his relatives. Two Pima then sold him for thirty silver dollars to an Italian photographer, Carlos Gentile, who named the boy Carlos Montezuma and raised him as best he could. (Montezuma's original name was Wassaja, meaning Beckoning or Signaling.) Gentile and young Montezuma traveled the country until Gentile, realizing his ward required more stability, entrusted the boy to a Baptist minister, William H. Steadman, and his family, in Urbana, Illinois. There Montezuma began to study in earnest, and in 1889 he earned a degree from Chicago Medical College. When his initial attempts at private practice failed, the doctor began work in the Indian Service, tending to patients on reservations in North Dakota, Nevada, and Washington

State. The experience left him outraged at the Bureau of Indian Affairs' corrupt and inefficient administration, and the reservation system in general. After Montezuma quit in disgust, he moved on to Carlisle from 1893 to 1896, becoming life-long friends with Richard Henry Pratt and a steadfast supporter of his assimilationist goals. By the time he helped found the SAI, Montezuma was one of the most famous Native men in the United States. He lectured widely on the Indian question from his base in Chicago, where he practiced medicine.[3] Sympathetic magazines touted him as the assimilationist ideal: an educated, urbanized, Christian Indian who was a valuable contributor to white society.[4]

Many among the SAI leadership bore similarities to both Carlos Montezuma and Philip Gordon. The Society boasted some of the most prominent Indians in the country, all of whom were largely Christian, assimilated, highly accomplished professionals educated in boarding schools and successful in the white world. Most used Native and English names interchangeably, and some had part-European heritage. In supporting the SAI, they had taken on the Progressive mantle of "a responsible elite" who would play intermediary between Native people, white society, and government institutions.[5] These luminaries included: the Seneca archeologist Arthur C. Parker; Yankton Dakota writer Gertrude Bonnin (better known as Zitkala-Ša); Santee Dakota physician Charles Alexander Eastman; Omaha lawyer Thomas L. Sloan; Oglala Lakota chief Henry Standing Bear; Peoria Indian Service supervisor of employment Charles E. Dagenett; Winnebago / Ho Chunk Yale graduate and Presbyterian minister Henry Roe Cloud; Ojibwe BIA accountant Marie Louise Bottineau Baldwin; and Arapahoe Episcopal priest and first SAI president Sherman Coolidge.[6] Gordon, with his mixed ancestry and knowledge of both the Ojibwe and white worlds, was at home among such company. He would establish relationships—sometimes fractious, but mostly friendly—with many of these figures during his tenure with the SAI, including two future presidents: Charles Eastman and Thomas Sloan.

Eastman, or Ohiyesa (Winner), was, like Gordon, of mixed lineage. His mother, half white, died in childbirth. His Santee Dakota father was imprisoned and presumed executed after the Sioux Outbreak of 1862 (which Hole in the Day the Younger had threatened to join). Ohiyesa's uncle raised him until he was fifteen, when his father, pardoned by Lincoln and convinced of the merits of Euro-American civilization and religion, suddenly appeared to collect him. At his father's insistence, Ohiyesa enrolled in the Santee Normal Training School, Nebraska, before ultimately completing Boston University Medical School.[7] While working as a physician on the Pine Ridge Reservation, South Dakota, Eastman witnessed the aftermath of the Wounded Knee Massacre in which approximately two hundred Lakota were killed by the Seventh Calvary.[8] Severely disillusioned, he resigned and began lecturing and writing of his formative experiences in books such as *Indian Boyhood* (1902), *The Soul of the Indian* (1911), and *From the Deep Woods to Civilization* (1916).[9]

Sloan, in turn, was born on the Omaha Reservation in Nebraska. As a young man, he was among a small group of Indians that graduated from Virginia's Hampton Institute, founded to educate freed slaves after the Civil War. Sloan graduated valedictorian but refused admission to Yale Law School, preferring to return home and read law with the Omaha lawyer Hiram Chase, another SAI founder. At age seventeen, Sloan was briefly jailed for protesting Omaha agency corruption. He and Chase devoted their practice to representing Indian interests, including the protection of the growing Peyote Religion.[10]

Indian interests were, of course, at the heart of the SAI's mission, and many of Gordon's later beliefs concerning Indian independence and racial pride matched the Society's stated philosophy. The original Society conference call highlighted the principle of fostering "self-help"—an objective that could be achieved "with the attainment of a race consciousness and a race leadership." This was a consciousness and leadership of a pan-Indian, or intertribal, nature, which bonded Native peoples from across the United States regardless of national affiliation, region, or cultural practice. Assimilation for the SAI therefore did not denote a complete reordering or erasure of indigenous identity, but a necessary adaptation to modernity anchored in the past. The founders duly stressed that the "Indian has certain contributions of value to offer our government and our people," while any policies that disregarded this fact would result in "immense losses" for Native societies.[11] Later on, the SAI highlighted the need to "present in a just light the true history of the race, to preserve its records, and emulate its distinguishing virtues."[12]

By 1913 (the year Gordon was ordained) the Society had grown considerably to over six hundred full and associate members. Full membership required indigenous origins, while white associates could join without voting rights. Membership costs totaled two dollars a year, plus one dollar for a subscription to the SAI's *Quarterly Journal*, later renamed the *American Indian Magazine* (AIM).[13] One especially active associate member was Gordon's acquaintance at Carlisle, Richard Henry Pratt. He appeared at the 1912 conference (again in Columbus) to denounce the BIA administration, on-reservation schooling, and Wild West shows as "wicked acts" intended to "prolong bureau domination."[14] Pratt by that time held a fierce vendetta against the bureau, having been pushed out of Carlisle in 1904 for his criticisms of the organ.[15] Also in attendance was director of the Catholic Bureau of Indian Missions (BCIM) Father William H. Ketcham, with whom Gordon had corresponded in 1909 while at St. Thomas's divinity school, St. Paul Seminary.

Father Ketcham had long played a role in Indian reform movements. As early as 1900, he had been appointed the third director of the Catholic Bureau in recognition of his work with the Choctaw, whose language Ketcham had studied intensively. President Taft awarded Ketcham a seat on the Board of Indian Commissioners in 1912 in recognition of his work. In both capacities the priest traversed Indian territories, investigating conditions and advocating improvements in bureau policy.[16] At the 1912 SAI conference, Ketcham spoke on the need for Indian citizenship and expressed hope that the organization would encourage an "awakening" among the white population "on the Indian subject."[17] His presence in Columbus showed not only his support for Indian peoples but the Catholic Bureau's interest in the Society.

Philip Gordon, too, was interested in the SAI, and they were interested in Philip Gordon. In December 1913, Gordon invited Arthur C. Parker, then SAI secretary-treasurer, to witness his first mass in Odanah.[18] Like Gordon, Parker was of European and indigenous lineage and had even considered becoming a clergyman while growing up on the Cattaraugus Reservation in New York. Instead, he made a career as an archeologist with the New York State Museum, concentrating on the Iroquois. (His great uncle, Ely S. Parker, had been the first Native commissioner of Indian Affairs, under Grant.)[19] Parker was "deeply obliged" by Gordon's "beautiful invitation" to Odanah, and certain that if he could find time to come it would bring him "great pleasure and spiritual benefit." Gordon's planned work as a missionary, Parker commented, would undoubtedly be "crowned with great results" for the Ojibwe if permeated by a "true spirit of reform." Parker ended his letter trusting that he and Gordon would "be able to work mutually for the honor of the race and the good of mankind."[20] This potential partnership would continue to develop, despite occasional tension. For now, however, Gordon had other pressing duties. Under his new appointment by Bishop Koudelka, in the winter of 1914 he commenced work as assistant missionary to Father Odoric Derenthal. Ministering on reservations throughout Wisconsin would prove a very difficult experience for the young man.[21] His efforts would quickly bring him into conflict with Odoric, and ultimately the Catholic hierarchy.

When Gordon began his mission, conditions on Wisconsin's Ojibwe reservations were dire. Most of the allotment process had been completed, leaving many residents with one foot in traditional tribal life and another in the individualistic world of American capitalism. The reservations had also become surrounded by whites who often took advantage of their indigenous neighbors, whether economically or through the liquor trade. On the Bad River Reservation, Gordon's former home, the superintendent reported that alcoholism was the most prominent ill afflicting the population. Starting in 1915, he sent policemen to patrol the roads. In just the first week they seized twenty quarts of liquor from bootleggers. This was hardly the only problem. Though each of the reservations in northern Wisconsin had a doctor and nurse on duty, there were no hospitals to deal with the prevalence of trachoma (which could lead to blindness) and tuberculosis (which could lead to death). At Lac Court Oreilles, a majority of the children were found to have trachoma, caused by a bacterium that thrives in unsanitary, overcrowded conditions. Tuberculosis, an incurable disease associated with poverty and malnutrition, affected many of the elderly.[22] Ojibwe boarding-school students off-reservation likewise suffered from these diseases due to poor living conditions, bed sharing, and communal use of items like towels.[23] Gordon, who saw the Catholic faith as a potential salve for his beleaguered people, tried his best to wrest support from the church in hopes of instituting beneficial changes and

expanding their influence. Instead, he mostly endured frustrations stem-
ming from underfunding, accounting mishaps, and a lack of resources.

In March 1914, Gordon arrived at the Catholic mission on the Lac
Court Oreilles Reservation, where he took up residence. At the end of the
month he filed a report with Odoric. In it, Gordon warned that those
on the reservation, especially the elderly, "are escaping us" due to the lack
of attention and support for missionary activities. He suggested that
Odoric come and visit an ailing woman who had requested a baptism,
because Gordon himself could not reach her without a team of horses.
There appeared to be some interest in Catholicism on the reservation,
which would wane if not consistently fostered. Until then, not much was
possible because, as Gordon put it, "Indians are Indians." Still, he had
heard that "three big Pagans" had "expressed a desire to hear about the
Church." This news possibly meant they were "drifting in our direction."
Gordon asked Odoric if he could remain at Lac Court Oreilles for the
next six weeks, a period that would allow him to get acquainted with the
residents, preach effectively, and take a much-needed census.[24]

Odoric, for whatever reason, denied Gordon's request to stay on at Lac
Court Oreilles. A few days later, Gordon found himself back in Odanah,
at Bad River, on his way to St. Joseph's Rectory in Hayward. In Odanah,
he performed four communions and again complained to Odoric that
without a team of horses his movements were severely restricted. To make
matters worse, the meagre donations he was collecting were barely enough
to pay for his travel fares. Gordon inquired whether the church would
provide him a livery, or if he should hire one himself. In the latter case, he
would charge it to Odoric personally.[25] Unsurprisingly, such letters displeased Odoric. He bristled at his importunate underling's complaints,
responding that Gordon seemed only to "contradict, criticize, [and] find
fault." Nonetheless, Odoric relented and supplied a "poor old buggy."
Gordon in turn deemed the conveyance inadequate, writing that one of
its wheels was "liable to collapse at any time." He was also chagrined at his
superior's having taken umbrage, insisting that if Odoric took his letters
less personally he would see that blame had not been directed at him. And
if Odoric continued to take such suggestions "amiss," there was nothing
more Gordon could do "but say more in sorrow than in anger 'tua culpa,

tua culpa.'" Gordon concluded his arguments by likening Odoric's supervision of him to "a lion watching a mosquito," ironically conceding that
Odoric was neither "sneak" nor "hypocrite," and that there had to be valid
"reasons for putting a damper on [his] well-meant zeal."

It is doubtful that Odoric had much time to contemplate Gordon's declared admiration. Over the following months, he would receive a stream
of grievances relating to almost every aspect of his young charge's missionary work. Two sore points were the church's failure to pay Gordon's salary,
and his feeling that he was being burdened by demands outside his job
description. "I hardly think that you will expect me to do your work on
the Missions," Gordon complained; but once his salary was "assured" he
would be "ready to do [his] best for the salvation of souls." These issues
frustrated Odoric, especially because Gordon kept reporting the paltriest
collections at mass—a mere ninety cents at Odanah.[26] Additionally, Gordon would not cease in pointing out various deficiencies. His subsequent
letter cited an insufficient supply of oats for his horses—which forced him
to charge several pails to the church's account—a shortage of mass wine
and hosts, and of course the "poor old buggy," which Gordon abandoned
after it was "pronounced unsafe by experts." He however persisted in his
duties, visiting sick women and children and hearing confessions. "You
see," he reminded Odoric, "there is work."[27]

In June, Gordon submitted his statement of revenues. Odoric found
them suspicious, as did Father Bernadine Veis, in Ashland. Together, they
requested immediate clarification. Gordon explained that he had misun-
derstood his instructions, listing only monies taken in collections. He
disclosed that he had profited from "personal" sources of revenue, including lectures and a leftover fifteen dollars that Father Optatus Loeffler, in
Odanah, had given him on the day of first mass. Loeffler, Gordon admitted, had given him another fifteen dollars after he confided that his salary
was "very poor." Gordon also made the point that he had not included
his "personal expenses." He then listed a series of items totaling over fifty
dollars, including candy, newspapers, tobacco, rosaries, bookcases, and
costs incurred from attending the funerals of two priests.[28]

Regrettably, more difficulties were in store for Gordon. The clamor
surrounding his incomplete list of revenues soon made it into the diocese

rumor mill, drawing the attention of Koudelka. The bishop came to believe—erroneously—that Gordon had taken in the princely sum of $250 during his first summer of missionary work. There was also a suspicion, unaccounted for, that he had received a large donation while briefly at Superior. Gordon was alarmed. He accused Odoric of ignorantly sharing incorrect information without "knowing the exact figure." Bishop Koudelka now believed Gordon to be "rolling in luxury," a "bias" that would negatively affect decisions concerning his future. Gordon wanted badly to get out the truth, asking Odoric if he was the source of the rumors or if he had "inadvertently made a mistake."[29] Odoric responded with his own calculations, which Gordon furiously tried to correct. He countered that the $250 figure did not include a deduction for his salary, and that Odoric had accidently added one $100 figure twice. Odoric was either "rattled by too much travelling," or he was "playing with the truth."[30]

Eventually, Gordon's misfortunes abated, and any perceived financial improprieties were dismissed. More miraculously, despite the difficulties surrounding his missionary work and his growing reputation for being openly critical, Gordon managed to stay on good terms with Odoric.[31] Odoric did, however, complain to the vicar general of the Superior Diocese, C. F. Schmit, that Gordon was often unprepared for his sermons. In the autumn of 1914, Gordon requested and received a leave of absence from the diocese, likely out of sheer frustration with his new post.[32] Without even informing Odoric, he made his way to Washington, DC, to enroll in the Catholic University of America. Settling in at the church's Apostolic Mission House, he began courses in history and sociology.[33] After being granted an extension of his leave in October, he continued his studies and started work as part-time chaplain at the Carlisle Indian Industrial School in Pennsylvania, meeting Charles Eastman on one of his visits.[34]

Gordon's presence in Washington afforded opportunities to meet important persons in the Bureau of Indian Affairs' apparatus, such as Commissioner of Indian Affairs Cato Sells and Assistant Commissioner E. B. Merritt.[35] It was also possible to reach more influential audiences. In 1914, Gordon spoke at the Federation of Catholic Societies Convention in Baltimore, garnering highly positive (if inherently racist) press coverage. The *Sun* described the event: "Father Gordon could not deny his Indian ancestry. Every line of his face revealed the red-skin, while his jet-black hair added to the picture of the aborigines of America. However, imagine the surprise of the assembled delegates when Father Gordon entered into a most interesting discussion of the Indian missions in the most faultless English you could have heard. But what was even more striking than his unexpected pure English was his unusual wit, with which he kept his audience in almost continuous convulsions of laughter. He was living proof of what real civilization has meant to the former wild tribes of our soil."[36] Though he might have been a curiosity to some, Gordon attracted more serious attention from William H. Ketcham.[37] In the young man, Ketcham saw the potential conversions reaped from having a Native priest working for his Bureau of Catholic Indian Missions. He decided to procure Gordon.

When Gordon was close to finishing his studies in Washington in March 1915, Ketcham wrote Bishop Koudelka. He related that Gordon had "accomplished a great deal of good" at Carlisle, and that those he studied with deemed him "equipped to do efficient missionary work." These facts, along with his indigenous ancestry, made Gordon a natural choice for missions among the Indians. Ketcham asked Koudelka if the Catholic Bureau could employ him for the next two years in Indian schools, so that "a great many Indian children would be saved to the Faith and an impetus given our work in these institutions."[38] Recalling his experiences with Gordon, Koudelka expressed skepticism. He replied that Gordon possessed a difficult personality and exhibited a lack of diligence in "fulfilling his duties"—certainly an allusion to the botched statement of revenues. Ketcham was "surprised" but not discouraged. Seeking to explain away Koudelka's reservations, he wondered if it were "possible that in a matter of this kind the Indian disposition and character has to be taken into consideration." Only if Koudelka agreed to the loan could Gordon have "a fair chance to do some very good work" and perhaps "prove his mettle."[39] (Ketcham, in the end, would regret ignoring Koudelka's warnings.)

In Washington, Gordon was also given the chance to "prove his mettle" to the Society of American Indians' leadership. At the 1914 conference in Madison, Wisconsin, the Society membership resolved to petition President Wilson via a Memorial Committee in hopes of spurring their agenda, which included ameliorating reservation conditions and allowing for a greater Society role in representing disparate tribes before the government. The leadership, quite impressively, managed to schedule an audience with Wilson for December of that year.[40] Conscious of Gordon's presence in Washington, Arthur C. Parker extended an invitation, asking him to speak at the meeting. Gordon instantly assented, effusively thanking Parker for the grand opportunity.[41] At the planned banquet, the young priest gave an address on the Indian's "moral responsibility"—a performance that, according to Parker, made a "considerable impression."[42] The larger event, too, was considered a smashing success, though Wilson admitted having given no prior thought to Indian affairs whatsoever. The president nonetheless promised the delegation to give their concerns "very serious consideration" in the near future.[43] The SAI *Quarterly Journal*, with striking optimism, described the meeting as "a new beginning in Indian progress" and "a new day for the red race."[44]

Though Gordon had pleased Parker at the Washington gathering, a minor conflict soon followed concerning Gordon's new mentor, Father Ketcham. Throughout 1914, Parker and *Quarterly* had put forth several criticisms of the Board of Indian Commissioners, questioning the need for its existence and suggesting it be replaced by "an independent citizen commission" that would oversee BIA activities on the reservations.[45] Ketcham, a member of the board, quit the Society in reaction. His departure as an associate member disturbed Marie Baldwin, who, having made Gordon's acquaintance, urged him to intercede. It was little surprise that Baldwin enlisted Gordon in her effort. Like him, she was of Ojibwe (Turtle Mountain Band) and French descent, and also Catholic. Since 1904, she had worked as accountant in the Education Division of the Indian Bureau. On the basis of her skills, Baldwin would soon become SAI treasurer.[46]

On January 8, 1915, Gordon wrote Parker at "the earnest request of Mrs. Baldwin" to ascertain whether Parker would support Ketcham's return to the SAI. Gordon, rather impolitely, suggested that Parker knew "just what drove" Ketcham away, adding that it "was hard to reconcile" Ketcham's absence due to his "well-established friendship for all movements that have the true interests of the Indian at heart." Still, Parker's attacks had put Ketcham in an awkward position. Being on the board and in the SAI was "as if a German officer might at present be serving the

French at the front." (The reference was fresh. In July 1914 the Great War had broken out in Europe.) Gordon asked whether Parker had deliberately insulted the Board of Indian Commissioners "by a liberal use of sarcasm" and if so, was his just a personal impolitic view or an official SAI position. Should Parker "enlighten" him on the matter, perhaps the Society could mend relations with both Ketcham and the board. "I have naught but the honor of the race and the good of the country as my aim," Gordon closed.[47]

Parker replied within a week, telling Gordon that he doubted Father Ketcham resigned from the Society due to his statements. Parker reminded Gordon that no other board members had resigned, and that the *Quarterly* was a free arena to voice opinions not necessarily representative of SAI official policy. After all, were the Society "held for everything said at the conferences, a single session would destroy it." If anyone was at fault it was Ketcham, who had abandoned the Society over little more than a disagreement with a single member. And though Parker admitted it was "quite possible" that he had "made serious errors," this was a small issue that should not interrupt SAI business or interfere with the larger picture of what they were trying to accomplish.[48] Apparently, no response from Gordon has survived.

Fortunately, any friction between Gordon and Parker caused by Ketcham's departure was smoothed over by the spring. In May, Parker contacted Gordon about the upcoming SAI conference, to be held in Lawrence, Kansas; its theme: "Responsibility for the Red Man." Parker again requested that Gordon "deliver an address upon the subject of moral responsibility, how the Indian may understand what this means and how he may equip himself to assume it."[49] When Gordon received the letter he had little idea that Kansas would soon be his new home. In July, Koudelka granted him, per Ketcham's request, a two-year leave of absence to join the Bureau of Catholic Indian Missions.[50] His first appointment was chaplain at the famous Indian boarding school, Haskell Institute, located in Lawrence, Kansas.

CHAPTER 4

A Conference and a Scandal at Haskell

In 1884, the United States Indian Training School opened in Lawrence, Kansas, modeled after Richard Henry Pratt's ideal of assimilation through off-reservation schooling. It was renamed the Haskell Institute in 1890 as an homage to Congressman Dudley Haskell, an early key supporter. The original curriculum encompassed grades one through five, with an emphasis on English instruction for the student body of just twenty-two. Despite these humble beginnings, Haskell grew rapidly, becoming the second largest Indian off-reservation school in the country after Pratt's Carlisle. At the beginning of the twentieth century, school grounds measured 650 acres, while the rolls boasted over six hundred students—the majority of whom were, like Gordon, Ojibwe.[1] School ceremonies, such as commencement, showed off the military discipline instilled in the students with elaborate marches and drills.[2]

Such outer indicators of success masked an unfolding tragedy manifested in family separation, cultural dislocation, anguished homesickness, and premature death. In the baldest terms, Haskell regimented both assimilationist schooling and institutionalized neglect. Food was poor, disease was rampant, quarters were cramped, and children were issued just one pair of clothes, a uniform, for the whole year.[3] Four years into the school's operation, 1888, nineteen of Haskell's male students from ten different tribes submitted a petition demanding to know why so many of their fellow classmates were dying. In response, the superintendent fired a nurse who had been stealing rations and replaced the school doctor. Even so, deaths continued unabated from diseases such as pneumonia

45

and measles. The Haskell cemetery, which still exists today, is filled with the graves of boys and girls who attended the school for as little as a few months before succumbing to the unhealthy environment.[4] President Taft visited the school in 1909, telling the assembled children, "You are under the guardianship of the United States which is trying in every legitimate way to fit you to meet what you have to meet in future life."[5]

During the 1910s, conditions at Haskell remained largely unsatisfactory. In 1912, the acting superintendent, John R. Wise, suffered deep embarrassment when a group of students sent another petition to then-commissioner of Indian Affairs, Robert Valentine, requesting that the school be closed. Seeking to retain his post and muffle criticism, Wise claimed to the BIA that the petition was merely a ruse perpetrated by a small group of unappreciative pupils. He nonetheless interrogated the student body following the humiliation, finally concluding that the petition had likely been circulated by a student held there against his will.[6] The incident therefore did not beg reflection.

Philip Gordon arrived at Haskell on August 28, 1915. The school paper, the *Indian Leader*, announced that he had come from Washington "assigned to take charge of the religious work among the Catholic students at Haskell." The new chaplain's duties would not be limited to Haskell school grounds. The *Leader* reported that the Bureau of Catholic Indian Missions' director, William H. Ketcham, had also charged Gordon with ministering to all Indians within a hundred-mile radius of the city. Such work would bring Gordon into contact with the Pottawatomi, Sac and Fox, and Kickapoo Nations. The young priest was to live in Lawrence with Father Eckert, who oversaw the city's St. John's Catholic Church.[7]

Once in his new "missionary headquarters," as he called it, Gordon wasted little time in contacting SAI secretary-treasurer, Arthur C. Parker. He wrote that Parker should not "fail to command" him, because he was now able to assist meaningfully with the upcoming Society conference. Gordon also extended the invitation of Father Eckart, who was ready to host the SAI delegates at a special Sunday mass before the conference, the church being "one of the Indian's staunchest friends."[8] Parker thanked Gordon, assuring him that he would attend. Gordon's lecture on moral conditions had also been written into the preliminary program. Parker requested that Gordon send a list of hotels and better boarding houses.[9] Gordon set to work finding accommodation but had to apologize for a lack of progress on his conference paper. Duties had precluded him thinking "more deeply on this tremendous subject," so it was hardly his fault. "I am so much on the road which with bad cigars makes me dizzy," he explained. "I must visit all Kansas before November."[10]

The fifth annual SAI conference took place from September 28 to October 3, 1915, with representatives from twenty-five tribes in attendance. The turnout totaled eight-five members—fewer than previous years—but almost all the SAI leaders appeared: Gertrude Bonnin, Marie Baldwin, Carlos Montezuma, Charles Dagenett, Thomas Sloan, Henry Roe Cloud, Sherman Coolidge, and, of course, Arthur C. Parker. Only Eastman was absent.[11] President Wilson and Father Ketcham were invited; each declined to attend.[12] Ever-dedicated associate member Richard Henry Pratt, however, made the long trip to Kansas.[13] Once there, he and the others gave their support to the Lawrence conference platform, which called for the creation of a United States court of tribal claims, defined legal status for the Indian, the suppression of alcohol on reservations, and improvements in schooling and hygiene inspection.[14] These were uncontroversial demands on which all could agree. The organization's stance on the Bureau of Indian Affairs, however, quickly became a source of serious disagreement among the membership.[15]

On the list of controversial SAI members, Carlos Montezuma took first place at Lawrence. His address, "Let My People Go," called for the abolishment of the BIA and criticized the Society for its acquiescence in the face of a corrupt and demoralizing reservation system that kept Indians as "prisoners" who could not "do anything for themselves." Only eliminating reservations and BIA wardship could ensure liberty and progress. This was a view anchored in the total belief that Indians, once free, would thrive in American society—just as Montezuma and his SAI compatriots had. Montezuma closed by warning those present that Indians had "a running chance with the public, but no chance with the Indian Bureau."[16] While some like Parker and Coolidge were generally unconvinced, Gordon was enamored.[17] He joined Montezuma in condemnation of the bureau and nominated Thomas Sloan for SAI president—likely due to his position on democratic elections for reservation superintendents.[18] In the voting Sherman Coolidge again won out, retaining his position. Sloan was elected vice president on legislation in recognition of his legal expertise; Parker was elected SAI secretary, his dual role as treasurer split, falling to Marie Baldwin.[19]

Despite the liveliness of the conference, Parker left Lawrence concerned. He had immediately recognized the danger of divisions concerning bureau abolition. In a subsequent editorial for the SAI's *Quarterly Journal*, he acknowledged the reality of the diverse views but recommended "harmonious action along the lines of great principles." The statement included a call for caution. "Insistence on a certain political policy not general in its application," Parker presaged, "will prove fatal."[20] Such tepid support for the BIA did not pacify the commissioner of Indian Affairs, Cato Sells. Soon after Lawrence, Parker met Sells at the Indian Rights Association Lake Mohonk conference in upstate New York. Parker discovered that— to his delight—Sells had suddenly become "very anxious about the publicity" generated by the SAI *Quarterly*.[21]

Though the Lawrence conference saw the beginnings of serious discord within the SAI, it did unify Gordon and Montezuma. They became fast friends with common aims, who would cooperate intensely over the coming years. Gordon also established relations with fellow Catholic Gertrude Bonnin, who would soon become a formidable force within the Society. Her personal history indicated the depths of her talent and perseverance. Born Gertrude Simmons on the Yankton Reservation, South Dakota, to an impoverished Yankton woman and a white father who disappeared before her birth, Bonnin, at age eight, had left for White's Manual Labor Institute, a Quaker-run boarding school in Wabash, Indiana. There she endured separation from her mother and a long course of white schooling. She eventually ended up teaching at Carlisle, an experience that left her embittered against the ideals of Indian assimilation through education. She promptly removed to Boston, where she penned a set of semi-autobiographical articles for the *Atlantic Monthly* that condemned Indian boarding schools. Adopting the penname Zitkala-Ša (or Red Bird, in Lakota), she continued to write critical tracts against white society. During this period, she suffered a brief, conflict-ridden engagement to Carlos

Montezuma. Upon Joining the SAI in 1914, Bonnin had largely rejected the East, having married Raymond Bonnin (of French and Sioux ancestry) and taken up residence on the Uintah and Ouray Reservation in Utah, home to the Ute Indians. At Uintah, the Bonnins, both Catholics, put considerable effort into aiding the tribe, encountering frustration with the BIA at every turn.[22] Bonnin's tales of poverty and neglect on the Uintah Reservation moved Gordon greatly.[23] Just a few months before, in August, he had visited her birthplace in the Yankton Reservation in South Dakota, where he participated in the Bureau of Catholic Indian Missions' Catholic Sioux Congress.[24] He would be a regular attendee thereafter, and even be formally adopted into the tribe at Standing Rock.[25]

A day after the Lawrence conference closed, Gordon wrote the Bureau of Catholic Indian Missions secretary, Charles Lusk, in Washington, DC. Perhaps exhibiting some premature paranoia or just wanting to head off any criticism from the BCIM, he cautioned Lusk of the following: "The Society of American Indians have just closed their annual conference here. During the Conference, I took an active part. I also came out quite strongly on the early abolishment of the Indian Bureau. No doubt, you will hear echoes of this and I am sure that it will be used against me by people who heard me and who are in the government service. They will say that I am not a safe man to have around a government school since I teach anarchy." These fears indicated the radical nature of Gordon's views, and the possible consequences that came with expressing them. The notion of bureau abolition, like the nascent Indian reform movement itself, was something that Sells's bureau found deeply discomforting.

Yet with the excitement of the conference over, Gordon was easing into his new post as Haskell chaplain—despite certain difficulties. He complained to Lusk of obstacles in obtaining a list of the school's Catholic students. Numerous requests to the institute's authorities had gone unanswered, and Gordon felt similarly irked by a lack of attendance at church services and what seemed to him Protestant interference in his work. When the children attended mass, they were supervised by Protestant chaperones who suspiciously took notes on everything Gordon said.[26] Gordon certainly had a right to his own suspicions. The legacy of anti-Catholicism he believed to be witnessing was long, fueled by the religion's relatively recent growth in the United States, brought on by Irish, German, and Polish immigration in the nineteenth century. Protestant nativists had responded to these new arrivals with ethnic prejudice and, quite frankly, alarm. Numerous anti-Catholic tracts accused the Vatican of a conspiracy aimed at world domination and painted Catholicism as a secretive, often sexually perverse sect working to subvert the Protestant values of domesticity and American freedoms in general.[27]

The Protestants at Haskell belonged to the Young Men's Christian Association (YMCA), which Gordon surmised was dominating religious life at the school. Upset, he sent a telegram to Commissioner Sells concerning the lack of attention to Haskell's Catholic students. Sells promised to respond, then went silent.[28] Gordon kept Lusk informed on the situation, calling Haskell's superintendent, John R. Wise, "a sort of spineless creature" in one of his letters. In a meeting, Gordon had demanded to see all the Catholic boys and girls on Sunday evening and hold a supervised mass twice a month in downtown Lawrence. Wise suggested a mass once a month and refused to allow integrated worship. Gordon found this absurd, because the boys and girls already dined together three times a day. Here again, the YMCA was the culprit. *They* allowed only segregated activities, therefore Catholics had to "follow suit."[29]

True to his character, Gordon would not let Sells ignore him. He composed a long, strongly worded letter to the commissioner that attacked two school employees, Mr. Birch, and a former Baptist missionary, Miss Stilwell, who had heaped "abuse and ridicule" on Catholic beliefs. Gordon asked if such bigotry was to be "tolerated," stating in earnestness that his query was not that of "an anti-Bureau fiend." Still, while begging "pardon and indulgence" for his "bald manner" of expression, he threatened to go to the press with "every detail" he had related lest Sells fail to respond adequately. Shortly after, Gordon received his list of Catholic students. It brought no gratification. He once more petitioned Sells, insisting that the list was as "inaccurate" as the previous one.

The list was only one issue in what was becoming an explosive situation born of the YMCA's influence over Haskell policy. Gordon informed Sells of the following: the YMCA secretary was living at the school rent-free and encroaching on dormitory space; the YMCA had access to special rooms for exclusive use; Catholics were barred from union meetings on Sunday evenings; Wise had reneged on his promise to allow students to attend mass downtown; Catholic pupils had—as a result of persecution—asked for a change in religious affiliation; Protestants were monopolizing all the unbaptized "pagan" children as converts; and finally, Gordon felt personally smeared in his efforts as chaplain. Rumors abounded that he was "bringing a religious war on at Haskell" by being untruthful and "personally quarrelsome"—a consequence of his requesting nothing more than "a proper balance." Gordon had made Wise aware of his discontent, yet no changes were forthcoming. The only recourse to "satisfaction" was a Congressional investigation.[30] Gordon sent copies of these letters to Catholic Bureau secretary Lusk, ensuring that his grievances were recorded in official channels.[31]

While haranguing Wise and Sells, Gordon also acquainted Father Ketcham with the Haskell situation. He wrote that in the face of prejudice and compromised services in the Protestant chapel, he had galvanized the Catholic students to "be more united." Yet if conditions did not change, Gordon saw only one "ultimate solution"—that Catholic parents not send their children to the school.[32] The root of the difficulties lay in Superintendent Wise's "very spineless" administration. His lack of "firmness" had resulted in "chaos," because Mr. Birch and Miss Stilwell were allowed to run wild, "making fun of our doctrine of the Real Presence, of going down-town to Mass, etc."[33] Then in November, an irate Gordon sent out a general letter to the parents of Catholic students, urging them to petition Superintendent Wise and Commissioner Sells for better treatment at Haskell. He informed them "that unless Catholics are allowed to worship in their own way and unless they receive at least as much encouragement as Protestants," parents should "consider the advisability of removing your child." Otherwise, the children were in danger of "losing their Catholic Faith."[34]

As the New Year approached, Gordon's anger and suspicion remained all-consuming. Even when sending Christmas greetings to the sisters in Odanah, he could not help speaking of the "awful" situation in Lawrence. "Just imagine!" he wondered, "Bigotry has prevented me from making arrangements to hear confessions for Christmas. The children clamor, so to speak, for the Bread of Life, but the officials sit mute and determined that Catholics shall not 'run' their school."[35] This "bigotry" had even marred a recent spelling bee. A "very popular" Catholic pupil named Ella had entered in good faith, only to be derailed by Birch. Gordon detailed the sabotage: "Ella stood up until about seven out of forty were left. Then she fell. I do not recollect the word she misspelled. Mr. Birch, Principal Teacher here is a confirmed bigot. . . . He had the pronouncing of the words in this match and I do believe when he came to children he knew were Catholic, he gave them 'jaw-breakers.'"[36] By this point Ketcham had taken a greater interest in Gordon's protests. He visited Haskell at the beginning of January but made little effect.[37] His options dwindling, Gordon contacted Cardinals James Gibbons and John Farley and Archbishop Edmund Francis Prendergast, members of the Bureau of Catholic Indian Missions. Together, they requested that Secretary of the Interior Franklin Knight Lane house Gordon on Haskell grounds without charge— an illegal request that got the YMCA secretary expelled from government housing posthaste.[38] Soon after, Gordon hit his breaking point. A massive row with Wise ensued. Finding at least some spine, the superintendent shouted that if Gordon persisted in being "objectionable," he would be barred from school grounds. With no other choice, Gordon went to the press.

In the beginning of February 1916, an extensive article appeared in Kansas City's *Catholic Register*. Penned by Gordon himself, it leveled "serious charges of bigoted discrimination" against the Haskell authorities and Superintendent Wise. The article listed the issues Gordon had complained of for months, stating that although Sells had intervened conditions had barely improved. Gordon gave accounts that must have infuriated Catholic readers. Four Catholic girls had taken Holy Communion one morning, went to the dining room, and were "told their breakfast was in the slop barrel." Another employee had "cast aspersions in a public manner of the Catholic doctrine of Confession." Superintendent Wise had insisted that Catholic gatherings be exclusively religious in character, making it impossible for the church to hold socials for all pupils at the school. Like the *Catholic Register*, the *Indian Sentinel* commented on the "wretched religious conditions" at Haskell, simultaneously praising Gordon's "zealous efforts to secure the rights of conscience for his protégées."[39] Spurred to action by these reports, Lawrence's Federation of Catholic Societies insisted upon a government investigation.[40]

A government team made up of E. B. Linnen, chief inspector of the Bureau of Indian Affairs, and Rev. S. A. Eliot, President Wilson's "personal representative," arrived at Haskell in the third week of February.[41] The two men went about determining whether the two hundred Catholic students enrolled faced prejudice and whether the YMCA Protestants were governing the school's religious life and improperly using government property for their own ends.[42] On February 18, the investigation concluded. The two-man committee entirely vindicated Gordon. The *Catholic Register* announced triumphantly that "practically every charge put forth . . . had been deemed true," save a few still under consideration by Secretary Lane. In desperation, the YMCA had done its best to protect their reputation, sending a special officer from New York to observe. The beleaguered representative, boasted the *Catholic Register*, was forced to watch powerlessly while his organization went down in "ignominious defeat." The *Register* also took delight in the YMCA secretary's removal from school housing, noting that it was "the shortest cut out of a ticklish position." Mr. Birch and Miss Stilwell met a worse fate, being "dropped outright." As a result of the scandal, the government ordered Haskell to make sweeping personnel changes over the subsequent months and institute a set of regulations ensuring that Catholic students would not face discrimination. The new regulations later became standard in all government Indian schools.

The Haskell investigation was an overwhelming victory for Gordon. Catholic students could now attend mass in a well-lighted and heated building; those children wishing to take communion would be provided breakfast after the service; Catholic pupils were as a rule barred from membership in the YMCA unless their parents requested such; the YMCA was denied the right to have a room set aside for their activities; Haskell's public book rack would feature non-denominational literature; neither Catholic nor Protestant Bibles would be placed in recreation rooms; Gordon was to be informed immediately if any Catholic student took ill; and Catholic rituals such as confession, communion, and mass were to be respected.[43] The government investigation had another lingering effect. Superintendent Wise found himself replaced less than a year later.[44]

From a secular perspective, it is tempting to view the scandal at Haskell as a denominational war motivated by Gordon's own sectarianism. But more pertinently, one must note how he seemed entirely oblivious to the wrongs embedded in the school's mission of separating children from their parents, extended families, cultures, and peoples. Indeed, Gordon appeared so out of touch with the pain and injustice surrounding him that he did not see the coming rebellion. Not long after his departure, in 1919, Haskell's pupils staged an insurrection at an assembly. After cutting the school's electricity supply, the students rioted, one threatening to lynch the superintendent. They destroyed much school property until order was restored. In the aftermath, four boys and five girls were expelled for their roles in the rebellion. The desperate actions of the students speak volumes about Haskell's atmosphere and the overwhelming frustrations that came with boarding-school life. Had he been there, would Gordon have been shocked by the riot? And as an Indian dedicated to assimilation, would he have sided with the students or the administration? Likely the latter, one fears.

How, one might ask, was Gordon so blind to wrongs and dangers that boarding schools like Haskell entailed? Because so many of the children were Ojibwe, he must have known that their parents preferred day schools, and that those children at Haskell had been sent there reluctantly. He must have known that in boarding-school history books Native peoples, the Ojibwe among them, were depicted as roaming savages who attacked whites with unparalleled brutality. He must have known that traditional Ojibwe ways—the cultural traditions of his mother—were being denigrated.[45] And finally, he must have known how personal Ojibwe names were to their holders—that they had secret and spiritual meanings, which gave direction in life.[46] Schools like Haskell disregarded these names, replacing them with meaningless monikers like Charles Dickens.[47] Did any of this matter to Gordon? Why did he approve of Haskell at all? Perhaps historical circumstances offer some insight.

The boarding-school experience had begun for the Ojibwe just after their land base and lifeways had been destroyed by the Dawes Act.

Remaining lands had been given over to whites, creating a new wave of financial hardship. Diseases such as tuberculosis had meanwhile ravaged the Ojibwe reservations, leaving many widows and orphans in their wake. Though tribal bonds and extended families mitigated some of this horror by providing homes for parentless children, economic realities often forced caregivers to send the young away. To some, boarding schools—with all their faults—appeared a haven from poverty and sickness. Perhaps for this reason Gordon could have justified Haskell's mission. Given conditions at home, the school perhaps seemed a service done to his people. Still, he must have seen the Haskell cemetery, where one hundred Indian students from thirty-seven tribes lay, some as young as six and seven. They lay there dead from neglect, representing an unnecessary sacrifice in the name of Christian civilization.[48] Why not reflect on this cold fact? Why not confront Wise about the matter of student mortality? Several of Gordon's contemporaries in the Society of American Indians, such as Gertrude Bonnin, the Wisconsin Oneida activist Laura Cornelius Kellogg, and Henry Roe Cloud, wrote critically of Indian assimilation through white education. Together, they questioned the boarding-school model's basis, efficacy, humanity, and goals, pointing out the detrimental effects and sometimes deadly consequences born of separation from parents and birth cultures.[49] Why not Gordon?

Still, in his own way Gordon cared—if narrowly—for the well-being of his Catholic wards. A letter to Sister Mary Macaria in Odanah from February 1916 makes evident how he knew each student, and how his concern continued even after they had left his supervision:

I wanted to see whether you could talk to Frank Holmes, an Odanah boy who left Haskell last week to visit a sick mother. I wish Frank would stay home for the sake of his Catholic faith. Now that he is home, I thought that if someone could see him and talk to him, telling him the risks he runs while at Haskell in the matter of losing his Faith, perhaps Frank will decide not to come back. The YMCA people have been after Frank for the reason that he sings well and is generally popular. Those are the kind that the YMCA singles out to work upon. During Frank's short stay with us, the YMCA took him on a Gospel Team trip to a neighboring town.

While the boys were away, they were entertained by Protestant preachers, etc. Naturally, this makes them feel kindly toward the people. Eventually they become very luke-warm Catholics. I have been very active lately, making up a census of "fallen-away" Catholics at Haskell. To date, I have discovered over 20. Just think of it! 20 souls![50]

While Gordon's letter betrays the strict sectarianism that motivated his war against the YMCA and Superintendent Wise, it also reveals his caring, however precisely targeted. Defending the interests of Catholics and their right to worship was his duty as chaplain, and Haskell's Catholic students were, unquestionably, experiencing discrimination. To his credit, exposing these wrongs at Haskell so publicly had come with risks that Gordon willingly hazarded. Commissioner Sells had come to see him as a nuisance, and he had generated much ill-will within the Bureau of Indian Affairs.[51] Gordon, in turn, was eyeing this larger giant to slay.

CHAPTER 5

Carlos Montezuma, *War-Whoop*, and the Bureau

While embroiled in his scandal at Haskell, Philip Gordon did not neglect his affiliation with the Society of American Indians or his growing desire to see the Bureau of Indian Affairs unceremoniously liquidated. This stance against the bureau involved genuine perils. Disapproval had been heaped upon Gordon from officialdom, even before he had pestered Sells about the Catholic students at Haskell. In early November 1915, Gordon wrote Arthur C. Parker from Lawrence. He had received word from the Catholic Bureau secretary, Charles Lusk, concerning his growing reputation in Washington. Commissioner Sells, "very much agitated," had harshly criticized Gordon for nominating Thomas Sloan for SAI president and advocating bureau abolishment. This was, in Gordon's mind, close to an infringement on free speech. "Now," he told Parker, "I was under the impression that at our Conferences, our members were at perfect liberty to discuss all questions pertaining to Indian Affairs. . . . I believed we had a 'free discussion' and I did not think that anyone could ever take issue with us after the Conference was ended. Here comes Mr. Sells, ready to intimidate, so to speak, with frowns and wry faces." Gordon refused to apologize for his exercise of "absolute freedom of expression," but regretted that Sells would never support the Society unless it toed the line dictated by the BIA. Gordon's letter closed with a bit of hyperbole, "A word of enlightenment may clear my case up, otherwise I may commit suicide."[1]

Parker responded by offering support for Gordon's ideals. His advocacy of Thomas Sloan for SAI president was another matter. Though Gordon had a "perfect right" to nominate Sloan, the Society would have been in "sore straights" had he been elected. Sloan was better as the attorney, and it was unwise to have a lawyer as executive officer. Why was unclear. Parker went on to say that, while the Indian Bureau disliked interference, there might soon be "a considerable shake up for all concerned." At the recent Friends of the Indian conference at Lake Mohonk, Parker and other delegates had insisted upon better organization and efficiency within the BIA. As for its abolishment, such a radical step first meant abolishing the "moral, social, educational and economic causes that the people of the country deem sufficient for requiring the Bureau." The SAI nonetheless had no duty to support the bureau or agree with Sells—quite the opposite. "If you agitated Mr. Sells," Parker confided, "you should congratulate yourself for if he has the good of the Indian at heart your criticism will make him more determined to demonstrate his integrity and to make straight the paths that have been shown up as crooked." Parker closed encouraging Gordon to think more on the matter and formulate arguments "to strike with added effectiveness" when the "psychological time comes."[2]

Parker's letter soothed Gordon, even if he remained confused regarding the Society's attitude toward Sloan. He remarked to Parker that Sloan garnered "scant notice" in both newspapers and the SAI *Quarterly Journal*. "Is this because he is persona non grata with Mr. Sells?" Gordon inquired. The situation was much the same with Montezuma. After Lawrence, the Haskell *Indian Leader* had made no mention of his stirring speech, "Let My People Go," which was delivered in the school's auditorium. This omission was shameful, because to Gordon it was "a matter of truth or no truth."[3] No response from Parker seems to have survived.

Acting on his principles, Gordon had already taken the "matter of truth" into his own hands. In January 1916, his new Indian-rights newsletter debuted, dubbed *War-Whoop*. The four-leaf magazine, "devoted to securing a decent management of Indian Affairs," sought to ensure integrity and humanity in government policy. In an editorial, Gordon explained that *War-Whoop* would strive to be "the expression in the United States of a new movement among Indians themselves," aimed directly at the bureau. He similarly condemned the "bungling" and "dishonesty" of the

BIA, stating that *War-Whoop* would provide reliable information on Indian issues and "sound a new battle-cry for the awakened Indian."[4]

This "battle-cry" was emitted not long after at the Kansas City Council Club House, where, on February 15, 1916, Gordon and his invited guest, Dr. Carlos Montezuma, held a public lecture on bureau abolition. The publicity flyer advertised Gordon as a "full-blooded Chippewa" and Montezuma as a "full-blooded Apache," while kindly noting that ladies were most welcome to attend. Montezuma's speech, "Let My People Go," was billed as the main attraction.[5] The Gordon-Montezuma venture was written up, like Gordon's besting of Wise and the YMCA, in Kansas City's *Catholic Register*. "Apache Condemns Federal Indian Bureau" recorded that Gordon gave a short talk on the situation developing at Haskell, declaring that any wrongs would soon be righted. He then left for Lawrence because the investigation he had spurred was ongoing. The *Register* described him as "a man of charming personality, highly educated," with "a natural humor which makes his remarks entertaining as well as interesting and instructive." With Gordon gone, Montezuma was left to dominate the proceedings. Forcefully detailing the "Indian's perspective," he described the reservation as "a hothouse, the wrong 'melting pot,' a demoralizing prison of idleness, beggary, gambling, pauperism and ruin, where the Indians remain as Indians, a barrier against enlightenment and knowledge." The *Register* agreed that "keeping the Indians on the reservation as wards of the government is manifestly unfair to the red man," asking that Indians "be given their freedom and be permitted to work out their own salvation." The large audience in attendance heartily applauded Montezuma's address.[6]

The timing of Montezuma's trip to Kansas was fortuitous. Just after the appearance of *War-Whoop*, the Catholic Bureau pressured Gordon to discontinue the magazine.[7] Gordon, employing his usual passion, was able to convince Montezuma to take over as editor. *War-Whoop*'s subsequent and final issue, February 1916, announced the news with a cryptic explanation: "The change in management of the *War-Whoop* is entirely due (in the well-known words of Mr. Micawber) 'to circumstances over which the Editor had no control.' Let it be known that it was not due to a diminution of interest on the part of the Editor." But Gordon, no

surprise, went down fighting. In a final gesture of contempt, he charged
that Superintendent Wise came "close to fulfilling par excellence the defi-
nition of the bigot," whose dealings contained "a little bit of the 'cheap
white trash' element." "It hurts your Editor," Gordon continued, "to think
that Indians are guided by such creatures—misguided would be better."
Even more unbearable was the fact that Wise made $2,000 a year plus
"grocery bills paid."

The sudden termination of *War-Whoop* was in some ways unexpected,
for it had already attracted sympathetic donors. Gordon hoped that none
would object to Montezuma's new stewardship.[8] The doctor wasted no
time in continuing the project, renaming it *Wassaja, or Freedom's Signal
to the Indians*. In a letter to Pratt, Montezuma vowed to "down the Indian
Bureau" and only "cease when that is accomplished." The maiden issue
of *Wassaja* debuted in April 1916.[9] Like Pratt, Parker also heard of the
burgeoning Gordon-Montezuma partnership. Speaking prematurely, he
deemed *War-Whoop* a worthy publication that would become "an organ
of genuine influence for the uplift of our people." Parker likewise offered
his benediction to the Montezuma-Gordon lecture in Kansas City and
the continuing partnership, predicting their "joint venture will excite a
large amount of attention."[10] He was quite correct.

In the fall of 1916, the Society of American Indians held their annual
conference in Cedar Rapids, Iowa, September 26 to 30, sponsored in part
by the Quaker Oats Company.[11] Turnout was poor, as was the Society's
financial standing.[12] Two key members, Thomas Sloan and Charles Eastman, did not attend. SAI president Sherman Coolidge gave the opening
address, grimly stating, "As a race we are in a state of chaos." Still, he
trusted that the Society would serve as a "union of strength and harmony"
amidst such troubling circumstances.[13] The conference platform, while
making the usual references to improving conditions on reservations and
Indian legal status, for the first time called for an eventual dismantling of
the Indian Bureau. The BIA, explained the program, had been originally
intended to perform a "temporary function." Considering the progress in
Indian education, the time had come for Native peoples to "be invested
with the full privileges of citizens without burdensome restrictions." This
process could be facilitated by making segregated Indian schools "stepping

stones" to white schools, "where contact with other American youth makes for patriotic, competent citizenship." Another major addition to the SAI platform was a strong condemnation of peyote. Discounting any potential religious significance of its ingestion, the Society equated the mushroom with alcohol, urging "habits of total abstinence."[14]

This concern surrounding the Peyote Religion had been festering underneath the veneer of the SAI for some time, though peyote itself had a much longer history. The Spanish had recorded peyote use hundreds of years ago among the Chichmeca in present-day Mexico. Peyote use then moved north in the seventeenth and eighteenth centuries, being adopted by the Coahuitec, Hopi, and Taos, who employed the cactus to alleviate illnesses and bring on visions. The Peyote Religion, or Peyotism, developed near the end of the nineteenth century among the Comanche, Kiowa, and Wichita Plains Indians. Their use of peyote as a sacrament was in part a response to the dislocations that had come with white invasion.[15] Peyote featured in organized rituals that mixed Christian elements with Native beliefs as a peaceful panacea for white colonialism.[16] In this manner, Peyotism fostered solidarity among Native peoples regardless of tribal affiliation.[17] Graduates of Carlisle and Haskell were often the most visible promoters of the new religion—a fact that irritated many in the SAI. Parker, for instance, saw Peyotism as a threat to Native peoples. Ever cautious, he avoided the issue for fear of dividing the Society. Others, such as Sloan, supported the right of peyote ingestion.[18] Though Gordon supported Sloan for SAI president, he was against peyote and, of course, in favor of teetotaling.[19]

The antipeyote forces in Cedar Rapids were led by two persons with no sympathy for the religious movement: Gertrude Bonnin and Richard Henry Pratt. Both vocally supported the Gandy Bill (drawn up by South Dakota representative H. L. Gandy), which sought a nationwide ban on peyote possession and trade. Pratt admitted to knowing little about peyote, but gave a speech condemning it anyway. He capped his remarks with a striking, hortatory call for autocracy. "It takes too much talk, too much legislation to do things," he remonstrated. "We ought to have a czar who would say and do the thing that put an end to vodka in Russia; quit it right now. There should be more of that sort of government."[20] In contrast,

Bonnin had legitimate experience with peyote, having witnessed its spread on the Uintah Reservation. Feeling that peyote use encouraged sexual licentiousness, family breakup, and societal degeneration, she had lectured extensively to women's temperance groups throughout the Midwest while distributing a pamphlet branding peyote a "menace." With S. M. Brosius of the Indian Rights Association, she had also prepared antipeyote testimony for the IRA's 1916 *Annual Report*.[21] Only one voice stood up for the Peyote Religion at Cedar Rapids. Carlisle graduate Delos Lone Wolf, a Kiowa peyote leader from Oklahoma, stressed the connections between the movement and Christianity. A user of the cactus for the past fifteen years, Lone Wolf claimed that with the aid of peyote he had converted "the hardest cases that the missionary or anyone else could not reach."[22] Despite Lone Wolf's plea, most of the SAI membership remained unmoved. At the conference's end they passed a resolution in support of a federal ban.[23] The *American Indian Magazine* later prevailed upon Congress to pass the Gandy Bill to counter peyote's "baneful effects upon the users in mind and morals."[24] Despite these evidently strong, united sentiments, much would change regarding the SAI and peyote over the next few years.

True to Parker's prophecy, the Gordon-Montezuma partnership excited a great deal of attention at Cedar Rapids. The Ojibwe Nation, too, took center stage. Gordon introduced two representatives. The first, Ira Isham, an interpreter from the Lac Court Oreilles Reservation, reported that the Ojibwe had, in effect, lost their rights to hunt and fish on land ceded to the U.S. government under the treaty of 1854. Indians had been arrested while searching for game, though they correctly believed they had the right. Isham appealed to the SAI for help, describing the conditions on the reservation as experienced by a male family head: "He has now got nothing; practically everything has now gone from him and taken away from him, and he goes back. He has a family of grandchildren and children he has got to look after. He cannot go and get his grub the same as he used to, but he depends on this wild game that he thinks belongs to him, but the game warden takes the opportunity to come and stop him."[25] Isham's account was entirely true. Wisconsin officials had been harassing and arresting Ojibwe hunters since the turn of the century, just as courts had denied their claims to treaty rights.[26] In one case, a game warden had even murdered an Ojibwe chief, Cut-ear, who was hunting entirely within his rights. The warden was later found innocent by an all-white jury.[27] Unfortunately, all this was but a prelude. Ojibwe hunting, fishing, and gathering rights would be systematically denied for most of the twentieth century.[28]

These were not the only hardships existing at Lac Court Oreilles. Another representative invited by Gordon, Prosper Guibord, revealed how the Ojibwe had been cheated out of 75 percent of the lumber proceeds from logging on their lands. Commissioner Sells had been informed two years prior, but his promises to send inspectors had never materialized. Guibord also spoke of being denied his rightful allotment for over a decade and the widespread dissatisfaction with Lac Court Oreilles's corrupt Indian agent, who appropriated funds on the pretext that the Ojibwe "could not handle" their own finances and "would buy whisky with the money."[29] Such issues required direct and concentrated attention from the SAI. Unfortunately, seeking the solutions they demanded was quickly sidelined by infighting.

Later on in the conference, Montezuma provoked a divisive debate by declaring that "Indian employees in the service of the Indian Bureau could not be loyal to the Indian race and to their real interests." Sherman Coolidge, incensed, remarked, "I do not know how many times I must get up and say that I believe an Indian who is a government employee can be loyal to his race and at the same time be loyal to his government." Montezuma tried to clarify, "The Indian Bureau, not the Government." Coolidge shot back, "The Government is represented by the Indian Bureau." Montezuma, in turn, objected to being put in the "very embarrassing position" of seeming to condemn the entire government, while he was merely opposed to bureau "system." After some more heated back and forth, Gordon stood up and made perhaps the most controversial comments of the gathering. Quite outrageously, he insisted that Indian Service employees could not be considered loyal to the SAI. "I disagree some with President Coolidge who says a member in the employment of the Government is at the same time loyal to this Society," Gordon announced, "I do not want to cast any personal reflections but speaking generally I do not believe that is possible." Coolidge countered him, but Gordon stood his ground, stating that it was simply "not possible for an Indian in the employ of the Government to take a step so he can get rid of the Indian Bureau."

Gordon's heavy-handedness incurred further disapproval. Marie Baldwin, a BIA accountant, felt offended and joined the debate. Identifying herself as "one of those Government clerks that my brothers have been speaking of today," Baldwin explained that despite working for the government, she felt no restrictions in saying that many BIA employees would like to see the bureau abolished. For the moment, though, this was too hasty a measure. There were, in her estimation, still numerous Indians "who are not ready now to be put out in the world to take care of themselves." A gradual approach was needed, and with diligence all could work to the end that "some day there will be no need of an Indian Bureau." Gertrude Bonnin, whose husband was a BAI clerk at Uintah, also made herself heard. Angered at the idea that any person be branded disloyal for laboring on reservations, she pointed out that many educated Indians gave up remunerative work to aid their countrymen "from a sense of duty and by all ties of the heart." For such dedicated people, this calling meant living "in the wilderness" while attending to the "human beings there that need their sympathy, and their kindness, just the kind of help that money could never buy." Coolidge terminated the discussion, asking, "Is it right for us to act this way?" Everyone, after all, wanted to "do right in all these things," but no one had the right to cast aspersions of disloyalty upon Native peoples or the SAI.[30]

As it turned out, Gordon's remarks in the debate formed a prologue to his coming speech, "Opposition to the Indian Bureau." Taking the floor, he told those assembled that the time had come for "very definite" action regarding the BIA. Gordon recalled that at the previous conference he had said "several nasty things about the Indian Bureau," and had been "severely called to task" as a result. Then in what appears to be an attempt at humor, he stated that "whatever I say against the Bureau is not directed particularly at any individual unless he happens to be a member of the Indian Bureau and in that case it is not my fault." The contradictory comment may have been intended to cause either controversy or a laugh, but

Gordon's ultimate message was clear. The bureau "system" kept Indians in "bondage." It had to go:

> I say the Society ought to take some definite move. It ought to go on record as opposed to the system, as opposed to the idea of keeping us Indians, in making us to prolong our Indian life when if it were to remove all bounds some may fall by the way-side, when I say so I do not mean every Indian must be thrown out in the highway and run over with automobiles. When we look around and see poorhouses full of whites—I do not mean we have to break the constitution of the United States but I mean place us under those laws which every pure-blooded citizen enjoys and which we do not enjoy and let us go about and be white men legally speaking. I think if they will give us this favor we will hold our own. I think if they let us come and mingle with the whites we will become just as good as any white men.[31]

Gordon's argument expressed certainty that Indians—despite the disadvantages and privations thrust upon them—were inherently competent and capable. The BIA machinery, not its wards, was responsible for the destitution present on the reservations. With the rights of white men, most Indians would flourish.

Not to be outdone, Montezuma concluded the conference by leveling a series of criticisms against the Society he had helped found. Claiming that he had not come to Cedar Rapids to fight, he insisted on only the best for the Society. But when faced with the real need to do something "radical," the Society consistently faltered. "We cannot work side by side with the Indian Bureau and do any good for the Indians," Montezuma insisted. The only legitimate position was BIA abolition. The SAI had to "get into the right road" and do what was truly beneficial for Indians. Only then could it claim success.[32]

At the conference's end, Gordon and Montezuma were branded the "radicals." There were also some shakeups in the Society's leadership. Parker, though a young man in his thirties, was elected SAI president; Bonnin took his place as secretary; Baldwin stayed on as treasurer. Gordon, despite all his rancor, was elected chairman of the advisory board—in truth an unimportant role.[33] Montezuma, for his part, left Cedar Rapids disgusted, quitting the SAI soon after. Only Bonnin, his former fiancé, could persuade him to rejoin. In a pleading letter she implored the doctor to "be kind" and understand that despite disagreements the SAI was "true to our race" and had not "sold out to the Bureau."[34] Placated, Montezuma renewed his commitment to the Society.[35] Though Gordon may have departed Cedar Rapids similarly frustrated, he had no intention of abandoning the SAI. Just two months later he wrote to Parker, asking how he could help prepare for next year's conference. "I'm a bit hazy just what I am supposed to do," Gordon admitted, but he was already looking forward to the next fight.[36]

Philip Gordon pictured in military uniform while attending St. Thomas College. Courtesy of the Wisconsin Historical Society, Image WHi-140672.

A photo of young Gordon featured in the 1912 *Indian Sentinel*. Courtesy of Marquette University Special Collections and Archives, Image BCIM10852.

Philip Gordon's first mass at St. Mary's Church in Odanah, January 6, 1914. Gordon, in his new clerical collar, sits in the center row with his left shoulder leaning against the makeshift curtain. Bishop Joseph Koudelka, wearing a crucifix around his neck, sits next to Gordon toward the center. Odoric Derenthal, the bearded man in dark robes, sits inside the curtain one over left of Koudelka. St. Mary's Father Optatus Loeffler, the bald man with a dark beard, is seated in the first row, far left. A confidant of Gordon's, Chrysostom Verwyst, is the small white-haired gentleman seated one over right from Loeffler in the front row. Courtesy of Marquette University Special Collections and Archives, Image BCIM11375.

The Right Reverend
William H. Ketcham in
an undated portrait.
Courtesy of Marquette
University Special
Collections and Archives,
Image BCIM00084.

Arthur Caswell Parker in
portrait. The photograph
appeared in the 1919 pamphlet
American Indian Freemasonry.

Odoric Derenthal pictured with family at daughter's first communion, ca. 1920s. The child on his lap evidently refused to sit still for the photograph. Courtesy of Marquette University Special Collections and Archives, Image BCIM11046.

Gordon addressing those present at the 1923 Catholic Sioux Congress, held in Kenel, South Dakota, Standing Rock Reservation. Courtesy of Marquette University Special Collections and Archives, Image BCIM00483.

Attendees of the Society of American Indians conference in Cedar Rapids, Iowa, September 29, 1916. Gertrude Bonnin appears in the front row holding a large hat. Marie Baldwin is on her right. Gordon is directly behind Bonnin on the step. Episcopal priest Sherman Coolidge, wearing his white collar, stands third from the left in the same row as Gordon. Richard Henry Pratt stands at the far right. Henry Roe Cloud is the dapper man in the first row on the far left. Carlos Montezuma's head is just visible near the top of the stairs, above and to the right of Gordon, just below an unidentified woman wearing a hat. This image was featured in the *American Indian Magazine*.

An undated photograph of Bishop Koudelka in the middle of a large group of Ojibwe wearing traditional dress. Courtesy of Marquette University Special Collections and Archives, Image SHFR11533.

Gordon and Carlos Montezuma photographed in 1919 during their speaking tour of the Ojibwe reservations with Charles Eastman. Courtesy of Marquette University Special Collections and Archives, Image BCIM01238.

Gertrude Bonnin at the
Catholic Sioux Congress,
Standing Rock Reservation,
1922. Courtesy of Marquette
University Special
Collections and Archives,
Image BCIM00684.

Gordon in middle age.
Courtesy of Wisconsin
Historical Society, Image
WHi-140673.

Gordon photographed in 1935 with two sisters at St. Joseph's Mission in La Pointe, Wisconsin. Courtesy of Marquette University Special Collections and Archives, Image BCIM00883.

CHAPTER 6

War in Europe, Battles at Home

When on January 8, 1915, Philip Gordon wrote Arthur C. Parker to criticize him for ostensibly driving William Ketcham out of the Society of American Indians, he referenced, quite morbidly, the raging war in Europe that had begun months earlier in June 1914. Gordon insisted that Parker's censure of the Board of Indian Commissioners, on which Ketcham held a seat, had put Ketcham in a position similar to a German officer "serving the French at the front" because of his simultaneous support for the SAI.[1] At the time Gordon wrote his letter, Americans could look upon the conflict from afar, almost hypothetically, fairly certain that their nation would remain aloof. This was not the case. Instead, eventual U.S. involvement in World War I would reverberate throughout society, exposing divisions, causing discord, and provoking politically motivated persecution and even murder. The SAI and its Progressive membership played a part in these events; and Gordon, witness to all, came to see some among his friends and colleagues denounced as pro-German agents while the country and presidency of Woodrow Wilson devolved into rampant jingoism.

In 1914, U.S. intervention in Europe seemed unthinkable. Reacting to isolationist sentiment, President Wilson advocated neutrality, running for reelection in 1916 on the slogan: "He kept us out of war." This policy sharply reversed once Wilson won his second term. His inaugural speech deemed the conflict in Europe vital to American interests. "Our own fortunes as a nation are involved," Wilson asserted, "whether we would have it so or not." Kaiser Wilhelm II paid little heed. In February of 1917,

Germany expanded its use of submarine warfare in an attempt to end a blockade of their ports and the war itself, destroying several American vessels. The same month, tensions increased when the British intercepted and decoded the Zimmerman Telegram, in which Germany pledged financial support to Mexico if they declared war on the United States. On April 7, 1917, the United States Congress declared war on Germany. Much of the American electorate remained unconvinced.[2] (Gordon's immediate views on the declaration could not be unearthed.) In the six weeks that followed declaration of war, only a small fraction of the million men needed volunteered.[3] The Selective Service Act of 1917, passed in May, instituting the first military draft since the Civil War.[4]

Wilson countered domestic opposition by forming the Committee on Public Information (CPI), a propaganda organ that promoted the war as a necessary struggle to democratize Europe. Pro-war posters, pamphlets, and patriotic rallies with calls to be "100% American" became ubiquitous, and many Americans responded with violent enthusiasm.[5] Vigilantes attacked pacifists, labor organizers, and left-wing groups, and persecuted German Americans. One man of German descent, Robert Prager, was lynched by an Illinois mob in April 1918 under suspicion of holding socialist beliefs. Police stood by and observed; a jury promptly acquitted the murderers. After the reading of the verdict one member reportedly shouted, "Well, I guess nobody can say we aren't loyal now."[6] The *Washington Post* referred to the incident as "a healthful and wholesome awakening in the interior of the country."[7] This kind of anti-German persecution would also occur in Wisconsin, affecting Gordon on a personal level.

As the Wilson administration encouraged such hysteria, Congress put in place measures to restrict free speech and limit constitutional freedoms. The Espionage Act, passed June 15, 1917, imposed prison sentences for antiwar activities; the Sedition Act, passed May 6, 1918, outlawed any "disloyal, profane, scurrilous, or abusive language" that took aim at American institutions and symbols.[8] A volunteer organization, the American Protective League (APL), aided in policing the citizenry by conducting illegal searches and raids and spying on anyone deemed unpatriotic.[9] Loosely affiliated with the Ku Klux Klan, the APL numbered a quarter of a million

members. They reported their findings directly to the Bureau of Investigation (BOI), the precursor of the Federal Bureau of Investigation.[10]

Though seemingly counterintuitive, many if not most of those involved
in the Progressive movement ultimately supported American militarization
and the successive intervention in Europe.[11] Walter Lippmann, Committee on Public Information coarchitect and founding editor of the flagship
Progressive publication, *New Republic*, argued (in self-delusion or good
faith) that the war was an opportunity to purify American democracy
through collective effort. The endeavor, he hoped, would bring the nation
to a higher level of civilization. Many labor leaders and socialists advocated
this quixotic stance, thinking, as Lippmann, that the war would result in
government regulation, nationalization of private enterprise, beneficial
legislation, and the stamping out of lingering societal ills through reform.
Such Progressives eventually suffered disillusionment at Wilson's conducting of the war and its essentially nonexistent benefits for Americans.[12]
But much like their white Progressive brethren, the SAI looked upon the
war as a chance for the meaningful amelioration of the Indian's status on
a national scale. Their disillusionment, too, would be bitter, as would
Gordon's.

Within the SAI, the war, conscription, and the question of Indian participation immediately became contentious issues. Although half of the
Indian population were noncitizens, Commissioner Sells was eager to set
up draft boards on reservations throughout the country. Putting aside
their long history of oppression, Native Americans volunteered in droves—
the result of warrior traditions, patriotism, and the economic incentives
that came with military service. Those Indians who attended boarding
schools signed up in great numbers. This was little surprise considering
that Pratt's original model had been much like a military academy, replete
with marches, drills, and the constant promotion of American patriotism. Ultimately, 25 percent of male Indians over eighteen served in the
war, compared to just 15 percent of the white, male population.[13] How
these Native men were to serve was a pertinent question. Initially, Sells,
taking his cue from the Board of Indian Commissioners, proposed that
Indians fight in segregated units.[14] The idea caused an uproar in the SAI.

In an editorial for the *American Indian Magazine*, Parker argued for integration and dismissed segregated units as "walking reservations."[15] Gertrude Bonnin agreed, outraged at the possibility that Indian units would suffer casualties en masse if forced into battle. In a letter to Parker she condemned the "walking reservation" as a "scheme to utterly annihilate the Red Man, by a whole-sale slaughter!"[16] Gordon and Montezuma disagreed, confounding Parker and Bonnin greatly.[17]

When the War Department decided against segregated Indian units, the Society—publicly and unquestioningly—threw its meagre weight behind the war effort. Parker, sensing an opportunity, ordered Bonnin to promote war service in AIM. In retrospect, this was a shameful if understandable position. Both Parker and Bonnin (whose husband volunteered) felt that Indian service could boost chances for the granting of citizenship after the war. They had some cause. In the summer of 1917, Arizona representative Carl Hayden put a bill before Congress with just this aim. It failed to pass. A bill proposed in January 1918 by Oklahoma representative (and Chickasaw SAI member) Charles D. Carter met the same fate.[18] Such opportunism and blood-for-citizenship logic, however, had in mind an achievable and important goal of the Society: the protections of U.S. citizenship and the rights that came with it for all Native peoples. While today one may question whether an act imposing citizenship on what should have been considered sovereign Indian nations was the correct course, the SAI's logic was sound given the limiting historical circumstances that prevailed. Yet just as hope appeared that a step toward Indian citizenship could be made, the Society began to fall prey to the contentious issues of bureau abolition and peyote, personal animosities, and a failure of leadership on the part of Parker.

The annual SAI conference had been planned for July in Oklahoma City on the theme "The American Indian in Patriotism, Production, Progress." Gordon had suggested Minneapolis; Parker vetoed the idea on the pretext that the location precluded many Indians from attending due to geographical distance. In truth, Parker might have feared that a meeting in Gordon's Ojibwe stronghold would tip the Society toward voting for BIA abolition. Gordon had recently been active in that region.[19] In December 1916, he had left Haskell for a tour of Catholic missions throughout Oklahoma and Minnesota, finally ending up in Reserve, Wisconsin, on the Lac Court Oreilles Reservation.[20] During this period, his quest to abolish the bureau continued unabated. Gordon and Montezuma were planning a new pamphlet directed "against the cruel system that holds us in bondage," and enlisting Richard Henry Pratt in the fight. Pratt suggested the title, "The cruel bondage of the Indian to a miserable system."[21] Gordon responded favorably but warned Pratt to "beware" of the SAI. Though the Society was "apparently well-meaning," Parker and the rank and file were "too close to the Indian Bureau" to ensure any radical changes for the better. Gordon stopped short of condemning the SAI but remained "suspicious." Pratt's "method of handling the Indian problem"—bureau abolishment—remained "the only workable one." The SAI refused to do anything save "smilingly nod their heads and say: 'Yes, General, it's a fine day!'"[22]

Gordon, however, had slightly misjudged President Parker's stance. The Seneca archeologist had been moving toward BIA abolition for some time. Reluctance to declare so openly sprung from a fear of offending people in high places. In March 1917, Parker wrote Gordon expressing his private views. He confided the hope that the BIA would "stagger into a stall and expire." Meanwhile, there needed to be guarantees for the many Indians who still required government support. "I want the government to carry out its promises to my people," Parker explained, "and I want them secured in their freedom as well as in their possessions. I want them to live with their hearts joyous with hope and not crushed with despair." This outcome would not be possible without the protection the bureau offered. Parker continued:

> I do not want them to have their land and resources stolen because of their failure to understand "modern business ethics." I rather honor them for not becoming commercial hearted. But without some form of protection and property restriction their lands are going to go. The pauper Indian has no friends. The drifting tramp Indian is no better than any other tramp, except in ancestry. I, therefore, shrink from the thought of having the weak and poor, the ignorant and old thrust weaponless into a commercial sea filled with long fanged sharks. "They will learn to fight?"

No they won't, not that way. They must enter the fight with a blade in hand, which if not as sharp will acquire an edge soon enough. The favored and capable such as you and perhaps me, need no protection and no special mercy. We can get along with this "Civilization," defective as it is.

Thus, it was imperative to guarantee both freedom and "freedom from pillage." The statement was Parker's assurance to Gordon that he was not a blind BIA supporter.[23]

Still, if Parker had intended to avoid public embarrassment and weaken Gordon's influence by holding the conference in Oklahoma, he had shot himself in the proverbial foot. He realized too late that Oklahoma was a more dangerous spot, the territory of peyote defender Thomas Sloan. Faced with losing control of the SAI, Parker chose to cancel the conference entirely, disingenuously citing the war emergency.[24] In her capacity as secretary, Gertrude Bonnin informed the membership that because so many SAI members were busy serving their nation in the war effort, Oklahoma had been, euphemistically, "postponed."[25]

Along with these contentious ideological conflicts, personal conflicts within the SAI were also worsening. Gordon found himself (predictably) in the middle. Though he was happy to learn of Parker's aversion to the bureau, there were still more criticisms to make. Gordon began to hector Parker about once again reaching out to Father Ketcham to reobtain his membership. The Society simply needed "the Wisdom and Zeal of such a staunch friend of the Indian." In support of his argument, Gordon pointed out that there were one hundred thousand Catholic Indians in the United States. The SAI could not claim to be representative without their membership.[26] Gertrude Bonnin had her own view on the matter. She had recently relocated to Washington, DC, where she was fulfilling her duties as secretary with remarkable dedication. Parker predicted to Gordon that Bonnin's new role would produce "a livelier administration," and he was quite correct.[27] Though she was close to Ketcham, Bonnin had come to suspect that the Bureau of Catholic Indians Missions was antagonistic to the SAI. When Gordon asked for the official Society mailing list in the run up to the 1917 conference, she refused to furnish it.[28] Parker later received a note from Bonnin claiming that Gordon had offered her no support or appreciation, and was "liable to do mischief."[29] Unmoved, Parker wrested the list from her arms.[30] More problems soon appeared when Bonnin came into conflict with Gordon's ally in bureau abolition, Treasurer Marie Baldwin. Bonnin saw Baldwin as blatantly shirking her duties and a bitter fight erupted between the two women. This incident would trigger Baldwin's exit from the Society.[31]

As if these internecine battles were not enough, Gordon's radical friend, Montezuma, expressed sheer indignation at the Oklahoma conference's cancellation. Under the firm suspicion that the BIA had influenced Parker to silence debate on Indian participation in the war, Montezuma spoke out publicly. In *War-Whoop*'s successor, *Wassaja*, he insisted that Indians meeting to discuss their welfare was of far greater importance than the war effort itself.[32] This cannon shot was the beginning of a larger rhetorical barrage meant to expose the hypocrisy of the U.S. government in asking Natives to serve. To grapple with the issue, Montezuma founded the League for the Extension of American Democracy to the American Indians, which Gordon supported in the pages of *Wassaja*. After labeling the BIA "the Kaiserism of America toward the Indians" and questioning whether Indians should obey the draft, Montezuma found himself the target of a BOI investigation. Only then did he recant.[33]

One assumes that Gordon held similar views to Montezuma's, or perhaps even more critical opinions on the war. Unfortunately, there is little record of Gordon's thoughts on these matters. It is known that nine months into the war, in January 1918, he volunteered to be a military chaplain, but never performed the duty.[34] This fact indicates he generally supported the war, or simply saw an opportunity to do some good. The accusation that he favored Indian regiments, meanwhile, was made by Gertrude Bonnin in a letter to Parker.[35] In another letter to Marie Baldwin, Gordon commented that Washington must be in "a hubbub about the war," and for "good reason."[36] No more substantial statement exists to quote. Regardless, Gordon loathed and condemned President Wilson and the wartime propaganda promulgated by his administration. The basis for this statement is a March 1917 letter Gordon received from a Catholic Kansas friend, George K. Earnst. Earnst, reacting to Gordon's own criticisms of Wilson, lambasted the president as a vile enemy of democracy:

I am sorry you have not the mental acumen and perspicacity to appreciate that most holy, transparently sincere, and righteously just man,
Woodrow Wilson, "behind whom everybody stands." What is the use
of having a constitutional Government when we have such a heaven-
crowned and anointed Czar? There must be one Czar in the world; on
with the espionage-bill! There is a German spy behind each lamp-post
and in every crook of the fence. The Germans do not speak English very
correctly so the professor wants them interned. If you are not a bellicist,
you are lacking patriotism. I am wearing the English flag you left here
to keep me from being interned in a concentration camp. What do I
think of Wilson! Don't you know it is a crime to think anything different
of Wilson than what he thinks of himself?[37]

Given the wartime atmosphere, Earnst would not have written such
things to one who disagreed. Gordon must have been disillusioned, and
knowing his personality, even more caustic in his assessment of the president, the wartime measures that limited freedom, and the national fashion
for xenophobia. His attitude to the soldiers overseas was much different.
In 1920, the *Wisconsin Magazine of History* did a profile on Gordon, describing him as "an ardent advocate of Americanization." The magazine
reported that Gordon was "proud of his boys [Ojibwe men] who served
in the European War, five of whom lost their lives on the battle field of
France." His plan was to collect their letters for the Wisconsin War History Commission and write an article on Ojibwe contributions to the
war effort.[38]

Had Gordon compiled the letters and written his article, there would
have been much to boast about. Ojibwe contributions were impressive, and
worth briefly noting here. Half of all Ojibwe men volunteered rather than
be taken by the draft. The small Bad River Reservation alone supplied sixty
of its men. Those too old to enlist often bought war bonds and contributed to the Red Cross, as did one Ojibwe woman who walked seventeen
miles to a Red Cross center in one day to donate a dollar. Upon laying
down her bill she declared, "I want to do something for my country."
Many other Ojibwe women helped by knitting socks and sewing hospital

clothing for injured soldiers. There were also multiple instances of extreme bravery by Ojibwe in Europe. One young man, Francis Lequier, took out a German machine-gun nest single-handedly despite being wounded seventeen times during his charge. At the war's end, Lac du Flambeau held a massive celebration attended by Wisconsin's governor, Emanuel L. Phillip. Celebrating Memorial Day subsequently became an annual event on the Ojibwe reservations, marked by picnics and parades.[39]

Though he was proud of Ojibwe involvement in the war effort, Gordon was likely disgusted by the events that took place in the summer of 1918 concerning the man who ordained him, Bishop Joseph M. Koudelka. Of Austrian extraction, Koudelka had come under suspicion of disloyalty among his fellow clergymen. Someone within the church had written the Department of Justice, suggesting that Koudelka be incarcerated. "In case he is an alien enemy," the letter read, "I am inclined to think he should be interned, unless he is removed from his present position." After enduring two rounds of interrogation by investigators, Koudelka was exonerated. The incident, the department concluded, "should be attributed to differences of opinion founded upon nationality rather than on a question of patriotism." Ignoring such tensions within the Diocese of Superior was the prudent course.[40] The results could have been worse. Despite much antiwar sentiment expressed by the state's dominant Progressive and Socialist parties, Wisconsin was no stranger to vigilantism. A majority of those in the state were of German background, and those who kept up their connections to Germany or even German culture and language often suffered harassment.[41] A German professor at Northland College in Ashland (where Gordon had attended) was kidnapped and tarred and feathered merely for continuing to teach his subject.[42] The Wisconsin chapter of the American Protective League investigated ten thousand persons deemed "enemy aliens" during the war years, reporting 2,400 alleged acts of sedition to the Department of Justice.[43] Wisconsin's Progressive senator Robert Lafollette, despite his antiwar stance, managed to survive politically.[44] Regardless, open disapproval from Gordon on war matters would have been unwise—even when critical thoughts crossed his mind. One can imagine how hard it was for him to keep his mouth shut. Gordon's penchant for reproach had by this time already incurred wrath—though not that of the U.S. government. He would soon be dismissed from the Catholic Bureau, and the fault was entirely his own.

In December 1916, Gordon began a mission trip throughout Oklahoma, Minnesota, and Nebraska, visiting the Choctaw, Ojibwe, and Winnebago, respectively.[45] The Catholic Bureau oversaw the work, so Gordon kept Ketcham apprised of his activities. His letters were informative and generally friendly, dealing mostly with church business. Yet slowly, just as with Odoric, Gordon's tendency to criticize wore on Ketcham. In one letter, Gordon remarked bitterly that discipline at Haskell was "simply rotten," and that many students had deserted the Church. He spoke of "cases of gross immorality," including bigotry against Catholics and broken promises made by Cato Sells. Ketcham was used to hearing such ridicule of others, but suddenly and without warning Gordon's comments veered in his direction. Gordon informed Ketcham that he had written Theophile Meerschaert, the bishop of Oklahoma City, to ask why in his state, which boasted one hundred thousand Indians, less than 1 percent were Catholic. Gordon felt the question pertinent. In other parts of the country, "20% to 95% of the Indian inhabitants" were Catholics, a fact that signaled a clear misallocation of resources. There were Ojibwe in Minnesota, for instance, who would be more receptive. If the Catholic Bureau "spent as much time, money and energy" on the "Pagans" in Minnesota as it did on the "poor scattered Choctaws," many more "souls would gain heaven." The point was not to "abandon" the Choctaws, but to concentrate more on the "neglected Chippewas."[46]

Quite predictably, Ketcham found Gordon's comments deeply offensive because the Oklahoma Choctaws had been the center of his energies for a long time.[47] Gordon's open criticism of anything he deemed improper and constant suggestions about his appropriate role in the Catholic Bureau grated equally. Blissfully unaware that he was provoking ire, Gordon refused to understand why Ketcham would not accept his proposals or share his concerns. While in visiting missions he could demonstrate that "an Indian can become a real, live priest," it was best for him to assess "the actual conditions and future prospects of Catholic Indians." This

meant changing long-established means of conversion. Gordon admitted
that he felt "a kind of right to know all about Indians and to speak for
them," and that the "feeling probably is not just according to Canon Law."
Nevertheless, he had to "speak out conscientiously" whenever and wherever
white priests and the church were "not treating poor, ignorant Indians
right."[48] Ketcham found such letters exasperating, but this was only part
of the story. Gordon's correspondence with others in the church soon became the real issue. Unfortunately, he had been maligning Ketcham behind
his back since the summer of 1916—and to Bishop Meerschaert no less.

Beginning in July, Gordon began complaining in person and in writing to Meerschaert, calling the Oklahoma Indian missions a failure due
to Ketcham's poor leadership. The reservations, he insisted, had been
staffed by indifferent and unworthy missionaries who plainly lacked
"zeal." When rumors of Gordon's criticism reached Ketcham his reaction
was understandable. News of Gordon's insubordination soon reached
higher circles, compelling the president of the Bureau of Catholic Indian
Missions, Cardinal James Gibbons, to take swift action.[49] In mid-April,
Gibbons decided against renewing Gordon's contract with the BCIM
for the "good of the cause."[50] The missionary's association with the Catholic Bureau was to end on June 1, 1917.[51] The date fell approximately one
month before the close of Gordon's two-year leave of absence from the
Diocese of Superior, granted by Koudelka in July 1915.[52]

Considering the circumstances, Ketcham's letter to Koudelka showed
great restraint. He thanked the bishop for allowing Gordon to do his
"special work," describing him as "a young man of vast energy" who "pos-
sesses much talent."[53] Perhaps the generous estimation meant to convince
Koudelka to take Gordon back. The *Indian Sentinel* similarly papered
over the incident, announcing that though he had "accomplished much
good," Gordon's tenure with the Catholic Bureau of Indian Missions
had ended. His "talents and boundless energy," however, "should make
his work in any portion of the Lord's Vineyard a success."[54]

For his part, Gordon hoped to stay on at the Catholic Bureau and tend
to Indians through various missions. When news of his imminent dismissal reached him, he lashed out furiously at Ketcham. "I thought,"

Gordon wrote, "that a line or two on my activities in your behalf might make my retirement less of an expulsion and at the same time dispossess you of any unjust ideas as to my intentions." Gordon claimed that he had been instrumental in securing Ketcham's degree of doctor of laws from Fordham University (though he did not say how) and had lobbied church superiors to confer on Ketcham a monsignorship—examples of genuine magnanimity despite having received "little encouragement" in his mission work. Then the real recriminations began. Gordon accused Ketcham, outrageously, of "diverting some hundreds of dollars yearly for the benefit of a few Choctaws" in a secret bid to be named bishop of Oklahoma City. In defending himself, Gordon insisted that his suggestions on how to improve "several awkward situations obtaining on the Indian missions" had been made in earnest, while he remained "wholly astonished" at Ketcham's "resentment," which had "descended perilously close to actual vindictiveness." The matter was clear. Ketcham did not care as he should for Gordon's "fellow-Indians." "For a long time," Gordon added, "I cherished a high opinion of you and only recently have I been disillusioned by your petty conduct and your small-caliber tactics."[55] As a last flourish, he threatened to send his letter to Bishop Meerschaert, once and for all exposing Ketcham's reputed inadequacies.

The shameless threat left Ketcham no choice. On May 2, 1917, he wrote Meerschaert a lengthy letter devoid of any charitable renderings of Gordon's personality. Telling his side of the story, Ketcham deftly turned the tables, enlightening Meerschaert to the many criticisms Gordon had directed at the bishop for the state of the Oklahoma Diocese and its relations with the Indians. Ketcham even revealed that Gordon had briefly considered attacking the bishop publicly. Fortunately, he had shied away from the idea before Ketcham strongly forbade him. Gordon's condemnatory letter to him, meanwhile, showed "the activities of this presumptions young man" whose actions inspired "indignation and mortification." Lest Meerschaert make a premature judgment, Ketcham begged him to hold off on any contact with Gordon until he could see him personally. Ketcham also contended that he had always been supportive of Gordon, but his young, rambunctious charge had gotten spectacularly out of control. His account warrants quoting at length:

Naturally I was ready to do everything to make the career of an Indian priest a success. . . . Father Gordon was talented and active. I hoped he would be of great service to the work. I placed him, as you know, where I thought help was most needed and he in fact did quite an amount of work. I began to realize however that he stirred up a great deal of trouble and he eventually sent me so many complaints and charges that I was completely "snowed under." He observed keenly but believed, apparently, all the idle gossip he heard. When I tried to moderate him he became abusive to me and accused me of neglecting my duty.

Not wanting to cause greater commotion, Ketcham had counselled Gordon the best he could. Yet ruinously, in all cases the errant missionary had "sharply resented advice."[56]

Cardinal John Farley of the BCIM received a similar letter from Ketcham, regretting that he had done "everything in [his] power to make the career of an Indian priest a success." The sad results had been nothing but "confusion and humiliation."[57] With his good name restored, Ketcham prevailed. Gordon was humiliated. He wrote to a sympathetic friend on the subject, ruefully admitting that he had been "called 'liar,' 'abominable liar,' etc." by his colleagues.[58] From his perspective, he had merely tried to do his best for the Catholic Bureau and the Indians. Articulating his thoughts with candor was normal. From Ketcham's perspective, Gordon had been little but a disobliging backstabber.

When Gordon's tenure with the Catholic Bureau abruptly ended in the summer of 1917, he found himself without post or salary, again under the charge of Bishop Koudelka in Superior. The position was awkward, the future uncertain. The incident also ended any relationship with Gordon's former mentor and supporter, William H. Ketcham. It appears that the two never spoke again. Ketcham would only live four more years, dying of a heart attack at age fifty-three while ministering to the Choctaw in Mississippi.[59]

CHAPTER 7

A New Appointment at Reserve

In July 1917, Bishop Koudelka put Philip Gordon to work collecting funds for his signature project, St. Joseph's orphanage in Superior.[1] The task required a great deal of traveling throughout the East Coast and Midwest.[2] In Gordon's estimation, the assignment was not "a very pleasant piece of work."[3] Unhappy with Koudelka's demands, Gordon turned to Father Chrysostom Verwyst, a friend who had worked among the Ojibwe as a missionary since 1878.[4] Both Verwyst and Gordon (as did many other priests) felt it proper that Gordon be assigned to a Wisconsin mission where he could minister to his own people. Gordon hoped that Verwyst could convince Koudelka of this fact, especially because he believed that "pagan Indians" were often "turned against Mother Church by too harsh methods of evangelization." The culprits were white priests, who were "too strict with the Redman." After all, Gordon pointed out, "It took several hundred years to make good people out of the Germans and I know some who condemn the Indian because he is not a saint in a generation!!"[5] Whether Verwyst interceded with Koudelka is unknown. If he did, it made no effect.

In October, Gordon decided that raising money for Koudelka's orphanage was not only onerous but pointless. Upon returning to the White Earth Reservation following a long trip, he protested. His letter to Koudelka deemed the "collecting-tour" a grand failure. In each city, Gordon could "secure no audiences or having secured a hearing was repulsed." His only option was to resign, and his reasons were valid. First, all the "rich Americans" were busy donating to the war effort. Few saw a Wisconsin orphanage as a priority. Second, the only work that suited Gordon was that among the Ojibwe. Being an Indian missionary was obviously the "prudent and feasible" path for his life. There was reason for Gordon to protest. Rumors circulated that he might be made, once again, assistant missionary to Father Odoric. This Gordon deemed "unworkable." He preferred a position with a reliable salary and clear duties. "The Indians need me," he reminded Koudelka, "and you are not the one to allow the call of the Redman to go unheeded."[6]

Koudelka addressed Gordon's concerns a little under two months later in early December 1917. Ignoring Gordon's wishes, the bishop assigned him to assist Father Odoric by taking over some of his missions "at once." The curt note gave special orders, partly in caps, meant to preclude any foreseeable trouble. "A conscientious discharge of your many duties as pastor of these missions will make it necessary for you constantly to remain on your post," stressed Koudelka, "and I therefore strictly forbid you to leave the diocese on any pretence without first obtaining my WRITTEN permission." Gordon was also bid to return all papers and documentation relating to his former role as collector.[7] Infuriated, Gordon requested a leave of absence. Koudelka—probably happy to be rid of a wearisome subordinate—assented.[8] What happened next must have shocked everyone in the Wisconsin Diocese. Deduced from archival sources, it appears that Gordon, determined to be assigned to a parish on Ojibwe lands, immediately traveled to Washington, DC. On the morning of December 14, he appealed in person to Father Giovanni (or John) Bonzano, archbishop of Melitene and Apostolic Delegate to the United States, for a proper church appointment in upper Wisconsin. The meeting left Bonzano very impressed. The very next day he posted a sternly toned letter to Koudelka, questioning whether it had been "an act of prudence to send around to collect a young priest who is ordained only four years." It was much more favorable, Bonzano instructed, that Gordon "be employed in a Sacred Ministry for which he was raised to the priesthood." Forthwith, Koudelka was to assign Gordon a parish in the Superior Diocese.[9] Utterly defeated, the bishop agreed. In January, he gave Gordon oversight of six Indian missions on the Lac du Flambeau and Lac Courte Oreilles Reservations, including Mud Lake and Post. His headquarters

would be Reserve, at Lac Courte Oreilles.[10] After his stinging humiliation by Ketcham and the Catholic Bureau, Gordon had come back with
a smashing victory.

Being appointed to Reserve satisfied Gordon tremendously. He later
wrote that as "a Chippewa Indian, an enrolled member of the tribe,
speaking the language, related by blood to many members of the tribe,
reared with the Indians in their own haunts, the appointment seemed fit-
ting and in keeping with the idea of a native clergy for the aborigines of
the country."[11] The church at Reserve, a handsome wooden structure with
a tall steeple, had been built in 1882 by the Franciscans. Since its inception
it had attracted a congregation of one thousand Ojibwe.[12] Wasting no
time, Gordon set about organizational matters, writing Odoric for advice,
documentation, and support.[13] Despite such eagerness, troubles began
immediately. The mission at Post came under threat when the part of the
land it sat on was allotted to a local woman, Lucy Thayer.[14] Lac Court
Oreilles Reservation superintendent Henry McQuigg informed Gordon
of the issue in February, forcing him to scramble for a solution.[15] Gordon
enlisted Odoric's aid and set off for Post, hoping to retain the land.[16] On
arrival, he learned that the mission had been built outside the tract owned
by the Catholic Church. Despite this, the Ojibwe there remained opposed
to deeding Thayer the land.[17] After more investigation, it turned out
that Odoric had purchased the land years ago from "old Indian Jim," for
thirty-five dollars—but the title could not be located. Meanwhile, the
local Ojibwe continued to protest, blocking Thayer from using part of
the allotment.[18] An ensuing council with the resident Indian agent sealed
the impasse.[19] Gordon later found Odoric's deed, though it had never
been registered. Whether the government accepted it as proof of owner-
ship is not revealed in any subsequent letters. Toward the end of March,
Gordon wrote Odoric of more interesting news: "Weather very Spring-
like now. Sleighing is all done for, I think. . . . In a few days, you will
receive a copy of *Anishinabe Enamiad*. It has come back to life and I am
the editor."[20]

Anishinabe Enamiad, or *A-ni-shi-na-be E-na-mi-ad,* as written in the
original, was Gordon's resurrection of *War-Whoop,* specifically published

for the Ojibwe. (Enamiad is Anishinaabemowin for Christian.)[21] Bearing the subtitle "Devoted to the Catholic Indian Missions," the newsletter debuted in April 1918. An editorial for the May edition announced that *Anishinabe Enamiad's* purpose was to bring Catholic missionaries in greater contact with the Ojibwe "for the sake of Jesus Christ." This heavy emphasis on Catholicism was a core theme. "Ere the sun sets on a vanishing race," read the May issue, "cannot we speed up our drives against the vestiges of paganism still noticeable on our Chippewa Reservations? We say mildly 'still noticeable.' In some portions of our field, paganism still holds notable sway."

Anishinabe Enamiad kept readers informed of all the Catholic doings at Gordon's missions, listing baptisms and events like a St. Patrick's eve party Gordon held in his home. A group of boys from Lake Flambeau Indian School attended, refreshments were served, and "a generally pleasant evening was spent." The magazine also heartily promoted teetotaling through the St. Joseph's Temperance Society, which Gordon had energized with a fund-raising effort that had collected seventy-five dollars.[22] (The Volstead Act, or Prohibition, would be passed in 1919, turning many of Wisconsin's famed breweries into producers of soda water.)[23] At temperance meetings, attendees sang religious songs and pledged to fight the "powers of evil on the Reservation," such as alcoholism, unsanctioned marriage, and paganism. As the last "evil" indicates, Gordon was insistent that all Ojibwe convert to Catholicism, lest immorality persist.

Whatever one's feelings on alcohol consumption or the kinds of sexual "immorality" to which Gordon referred, intoxication at times caused serious problems on the Ojibwe reservations. One government inspector found that many girls had been "debauched before arriving at the age of earliest womanhood," or put more bluntly, puberty. Such forced unions, when perpetrated by white men, had resulted in a rapid decline in "fullblooded" tribe members. Alcohol use also produced crime, and worse, deaths. Drunken fighting was commonplace. One young man from Odanah disappeared and was found with his skull smashed in; another Ojibwe man under the influence of spirits attacked his wife, incinerated his own home, and threatened to shoot the police that came to arrest him.[24] In this context, Gordon's hope that Catholicism and its moral beliefs—as expressed in *Anishinabe Enamiad*—could act as a palliative for societal discord appears understandable.

Focusing only on such naked proselytizing, however, diminishes the significance of *Anishinabe Enamiad* and Gordon's activities at his missions. The same May issue discussed a large tribal council held by Gordon at the church's expense, which sought medical care, the dismissal of incompetent BIA employees, and better schooling from reservation authorities. Gordon suggested petitioning Secretary of the Interior Lane so that the Indian Bureau might recognize these demands and the legitimacy of the council. The issue also listed the number of sick, condemned the reservation's "wretched medical service," and highlighted the need for an investigation into these poor conditions.

Gordon voiced his displeasure with the Indian Bureau in an article titled "The Anvil." Noting the recent propagandistic calls for democracy in Europe, he asked if Indians would ever enjoy "self-determination" themselves. Referencing the treaties that had plunged Europe into war, he wrote of the "scraps of paper" that had been systematically ignored by the U.S. government—the "350 solemn covenants between Uncle Sam and Poor Lo." The comparison was pertinent. Indians, whose treaty rights had been trampled on for over a century, now lived confined on reservations supervised by a total of seven thousand whites. Yet unlike Europeans, Indians did not make war over their treaties. Instead, they suffered a "continual current of uneasiness" and a "chronic spirit of discontent." In his own dealings with BIA officials, Gordon admitted that some were upright. Others were severely bigoted.[25] These were bold sentiments, and in print.

Aside from the publication of his news bulletin, Gordon's activities at the missions were related to Father Odoric in letters posted from the Ojibwe reservations. They detail various sick-calls, collections, mass attendances, deaths, and news on St. Joseph's Temperance Society, which had swelled to sixty members.[26] Gordon also mentioned that he was overseeing eight sisters, though he was unhappy with their work.[27] Then, in early May, a shocking rumor erupted in the Superior Diocese. Father Odoric (born in Prussia) had reputedly been imprisoned for sending financial support to Germany. Inundated by inquiries regarding Odoric's whereabouts, Gordon begged him to pen a statement denying the false claims, which he would read before his congregation.[28] Odoric requested that Gordon simply ignore the matter; he refused. After some investigating, Gordon identified the sources of the rumor: local "whites." A preacher at Lac du Flambeau, Mr. Murry, had claimed that Odoric was sent to the notorious Leavenworth Prison in Kansas for a twenty-year sentence. A logger, Mr. Smith, told Gordon that Odoric was so "intensely pro-German" that he had a "picture of Kaiser Bill" displayed proudly in his room. Odoric's German citizenship was the cause of such "foolish and silly" stories. In other news, Gordon's Ford was consuming "lots of oats" on his constant travels.[29] Mention should also be given to the effect Gordon had on some of those he served. A letter from Benedict and Margaret Gauthier shows the impact of one of his visits to Lac du Flambeau. Regretting the loss of his presence, the Gauthiers wrote that "we think of you so much," praying that Gordon would one day return to his "poor Flambeau People."[30]

An impact on people's lives is precisely what Gordon meant to accomplish. In June, he hosted Carlos Montezuma at Reserve. Montezuma surveyed reservation conditions and visited several missions. The experience moved him, and he departed for home deeply impressed by Gordon's work. A subsequent letter expressed as much:

> The meeting at Reserve was a picturesque scene on the lake by the dark woods. It is one that I shall never forget. Those gathered were fed spiritually, mentally and bodily. It was sad to see the once strong Chippewa race whose freedom was the freedom of the birds, free from care as children then but now under the burden of not knowing what to do, overwhelmed by the rush of surrounding encroachment and the new order of things. The tidal wave of civilization is surely coming on them. There need be no fear. Something always happens. God sends a man to clear away the crisis. When the Indians have such men as you who have seen the world and know the progress of advancement, they are fortunate. You are in a position to explain all things well for them. When we have a lantern to see our way step by step, there is no fear. Father, you are the lantern for these Indians. Aim well and lead in the right.

Montezuma's warm words of encouragement were intermingled with words of concern for Richard Henry Pratt. The doctor had recently seen Pratt at an Indian rights event at the Battle Creek Sanitarium in Michigan. Montezuma had spoken passionately in support of freedom for the Indians, a speech Pratt "enjoyed." Sadly, however, Pratt had become so elderly that he could not "do much on account of feebleness."[31]

Gordon's organizing out of Reserve, his running criticism of the Indian Bureau, his association with the outspoken Montezuma, and perhaps his views articulated in *Anishinabe Enamiad*, had by July 1918 drawn attention in Washington—both negative and positive. Commissioner Sells continued to look with misgivings upon Gordon's efforts, but Wisconsin senator Irvine Lenroot had befriended the priest. Following a visit to Reserve, Lenroot insisted to Sells that any dismissive estimation of Gordon was in error, and that he was "a Catholic priest of the very highest ideals." In matters concerning the Ojibwe reservations, Lenroot insisted that Sells consider Gordon "of very great value in giving to the Department disinterested information concerning the various problems that arise."[32]

For Sells, problems of a different sort soon arose at the 1918 SAI conference, held from September 25 to 28 in Pierre, South Dakota. The slogan, borrowed from the cancelled 1917 meeting, read "Indian Patriotism, Production, Progress." Gordon attended, as did Montezuma, Sherman Coolidge, Charles Eastman, and Gertrude Bonnin, who was in the process of taking over the Society from her position in Washington. Were it not for her steely perseverance, the conference would likely have never occurred. SAI president Parker, distracted by his duties at the New York State Museum, failed to appear. So did many others. Only about twenty-five to thirty active members came to debate, each largely ignoring Secretary Bonnin's motion to lobby President Wilson for an Indian delegation to the anticipated peace conference in France.[33] (The Great War would end two months later, in November.) Delegates did, however, take note of Montezuma's blistering address, "Abolish the Indian Bureau." With mostly the radicals like Gordon in attendance, a resolution passed to do just that. For the first time, the SAI came out in a (somewhat) unified voice to liquidate the bureau, aggrieving Commissioner Sells profoundly.[34] Members against the motion were upset, some even infuriated. Nevertheless, the conference ended with a unanimous call to improve the legal status of Natives following cessation of the European conflict.[35]

Unfortunately, nothing of Gordon's contributions at Pierre was written up in the *American Indian Magazine*, though his influence could be felt in an extract published post conference. AIM called upon the "country and congress to take immediate action for abolishing the Indian Bureau," explaining that the BIA had been "erected merely to perform a temporary function."[36] This was precisely the kind of statement Gordon and Montezuma had been pushing for since Lawrence. More fortuitously, in the Pierre conference's voting there had been another reorganization in leadership. Charles Eastman was elected SAI President in Parker's absence, while Bonnin forced Baldwin (also absent) out as treasurer. As the new secretary-treasurer, Bonnin soon after declared herself editor of the *American Indian Magazine*. None opposed her.[37] Gordon was elected vice president, moving up in the SAI hierarchy and going home to Reserve quite pleased. He should have given pause. The factionalism he and Montezuma had inspired within the Society would, in the next few years, lead to its unravelling.[38]

As Christmas neared, Gordon wrote Odoric with some complaints about Protestant "tricks" at Lac du Flambeau. The resident preacher, Mr. Murry (who had maligned Odoric with rumors of imprisonment) had circulated some anti-Catholic pamphlets and stolen a few Catholic converts. But Gordon was confident he could handle the situation. He had already visited Lac du Flambeau to acquire baptismal records in hopes of luring back twenty children who had been attending Protestant church. Concluding his first year as an Indian missionary at Reserve, Gordon wished Odoric "a Merry Christmas."[39]

CHAPTER 8

Struggles and Injustices

On March 11, 1919, Wisconsin's *Sawyer County Record* published the following letter submitted by Father Philip Gordon:

> To the Editor *Sawyer County Record*:
>
> Word has just reached my ears of the death of another of our old Indians from starvation and cold. Old Louis Martin who lived by himself about six miles from Reserve was found dead in his little log cabin last Wednesday. The body was completely frozen and lay in front of a stove with matches and shavings in his hands. It is presumed that he died during the cold spell of ten days ago. In the cabin was found no food whatsoever and very little wood. Mr. Martin, while alive, was a familiar sight about this Mission and although dressed in nothing better than rags came frequently to my house for the little tobacco I could afford to give him and other little helps. Had it not been for the extraordinary kindness of his neighbors, old man Martin would have died from starvation a long time ago. With his nearest neighbors three miles away, it was of course, impossible that they keep in close touch with the old man. Hence his death which, in this land of plenty, is truly a frightful thing. Where lies the blame, Mr. Editor? Our late Indian Agent appeared to have done his utmost in these cases of distress among our Indians. I herewith submit a typical letter submitted by Mr. McQuigg.

Superintendent McQuigg's letter, addressed to Commissioner of Indian Affairs Cato Sells, requested the immediate disbursal of relief funds to aid twenty-one "destitute and helpless Indians." The list included mainly the elderly, male and female, as well as a widowed woman with two children. McQuigg continued:

> In addition to the names mentioned above there are at least 30 more whose names could be given as they are in a condition almost as helpless. The names listed above, however, have absolutely no one to take care of them and have no trust funds or other income which they can use and it is a mystery how they can live. They have absolutely no visible means of support so far as I can learn and live in the most extreme and dire need. Some of them have only burlap sacks for bed clothing and their clothes are all in rags and of course are very dirty. The Indians under this jurisdiction are for the much greater part poverty stricken. In this country with the long, severe winters it is necessary as a rule for a person to eat substantial and nourishing food to keep warm, as well as have plenty of clothing.
>
> There is no available fund for the alleviation of the distress of the Indians mentioned. The rations on hand would not last any one of the above-mentioned Indians for a month and the Government Farmer who distributes the scant rations sent here doles them out little by little and tries to nurse it along through the winter.

Given such destitution, McQuigg respectfully requested the allocation of $500 "to assist these worthy and indigent people."

Gordon, in his characteristic bluntness, then commented on the letter:

> It would appear, my dear Sir, that the fault does not lie in any local official but at Headquarters in Washington and partially with the U.S. Congress. Mr. Cato Sells, Commissioner, although appealed to in behalf of our Sawyer County Indians many times, personally as well as otherwise, has not bestirred himself to any degree worth mentioning. Mr. Sells comes from Texas where until recently a statute made it a crime for an Indian to enter the State!
>
> Certain well known citizens of our County took considerable pains to telegraph to Washington in the matter of Superintendent McQuigg's transfer. Is it asking these illustrious gentlemen too great a favor to ask

them to evince as great an interest where it is a matter of humanity and
very fundamental Christianity?[1]

And Gordon was not done. On March 31, he wrote Secretary of the Interior Lane on the issue, enclosing the clipping from the *Sawyer County
Record*. "It is with excessive grief and not a little shame that I feel obliged
to address you relative to the most distressing conditions obtaining on
this Reservation," he began. "Fully a year has passed since I commenced
to call attention to the sad condition of the Lac Court Oreilles Indians
but as yet we have had no satisfaction outside of numerous stereotyped
letters." An investigation had taken place since that time, which Gordon
labeled "farcical and not far from a joke." Meanwhile, "three or four
deaths the past winter from nothing else than plain STARVATION" had
occurred. These were, frankly, "suggestive of murder." The letter concluded with Gordon insisting that Lane not send him "one of those formal replies which reads that the matter has been referred to the Indian
Office." He also reminded Lane that the Ojibwe had approximately sev-
enty men serving in the military, most overseas.[2]

Lane responded in early April, promising that Gordon's voice had been
heard and McQuigg's request for $500 dollars noted. The Spanish influ-
enza pandemic of 1918 and forest fires in Minnesota had, however, drained
the budget, while Congress had failed to appropriate enough money to
cover the needs of those at Lac Court Oreilles. As a result, McQuigg had
been instructed to be "liberal" in disbursing "individual funds." There
was simply no more that could be done.[3]

Such were the conditions that existed on the Ojibwe reservations. Such
were the responses from those responsible for their alleviation. The reasons
for the intense hardships were, unsurprisingly, a consequence of federal
policy and white exploitation of nature. The Dawes Act allotment process, the sale of "excess" lands to whites, and rampant land fraud had
destroyed communal Ojibwe landholding. These factors would result in
the eventual loss of 40 percent of the land base by 1934.[4] Meanwhile, logging companies—which had long ago replaced the fur trade—had devas-
tated the once-pristine environment, reducing the evergreen forests that
had dominated the region to a landscape of sorry stumps and brush that

served as tinder for forest fires. At Lac du Flambeau, the labor costs of removing the stumps and roots topped the value of the lands they dotted. White Earth in Minnesota had also been raped of its pines, and the Bad River Reservation had been so depleted of timber that logging operations were completely shut down in 1921, leaving most of Odanah unemployed. The BIA expected the Ojibwe to make farmers of themselves, but fertile parcels had generally fallen into the hands of whites. Most tribe members had such small landholdings that little more than maintaining a vegetable garden was possible. Families were forced to survive by working off-reservation in fishing and logging, unable to find work at home.[5]

Confronted with rapidly deteriorating circumstances, the Ojibwe continued traditional ways as best they could, harvesting rice and blueberries, making maple syrup, and hunting what was left of the game. Yet sickness stalked their communities. Tuberculosis rates increased in the first two decades of twentieth century, with 15 percent of Ojibwe falling victim and deaths multiplying. Venereal diseases such as syphilis and gonorrhea also became prevalent. The BIA blamed the Ojibwe themselves for the disease and high mortality rates, claiming they were "immoral" and too attached to traditional medicines. Even were this true, it would have mattered little in the face of the Spanish influenza pandemic, which hit the Ojibwe particularly hard while killing fifty million around the globe.[6]

Despite the gravity of the situation, aid offered the Ojibwe by the Catholic Church was paltry. In ministering to the impoverished and sick through the missions under his charge, Gordon faced severe financial constraints. His Ford, for instance, had died, and he required a new one. The purchase mandated a trip to Superior. In the interim, Gordon was using a horse supplied by an acquaintance because Father Odoric was refusing to pay for a new auto. Gordon asked him to be "a little more easy on a young priest whose heart is with the Indian," mentioning that Odoric had just acquired $1,000. "So you see," he pointed out. "I am not asking for what you have not."[7]

Though Gordon found time to badger Odoric about funding his Ford, by the spring of 1919 he had become involved in a more important endeavor. In cooperation with Carlos Montezuma and Charles Eastman, Gordon was planning a three-month lecture tour throughout Ojibwe country. The issues discussed would be citizenship and BIA abolition.[8] He explained to Odoric that the purpose of the meetings was to encourage "independent thinking" among Indians, who appeared "like babies, badly over-nursed." With encouragement "along the line of progressive living," Gordon believed they would ultimately do better for themselves.[9] This emphasis on self-help, one could easily note, appeared futile in light of the reservation conditions described by Gordon in his letter to the *Sawyer County Record.* Considering the lack of an appropriate official response from Washington, perhaps Gordon felt there was little Indians could do but rely on themselves. Personal responsibility and morality (of course) were issues Gordon took very seriously. When away from Reserve for some time, he once returned home to find that without his permission, some missionaries had begun to build housing on church grounds for several local "drunkards and gamblers." These characters included adulterers and other "pagans" who refused churchgoing and legal marriages. Gordon questioned whether Odoric had allowed this and indicated that the appalling circumstances had forced him to enlist the police in removing the resident reprobates. Gordon was also experiencing troubles with his eight sisters, who were "trying their best" to make him quit. He especially feared that Bishop Koudelka had become sympathetic to the idea.[10]

Near the end of May 1919, Eastman and Montezuma arrived for their tour. Gordon escorted them throughout the Wisconsin reservations, where they spoke against the BIA, argued for Indian citizenship, and attempted to recruit new members for the SAI.[11] They averaged three to four addresses a day.[12] All was going well until the group reached the Menominee Reservation in the northeast of the state. There the agent in charge, concerned about the content of the men's speeches, barred their entry and threatened to have them jailed.[13] Gordon managed to quickly arrange a meeting at the local Catholic school, as well as another at a U.S. government school. Montezuma later downplayed the Menominee episode in his Native rights journal, *Wassaja.*[14] In contrast, Bonnin denounced the incident. She declared in the *American Indian Magazine* that the "Indian Bureau autocracy forbade these educated, leading men to hold any meeting on the Indian reservation," while the "very scum of other races" entered Indian lands at will to homestead and appropriate everything they saw.[15]

Gordon, Montezuma, and Eastman met again in autumn for the SAI's 1919 conference, October 2 to 4; its slogan: "American Citizenship for Indians." Gordon and Montezuma had been the driving force behind the planning, choosing their bailiwick, Minneapolis, for the site. Though some in the SAI urged Parker to attend and counter the influence of the radicals, it was not to be. Parker again stayed away, having consciously withdrawn from the Society due to frustration over its direction. His place was filled by a pro-peyote contingent from Oklahoma led by Gordon's former choice for SAI president, Omaha lawyer Thomas Sloan.[16] Sherman Coolidge, a stalwart, was also present. President Eastman gave an opening address lauding the ideals that had animated Indians in the past. It was they, he insisted, who "laid the foundation of freedom and equality and democracy long before any white people."[17]

When Eastman concluded his remarks, Vice-President Gordon commanded the floor. In a call for action on abolishing the bureau, he stressed the need to be practical. "It is all right," he conceded, "to be idealistic," but there had been enough talk already about Indian ideals, virtues, and principles. Now was the time to put in the effort by drafting a bill to abolish the BIA, proposing a plan to replace it, and lobbying Washington to take legislative action. Gordon cited his own efforts and those of the Ojibwe as a model, claiming they had "given the Bureau such a jolt that the chairs in Washington are still shaking." Also key was raising awareness among the white population. Demonstrating no mean idealism himself, Gordon exhorted the Society to "enlighten the American public to the true status of the Indian." Once this had been accomplished, he was sure Congress would do the necessary work. The Indian had, after all, fought in France. Faced with this honorable fact, few Americans could deny that he had the right to a new system that ensured freedom. Gordon also spoke out on the Menominee Reservation incident with Montezuma and Eastman, revealing that the agent had threatened them once he learned they were to speak on Indian democracy. In view of such opposition, the bureau had to go. The enormity of this task demanded immediate care despite various challenges. All three thousand of the BIA's Indian employees, for instance, would have to be provided work. Nonetheless, the SAI had to "organize and fight to a finish."[18]

Gertrude Bonnin as well played a prominent role at the conference. Seconding Gordon's appeal to organize, in a long address she insisted the Society confront the "race that came from Europe" and "stand the test, true to the Indian blood."[19] Sloan also made an impression by stating that the Indian deserved citizenship regardless of notions of "competency," because it was "a universal rule of civilization that a person shall be a citizen of the country of which he is a native." Moreover, the "backward subject Indian" required citizenship "more than the advanced Indian." In this respect and others, America had failed utterly in its obligations. There was some irony in this fact. U.S. citizens had given the needy in Europe billions of dollars while ignoring the claims of Indians who deserved restitution for lost lands and resources.[20] Sloan's strong speech propelled him into the presidency in the subsequent voting for new officers. He handily defeated both Eastman and Bonnin's husband, Raymond. Many Minnesota Indians had attended thanks to Gordon's efforts in the region, meaning that he was also instrumental in getting Theodore D. Beaulieu, an Ojibwe, elected SAI vice-president. Gordon himself took a position on the advisory board.[21]

These events left Bonnin horrified. Unable to accept Sloan's pro-peyote stance, she immediately quit her work for the Society on the pretext of health issues, even though she was reelected to her posts. In leaving, she vowed that "if there is any Indian council in the United States that asks me to go there, in justice for the Indian, I will be there and I will not ask them to see that I will not go to jail."[22] The loss of Bonnin, with her indefatigable commitment, was one from which the SAI would never recover.[23] Eastman was equally unhappy with the election of Sloan as SAI president. He declared the Society "a political pressure group with patronage interests" and exited soon after.[24]

Following the 1919 SAI conference, Gordon returned to Reserve having achieved a small victory. There was little time to savor the moment. The number of missions he oversaw kept him on the move, and his work was often emotionally draining—particularly his ministering to the infirm and dying. Just one letter to Odoric in December 1919 mentions numerous sick calls, which included three deaths. Of a trip to Lac du

Flambeau, Gordon wrote that he was called to the deathbed of a young boy named Eddie LaCass. LaCass, who had been ill for some time, had resisted Gordon's offers of a visit. As a result, the priest arrived too late to administer last rites, and thus had not prepared the soul for death by the absolution of sins. Gordon feared that many Ojibwe at Lac du Flambeau would "die like Eddie LaCass" due to their lack of commitment to Catholicism. Such tragedies could be avoided if the church would change its methods in converting Natives. He told Odoric it was "a mistake to baptize these little pagans, that is, little at the time of their baptism, for as soon as they quit the Government School, good bye Catholic Church and good bye Catholic priest!" Even worse, once they matured they happily married outside of the Church. Aside from these aggravations, missionary work had its lighter moments. Gordon reported that he was making "grand preparations" for Christmas, with three deer in his basement waiting to be feasted upon by the societies he had organized. There would be a midnight mass accompanied by "a splendid choir," though the organist remained "a little weak." Gordon had furnished club rooms to the community replete with Catholic literature and newspapers, and even a new pool table. The main trouble remained his nuns and superiors. The sisters were still trying to have him removed, while Bishop Koudelka kept up his usual threats to have Gordon expelled from the diocese.[25]

It was true that some in the Catholic hierarchy in Superior wanted Gordon gone, and they would eventually succeed. The reasons were the very heart of his mission: his constant advocacy on behalf of the Natives in his region and his lobbying of those in government. (Gordon's acrid personality did him no favors, either.) In early 1920, Gordon and Montezuma once again made a tour of reservations, visiting the Potawatomi Indians in eastern Wisconsin. With the trip, Gordon hoped to draw attention to a people "so long neglected by both the government and by missionary agencies." He publicly announced his desire to establish a mission on their lands. Press coverage of the tour described Gordon as "an enthusiastic advocate of making the Indians citizens and responsible for their own development."[26] These concerted efforts to influence Indian policy took place not only at the grass roots; they extended to the highest reaches

of Washington. Following Republican Warren G. Harding's election in
1920, Gordon implored the president-elect to give the SAI an audience so
they could influence the appointment of the new commissioner of Indian
Affairs. He reminded Harding that the SAI was "non-partisan," though
"the record of the past eight years in Indian affairs is such" that it could be
considered "anarchist." He also complained that a Department of Agriculture veterinary position paid "more than the regular Indian Service
physician and surgeon receives."[27] Upon receiving this letter from a largely
nonvoting constituency, Harding's secretary declined the meeting some
two months later.[28]

The SAI's defeat in securing a meeting with the president-elect came
on the heels of its 1920 conference, November 15 to 19, held in St. Louis.
Sadly, only eight members bothered to appear. Montezuma led an Arizona
delegation. Coolidge, Sloan, and Gordon attended. It was a dismal affair
by all accounts. Without Eastman, Parker, and Bonnin, the Society had
become little but a shadow of itself. There were debates about the *American Indian Magazine*, which had been operating at a loss and would soon
expire. There was also a push to have Sloan nominated for commissioner
of Indian Affairs (though Harding showed no interest). The story was
much the same at the next annual meeting, October 26 to November 2,
1921, in Detroit. The SAI secretary, Thomas Bishop, called the meeting
an outright "fiasco." There, Sloan made an ineffectual call for BIA abolition, but little else occurred. Gordon returned home thoroughly dishear-
tened.[29] Back in Reserve, he telephoned Montezuma to commiserate. In
a letter the doctor described Gordon's mood to his wife, Marie: "Father
Gordon came back from Detroit. We had a long talk. I have not heard
from him so often. No wonder he is a little discouraged with the Indians.
The Indians change their minds. . . . He argued as though some of his
Indians need the supervision of the Indian Bureau. I would not give in
but opposed his ideas. After a while we spoke on some other subject. I
suppose he has been around and heard too much. He has been too enthusiastic and the results have not been what he expected. He is trying to
raise money for a new church."[30]

Chagrined by the daily poverty he witnessed on the reservations and the
lack of progress made by the SAI, Gordon was losing faith that conditions

could change as he wished. Throughout 1921, he had continued to push forcefully for bureau abolition in the Wisconsin press, writing in the *Bay-field Progress* of how the BIA unjustly wielded control over every aspect of the Indian's life, stealing his land for commercial exploitation and use as national parks.[31] Nothing had come of these protests, and as the last line Montezuma's letter mentioned, Gordon had other pressing distractions.

CHAPTER 9

Bitter Ends

In early August 1921, a massive electrical storm hit Reserve.[1] A bolt of
lightning struck the steeple of the Catholic mission and set it aflame.
The church, Gordon's residence, the parish hall, and everything within
was destroyed, including the pipe organ.[2] The damage was estimated at
$10,000, only partially covered by insurance.[3] Father Gordon was devas-
tated. With no other recourse, he set about raising money to rebuild. He
composed an open letter, distributed in pamphlet form. "My Dear Friend,"
it began, "I have never begged for money in all my life. In fact, I was once
severely reprimanded by my superiors for declining to beg for a charitable
institution. Times have changed, however, and I now feel obliged in conscience to ask of every friend of mine, aid, for myself and the destitute
Wisconsin Indians." The letter described the fate of the church and the
cases of death by "lack of nourishment" at Lac Courte Oreilles, a fact
"shameful and embarrassing to the white man." Asking for "a crumb from
ample tables," Gordon revealed the emotional cost of his missionary
work: "I am on my knees, so to speak, and though I am not easily moved,
tears do sometimes come as I witness and contemplate the rapid decima-
tion by disease and neglect of my poor Indian charges." At Bad River, as
much as 20 percent of the population were afflicted with tuberculosis.
The appeal, then, was not only for funds to resurrect the mission but also
to build a hospital and improve health care and schooling for the two
hundred children on the reservations.[4]

Though Gordon's efforts to raise funds for Koudelka's orphanage had
ended in disaster, his efforts at Reserve yielded much. Over the next two

years, he collected approximately $35,000 (almost $500,000 in today's terms) to rebuild the mission.[5] Some of those who donated were the Progressive senator from Wisconsin, Robert LaFollette, and Senator Lenroot, both of whom had befriended Gordon.[6] When the cornerstone of the new church was laid, Wisconsin governor John J. Blaine attended and gave an address. President Harding sent a congratulatory telegram.[7] The local Ojibwe assisted in the building and the new church was designed, in Gordon's words, to be a "connecting link which would sagely bring Indians from paganism to Catholicism," since "it is the only way to reach the Indian's heart."[8] This meant the inclusion of deerskins and altar cloths woven in the traditional manner by Ojibwe women. "Remember this is to be an Indian's place of worship, not a white man's church," he explained to the press.[9] Another local newspaper reported how "Indian psychology has been taken into consideration in working out the symbolic designs of the stained-glass windows." Because many of the Ojibwe Indian parishioners could not read, the church's windows depicted "the rising sun, many arrows, crossed calumets and tobacco, and above the pipes and arrows, the cross." Traditional Ojibwe dances were welcome at the mission, despite BIA displeasure. Gordon's mother, Ategekwe, would later attend these ceremonies in full regalia. Gordon's church residence, meanwhile, was designed to appear like a teepee. The rebuilding brought great satisfaction to Gordon. "I never want to leave Reserve," he was quoted saying. "This is the work I love and understand and I ask as my only reward greater appreciation on the part of the white men of the Indians' problems."[10] Though Gordon desired to remain where he was, a man-made disaster at Post—and his opposition to it—would shortly contribute to his dismissal.

In 1914, American Public Utilities approached the Ojibwe at Lac Courte Oreilles, hoping to obtain their lands around the ancient settlement of Pahquahwong, also known as Post, which had been a trading center since the early 1870s. The utility company planned to construct a massive dam to generate electricity, termed the Chippewa Flowage Project. At the time, approximately 180 people lived in Post, a mixed population of Ojibwe and Euro-Americans dwelling in a collection of traditional wigwams and newer houses surrounding a village center. Catholic and Presbyterian

churches had been established there in the nineteenth century.[11] Those at
Lac Courte Oreilles summarily rejected American Public Utilities' offer,
preferring not to see their homes and burial grounds submerged by the
waters of the Chippewa River. Rebuffed, American Public Utilities began
an intense lobbying campaign in Washington. Congress quickly authorized
the sale of the individual allotments and tribal lands needed for the project,
but stopped short of granting access without the Lac Courte Oreilles' agree-
ment. In 1916, the company again applied pressure, claiming the right of
eminent domain and insisting on three-party negotiations with the Ojibwe
and the BIA. American Public Utilities promised to pay for the relocation
of anyone affected onto newly purchased lands. The Catholic and Presbyterian churches to be flooded would also be replaced. At a council meeting,
Superintendent McQuigg informed the tribe that it was futile to resist the
dam project because American Public Utilities had "lots of money behind
them and can do anything they say." The Ojibwe resisted nonetheless.

In 1919, a new player, Wisconsin-Minnesota Light & Power, made its try.
Wisconsin-Minnesota Light & Power offered $20,000 in compensation
for 315 acres of land. The tribe, still determined to keep what was theirs,
voted against the proposal unanimously. McQuigg abetted the company
best he could, incurring the displeasure of the Ojibwe and leading to his
transfer. Then in June 1920, the Federal Power Act passed, authorizing
the building of dams on reservation lands and enabling the Federal Power
Commission (FPC) to set compensation amounts. The new Indian agent
at Lac Courte Oreilles, Robert Craige, informed the tribe of the dire situation in May 1921. If those at Pahquahwong did not accept Wisconsin-
Minnesota's offer, the company would proceed regardless. The tribe fought
the FPC on the grounds of the 1854 treaty, to no avail. On August 8, 1921,
work commenced.[12]

Like his fellow Ojibwe at Lac Courte Oreilles, Gordon was livid at the
progression of the dam project. He wrote to numerous officials in Washington and tried fruitlessly to enlist the help of the Bishop Koudelka.[13]
(Koudelka died in June 1921, just before the project's commencement).[14]
Gordon's concern was not only the Catholic mission and its cemetery but,
as he wrote, "the matter of proper redress for the poor Indians." His ultimate goal was a Senate investigation into the Chippewa Flowage Project,

leading the powerful interests pushing for the project to take notice. At a district convention of the General Federation of Women's Clubs, Gordon planned to speak on the matter. As he began, some women in the audience shouted him down. It later turned out that they had been planted by the Public Utilities Company at Eau Claire.[15]

The Chippewa Flowage Project was completed in March 1923. The Federal Power Commission ordered Wisconsin-Minnesota Light & Power to build a replacement village, named New Post, for the Ojibwe, with a school, a church, and stores. The company was also forced to pay an annual lease of $1,200 and disinter the remains of those resting in Ojibwe and Christian cemeteries to higher ground. Workers received $25 for each body they excavated and reburied upland. Not every grave could be located. Many who had lived in Post all their lives were slowly forced out over the course of several months by the rising water. They fled to New Post, still under construction. That summer, the dislocated Ojibwe gathered with other tribe members living off reservation to witness what was left of their old village. Women wept as they surveyed their flooded home. Even decades later, the remains of Ojibwe ancestors continued to wash up on the shores what is today Lake Chippewa.[16]

The cruel divestment at Lac Courte Oreilles was typical of the corrupt Harding administration. In 1921, the president had appointed Albert B. Fall as Secretary of the Interior. This would prove a disaster for indigenous rights. Fall, formerly a New Mexico senator, swiftly threw his support behind a bill to appropriate Pueblo lands for use by white squatters, then declared that reservations established by executive order (and not treaties) could be treated as "public lands." The decision opened twenty-two million acres of Indian territories to resource exploitation.[17] These actions were accompanied by the repressive Dance Order, yet another attempt by the U.S. government to quash Indian religious ceremonies.[18] Meanwhile in Oklahoma, members of the Five Civilized Tribes—the Chickasaw, Creek, Choctaw, Seminole, and Cherokee—found themselves beleaguered by a state-supported graft of their oil-rich lands under a "guardianship" system that entrusted Indian wards to white businessmen, who, more often than not, stole whatever profits they could with the help of corrupt judges. Not even children were spared in the orgy of exploitation, some

poisoned in order to acquire their allotments.[19] Fortunately, the Indian
Rights Association and General Federation of Women's Clubs became
involved in both the Pueblo and Oklahoma struggles, while also trying to
block the Dance Order. The IRA quickly organized the American Indian
Defense Association (AIDA), which sent an investigatory team to Oklahoma led by Gertrude Bonnin. The AIDA was headed by a young activist, John Collier, who would take the position of commissioner of Indian
Affairs during the Roosevelt administration.[20]

Back in Wisconsin, Gordon complained vigorously to the press about
the flooding at Lac Courte Oreilles, stating that many Ojibwe men had
served in France in order to highlight the injustice. He also continued to
take a very public stance on the Indian Bureau, giving interviews to major
papers in the region in which he condemned the system he felt was holding Indians back from achieving basic freedom and advancement in white
society. In 1923, the *Milwaukee Journal*, for one, had named Gordon "the
leader of a new deal for the Indian" for his criticisms of the BIA.[21] In a
long interview for the *Milwaukee Sentinel*, Gordon implored the government to create an impartial commission to investigate reservation conditions and suggest legislation to abolish the stifling "bureaucratic control"
over the Indian population. "I take it as my duty," he stated, "to expose
any official, elective, appointed or otherwise, who takes the extreme attitude that Indians cannot absolutely get along without the immense wire
pulling, un-American anomaly known as the Indian Bureau."[22] This was
another declaration of confidence in the inherent competence of his
people, though they had been made "sick" by the "virus of paternalism."[23]

As his frustrations mounted, 1923 became a very painful year for Philip
Gordon. The defeat at Lac Courte Oreilles was followed by new misfortunes. Toward the end of 1922, Montezuma, Gordon's oldest friend and
ally in the Society of American Indians, took gravely ill with tuberculosis.
In December, Gordon visited him in Chicago and witnessed his emaci-
ated condition. He and Marie Montezuma brought the doctor to the
city's central train station, where Montezuma boarded the Santa Fe Railroad to Phoenix, Arizona, the land of his birth. He died on January 31,
1923, in a small hut constructed by his fellow Yavapai twenty-three miles
northeast of Phoenix, on Fort McDowell Reservation. Over the past two

decades, Montezuma had reconnected with his tribe, fighting furiously for their land and water rights. Though he had attacked the SAI through-out most of its existence, one of his last wishes was for the 1923 conference to proceed. The 1922 conference in Kansas City had come to very little, but before Montezuma left Chicago on his last trip, he tearfully begged a schoolteacher friend, Ms. M. Augustine Stanley, to organize a gathering.[24] She consulted former SAI president Arthur C. Parker, who expressed no enthusiasm for the possibility. Stanley persevered regardless.

In September, the Society conference commenced in Chicago. Much less political in nature, the *Chicago Tribune* reported the event as a ban-quet to "entertain twenty-five Indian chiefs."[25] Sloan was there, speaking of the evils of the bureau and the hope of Indian citizenship. Gordon was elected president in the voting. It was a victory of severely diminished significance. Bureau abolishment was but a dream, and the intertribal bonds the organization meant to foster had been irretrievably frayed over the Peyote Religion and issue of BIA abolition. Gordon's partner and friend, Montezuma, had of course also died. The SAI would exist in name only for several more years. The Society had succumbed to infighting, though in truth the sweeping goals it had set for itself were likely doomed by Washington from the start.[26]

Gordon's opportunities to effect some meaningful change, however, received a boost in early 1923 when Secretary of the Interior Fall resigned his post in shame, implicated in taking bribes for oil leases in the Teapot Dome scandal.[27] Meanwhile, thanks to the work of the Indian Rights Association and the General Federation of Women's Clubs and its Indian Welfare Committee, the plan to divest the Pueblo failed and a Congres-sional investigation was launched regarding the Five Civilized Tribes' troubles in Oklahoma (though it yielded very little).[28] Secretary of the Interior Fall's replacement, Herbert W. Work, was eager to allay reformers' concerns. Work quickly formed the Committee of One Hundred, made up of both Native and white reformers who were to investigate reserva-tion conditions and submit a report on the state of indigenous peoples in America. Along with distinguished politicians and military figures such as General John J. Pershing and presidential candidate William Jennings Bryan, Work's committee included many SAI members: Parker, Sloan,

Eastman, Roe Cloud, and, naturally, Philip Gordon.[29] The committee would later recommend that Fall's decision to open Indians reservations created by executive order be reversed and a court of claims opened. They also suggested investments in reservation health care and sanitation, a loosening of restrictions on religious freedom, and the admission of Indian children to public schools.[30]

Yet when Gordon set to work under the committee's auspices, he immediately felt undermined by the bureau. A scandal erupted at Reserve in September, which he took as an engineered BIA campaign against him. The details are sparse, but Gordon was forced to hire legal counsel after some anti-Catholic Ojibwe, in his words, "filed absurd and ridiculous charges" concerning his "personal conduct" with the Indian Bureau. He was only exonerated after investigations by both the Catholic Church and government inspectors.[31] Disregarding all diplomacy and fear of censure from above, Gordon, in a nearly suicidal gesture of protest, wrote a letter to the Superior *Telegram* expressing his anger at the BIA. It was reprinted in the *Notre Dame University Bulletin*, as well other Catholic and mainstream newspapers. The statement read:

> It is an old trick of the Indian Office to blacken the character of any
> Indian that happens, notwithstanding the retardation caused by the Indian
> Bureau, to rise a little above the ranks. So as soon as an educated Indian
> begins to deplore the conditions of his brother Indians, the Indian Office
> dubs such a one as a disturber, an agitator, and lately he is placed in the
> Bolshevik class. The whole Indian Bureau system of managing Indian
> business to the detriment of the Indian but for the benefit of a few greedy
> and voracious whites, is the most dramatic autocracy in existence the world
> over. Gradually through assistance of the American press, the generous-
> hearted and justice-loving American people are learning something of this
> present-day Indian government humbuggery and deceit practiced by the
> Indian Office forces.

The letter drew the attention of Minnesota senator Henrik Shipstead, who made a trip to the Ojibwe reservations in November and met Father Gordon. The meeting disappointed Gordon and no changes ensued.

In January 1924, Gordon tried again to highlight the plight of the Ojibwe after a private survey of the White Earth Reservation. He presented his critical findings in lectures to women's groups and Catholic organizations in Minneapolis, beseeching both Minnesota's governor, J. A. O. Preus, and the Red Cross to intervene. The Red Cross offered some relief, but Gordon had incited much contentious publicity. The Catholic hierarchy in Superior was displeased.

Bishop Koudelka, despite his conflicts with Gordon, had always treated his missionary with some tolerance. Koudelka's replacement, Bishop Joseph Gabriel Pinten, had no patience for strident pleas for assistance at the missions by an Indian priest who did not know his place. The combination of Gordon's open opposition to the Chippewa Flowage Project and the BIA, his long-standing criticisms of public figures, and the various public scandals he caused with his outspokenness, finally spelled his end at Reserve. In the last days of January, Pinten disingenuously requested Gordon's resignation for "administrative reasons."[32] Friends in the church later told Gordon that 600 to 700 Ojibwe had signed a petition demanding his return, and sent four delegations to lobby Pinten, who ignored them.[33] Gordon questioned whether so many had sought his return, suggesting that he may have had middling support in the Ojibwe community. Most frustratingly, he resigned just before his church was completed. Gordon later claimed that he left Reserve "without controversy and without complaint and without bitterness." One doubts this was true.[34]

In March 1924, two weeks after his forced resignation, Gordon was contacted by the eminent anthropologist and member of the Committee of One Hundred, Warren C. Moorehead. Moorehead's letter concerned the findings of the committee, which he hoped to publish by the summer. Expressing optimism, the anthropologist was certain that the report would create "an unusual opportunity to do something worthwhile along constructive lines in the next Congress." "If we confine ourselves to facts," Moorehead suggested, "no controversy can arise." His idea was to submit a meticulous plan for reorganization, buttressed by supporting materials. Gordon was requested to secure photographic evidence of poverty and disease. The images would persuade Congress that reform was necessary, and that medical and housing appropriations had to be increased.[35] Gordon's

reply tersely expressed his disillusionment with the prospect of development under the BIA. "My dear Moorehead," he began,

> I wish I had time to give you part of my experience of ten years or so dura-
> tion as Catholic priest and Indian versus Indian Office and its policies.
> A summary of the whole experience is as follows:
> For the Indian Office: Ignorance, Stupidity and many times Dishonesty.
> For the Indians: Confusion, Misery, Distress, Misunderstanding, and
> frequently Rascality, Low Living.
> For the Ordinary Citizen: Indian welfare reports distorted, exagger-
> ated, half-told, dishonest, partial.
> For the Country at large: Shame and Disgrace and Dishonour.
> Very sincerely yours,
> Philip Gordon,
> Chippewa Indian and Catholic missionary[36]

At the time he penned his letter, Gordon was exhausted and considered
himself largely done fighting the bureau. Just as he was reaching age
forty, he had experienced the death of his friend Montezuma, witnessed
the destruction of Post and the breakdown of the Society of American
Indians, struggled bitterly and unsuccessfully against the BIA, and—with
his forced resignation—lost his entire purpose as Indian missionary at
Reserve. Much like in 1917 when Gordon was let go by the Bureau of
Catholic Indian Missions, fresh defeats lay behind him and uncertainty
lay ahead.

CHAPTER 10

Continuing the Fight from Centuria

In mid-May 1924, after several months of limbo, Bishop Joseph Gabriel Pinten in Superior appointed Philip Gordon to the largely Irish St. Patrick's Parish in Centuria, Wisconsin. It was an isolated, rural area dominated by Norwegians, where little trouble could be caused. His church and residence were located four miles from Centuria town, on Long Lake.[1] The local *Telegram* newspaper announced that after "six years of extraordinary activity" in Reserve, the famous Father Gordon had arrived.[2] Two weeks after he commenced work, Gordon officiated at the Feast of Saint Philip Neri. The Irish community's welcome was warm, and the experience touched him. He wrote of how "something most significant of the feelings of the real Catholic heart took place in the rectory." Families had come to wish him well, a townsperson read a poem, and those assembled sat down for lunch. According to Gordon, "All departed conscious of having performed a good deed." He thanked God for being "in the midst of a devout Catholic people."[3]

During the following twenty-four years in Centuria, Gordon would attain the mainstream respectability and recognition that had eluded him in Reserve. There would still be agitation for the Indian cause and other political activities in which to partake, but compared to his controversial years as an Indian missionary Gordon's tenure in Centuria was marked by a mellowing militancy, and increasing honors at home and abroad. Unfortunately, the rich epistolary record that exists from 1914 to 1919 dwindles precipitously in the 1920s, eventually becoming nonexistent. Scattered newspaper articles and other records however provide a concise, external

portrait of the last twenty-four years of Gordon's life against the backdrop
of historical events.

In January 1924, the month Gordon had suffered his greatest troubles
in Reserve, a House bill had reached the Senate proposing citizenship
for Indians who requested it. Gordon's friend, Wisconsin senator Robert
La Follette, helped rewrite the bill to grant citizenship without any pre-
requisites. By early June, the revised bill passed both the House and Senate
and was signed by President Coolidge. The Indian Citizenship Act (ICA)
was now law.[4] Montezuma had not lived to see the ICA passed, nor had
Richard Henry Pratt, who died several weeks before in an army hospital
in San Francisco, age eighty-three.[5] Although the act imposed, without
consultation or explicit assent, citizenship upon all indigenous persons in
the United States, Gordon certainly perceived the bill's passage as a great
step forward because of the legal protections it theoretically offered.[6]

In Centuria, Gordon's immediate concern was the anti-Catholic prejudice he felt from the greater Protestant community. At the time, many
non-Catholic Americans believed the Vatican to be a government that
asserted a higher loyalty than that of the United States. As a result, Catholics were often considered disloyal Americans. Conspiracy theories dis-
seminated by groups such as the America Protective League claimed that
the Vatican was attempting a takeover of the country.[7] Dismayed by such
conceptions, Gordon made efforts to engage anyone suspicious of Catholicism. He wrote later in life of how it was "evident from the attitude of some
of my brothers of the cloth that opposition to the Catholic Church was a
necessary evil and bound to exist." In response, Gordon lectured around
Wisconsin in the belief that "a great deal of the antipathy to anything
even remotely Catholic was due in large part to sheer ignorance." Such
appearances sought to counter "the stereotyped objections hurled against
the Catholic Church ever since the founding of the Republic in 1776."[8]
While such conflicts may appear less explosive today, a century ago they
had more sinister implications.

The 1920s saw a strong revival of the Ku Klux Klan not only in the
South but in the North and Midwest, where it became strongest. This
new incarnation of the Klan promoted itself as a reform movement based
on a platform of nativism (or 100 percent Americanism, a slogan held

over from the First World War), white supremacy, separation of church and state, Protestant fundamentalism, anti-Semitism, and anti-Catholicism. (Native Americans were not a group that the Klan felt worth persecuting because they were "safely" contained on reservations.) Between 1920 and 1926, the new Klan attracted millions of members and supporters, many of whom held posts as elected government officials.[9] Their burning crosses were meant to symbolize life, while Catholics worshipped the dead cross.[10] Though these public burnings did not usually target individuals, they asserted the Klan's presence through intimidation.[11]

In 1920, a group of Milwaukee businessmen founded the Knights of the Ku Klux Klan of Wisconsin. Slowly, they made membership gains in the state by encouraging "hate speakers" and alliances with Protestant churches. Because Wisconsin had Irish and Polish Catholic minorities, it was fertile ground for prejudice.[12] In 1924, the Wisconsin Klan reached its peak, publicly chartering their organization with the authorities in Madison and recruiting thirty-four thousand members.[13] The University of Wisconsin even boasted a popular Klan fraternity.[14] The Wisconsin Klan's activities mainly targeted Catholics, though very little physical violence transpired. Instead, Catholics endured incidents of public hate speech, such as the one that took place on June 25, 1926, in Marinette, Wisconsin. There, the Klan held an assembly to expose alleged truths about the Catholic Church. Due to advance publicity, many Catholics attended. After the Klan speakers denounced a group of Catholic nuns active in the area, several men related to the sisters attacked the Klan members, precipitating a riot. The Klan tent was burned to the ground and the five attackers imprisoned for incitement. The incident garnered widespread attention in the Wisconsin press. In the end, Wisconsin governor John J. Blaine pardoned the men.

Gordon, because he lived in a rural area, was highly aware of the Klan's activities in Wisconsin. The state's countryside was particularly receptive to the group's appeals. Grant County boasted one of the largest populations of supporters, who held large public celebrations marked by band music, parades, picnics, and speeches that denounced the three Ks: Koons, Kikes, and Katholics. Other hotbeds included Rusk County in northern Wisconsin, one county over from Gordon's pastorate in Centuria. There a Klan speaker and preacher, Pat Malone, made a specialty of attacking

Catholics.[15] Malone appeared in Centuria in April of that year. Gordon's response to his hate speech, and the Klan's antics in general, is an instructive gauge of his character. Deeply concerned, he contacted the Catholic Church in Ladysmith, Rusk County, to ascertain more information on Malone. The resident priest, L. J. Quigley, denounced the Klan speaker as "a professional mudslinger, out to wrest the people of their hard-earned money through his malicious fanaticism." Worse, a local Protestant minister had been supporting him. "It would do my heart good, and I would feel avenged," Father Quigley confided, "if a bunch of sturdy young lads would give him the fine duckling and a forceful egress from your town."[16] Two weeks after Gordon received this letter, a cross was found burning near the farms of two local Irish-Americans. Polk County's sheriff, George B. Mattson, was suspected of participating.[17] This was of little surprise. The Klan had infiltrated police departments across the state, in particular the one in Madison.[18] On May 11, Gordon interceded by writing Governor Blaine, who warned Mattson that if anyone in his office had been involved dismissal would ensue.[19] No further incidents occurred. Malone's career as a hate speaker concluded not long after when he was convicted of slander for claiming an area priest had fathered an illegitimate child.[20]

Gordon's opposition to the Klan was not only inspired by the organization's anti-Catholicism, but also his belief in racial equality. Several months prior to Malone's appearance in Centuria, Gordon had made a tour of Florida with Major J. Frank Quilty of the U.S. Army and his wife. The segregation they encountered under Jim Crow disgusted Gordon as much as the Klan, who, he stated, based their "degenerate" ideology "on racial and religious prejudice."[21] Wisconsin's surge of Klan activity finally ended around 1928 when membership dropped to just eight hundred—the Klan message having lost its appeal due to negative publicity, corruption scandals, and internal squabbling.[22] On a national scale, the Klan had all but disappeared by 1930, 99 percent of the members having abandoned its various fraternal organizations due to similar reasons.[23]

Though he was isolated at Centuria, Gordon remained as involved as he could in matters affecting Native rights. He hoped, ultimately, to return to Ojibwe lands. In a moving letter, he appealed to the Apostolic Delegate in Washington, DC, Pietro Fumasoni Biondi, for an appointment to an Indian mission:

> The fact that causes me personal grief is that I am an Indian and am deprived of the opportunity to work for my own. Work in the Indian mission field is one of great privation and bitter experience because of the childish prejudices, the ignorance, the illiteracy, the primitive conditions obtaining among the Indian people, the lack for financial support, and the general indifference and apathy of all concerned. I know all this and have experienced it. Nevertheless, I feel so affected by the present conditions that I am quite willing to forsake all else in life to render succor to the Indians whose faith is indeed in peril.[24]

Biondi, it appears, did not even reply.[25] As the titular president of the SAI, Gordon continued to speak out whenever he could on various issues, especially concerning the BIA prohibition on Indian dances on reservations. He lobbied Senator Lenroot to help lift the ban; and to make his point, in August 1926 Gordon organized a large Ojibwe dance at the Church of the Blessed Sacrament in St. Paul, which featured over a hundred dancers from Lac Courte Oreilles. The summer of that year, Gordon also made news when he appeared in Chicago for the Eucharistic Congress donning "full Indian costume, including war bonnet."[26]

According to the St. Paul *Daily News*, Gordon specifically included dances that "certain officials of the federal Indian Bureau are seeking to prohibit on the ground that their continuance only retards the complete civilization of the original Americans." He was defiant, insisting that the "American Indian will not abandon the tribal dances, at least not without stubborn resistance." And there was little reason he should. Gordon explained to the white audience that tribal dances remained "all there is left to the present-day Indians to connect them with their savage ancestors who roamed the prairies and woods of America before this continent was discovered." These dances were "a tradition with them," and "consequently dear to the heart of every Indian." While some were "ceremonial in nature," others had different functions, such as "recreation and entertainment," just as in white society. It was therefore an obvious wrong for the federal government "to deprive the Indians of this traditional cus-tom." And while Gordon conceded that the dancing associated with "late hours, décolleté, escorting, moonshine, etc.," was to be discouraged, he saw no more reason to abolish Indian dances than the Charleston.[27]

Such events and Gordon's role as president of the defunct SAI ensured that his reputation within the BIA lingered.[28] In the summer of 1928, President Coolidge chose to vacation at Cedar Island on the Brule River. Gordon tried in vain to arrange for an Ojibwe delegation to meet with Coolidge in Superior on a tour of Wisconsin that was to follow. The BIA took care to thwart his plans. After corresponding with Coolidge's secre-tary, Everett Sanders, Gordon suggested the meeting for late July.[29] Sand-ers then asked Charles H. Burke, the new commissioner of Indian Affairs, whether he could provide a reference in relation to Gordon's character. "My dear Mr. Sanders," Burke replied,

> I have yours of the 16th making an inquiry with reference to the Rev. Philip Gordon, Pastor of St. Patrick's Church at Centuria, and I have just wired you as follows:
>
>> "Party mentioned yours 16th an agitator, Bolshevist and trouble-maker. He is probably seeking publicity. Letter follows."
>
> I am returning his letter to you, that you may get the name of the society of which he appears to be the president and that you may know that the other officers, all of whom I know except the last one named, are of the same type that he is. It is a very much discredited organization, and I am very sure that the President will make no mistake in declining to participate in any function that the aforesaid organization or its president promotes.[30]

Burke's spiteful censure ensured that no meeting with Coolidge took place, though Gordon was, as a courtesy, given a brief audience with Sanders in Superior—of which nothing came.

Gordon's criticisms nonetheless continued. On a tour of the East Coast in 1929, he stated to the Trenton *Times* that the "poverty existing among the Indian tribes in the United States is simply appalling."[31] He cited the

recently released Meriam Report (1928), a survey of reservation conditions
funded by John D. Rockefeller, named after its director, Lewis Meriam.
The report confirmed and detailed what many already knew. Indians were
mired in an underfinanced trap created and preserved by the U.S. government.[32] Gordon noted how the report proved "widespread poverty,
which verges upon actual starvation, can be found on many Indian Reservations."[33] In 1930, he was still maintaining some connection to Native
activism, giving lectures in major cities arranged by a group called the
Indian Council Fire, and serving as president of the Indian Association of
America. The organization professed many of the goals sought by the
defunct SAI, but without the former's profile.[34] Gordon's own profile,
however, remained very high. In 1932, he traveled to Dublin, Ireland, with
a hundred St. Paul pilgrims, to the Eucharistic Congress. Gordon took
the opportunity, as he often did, to display his feathered headdress.[35] St.
Paul's *Pioneer Press* reported on how the "full-blooded Indian priest of
the Chippewa tribe" thoroughly upstaged "the conventionally dressed cardinals and the pope's legate who marched in the procession." The following year Gordon led another pilgrimage to Rome, where Pope Pius XI
graciously received him.[36] That same year, 1933, Gordon received an hon-
orary doctor of laws from the University of Notre Dame and another
from his alma mater, St. Thomas, each of which he accepted wearing his
headdress.[37] Gordon's life almost ended soon after. In 1934, he was diag-
nosed with malignant carcinoma and given only months to live. A major
operation to remove the tumor, performed by Dr. William Carroll, saved
his life.[38]

When the Great Depression hit in 1929, Gordon became increasingly
involved in Democratic politics and farmers union organizing through
the National Catholic Rural Life Conference, part of the Social Action
Department of the National Catholic Welfare Conference.[39] He felt that
ending rural poverty was a goal all in the Catholic Church should support
vigorously. "I am still waiting to see my brothers of the cloth to become
indignant over the woes of the farmer," he told one newspaper. "Some are
interested in foreign missions and take collections for the heathen in far-
off China. Others are interested in Madagascar or Manchuria, but Polk
County counts many farmers living in absolute insecurity, and few seem

interested. . . . Preachers preach 'Love Thy Neighbor' and promptly forget the neighbor, apparently." Gordon's approach to economics was much the same. He considered conflicts between socialists and capitalists "examples of modern man looking outside himself to explain the chaos that is gradually forming in the world." The key was to look inside and examine one's conscience. This way one could locate the "real answer" to the world's woes, which was "the almost universal rejection by mankind of Christian principles." Republicans, according to Gordon, often failed in the area of charity and good governance. He wrote a friend in 1943, condemning Wisconsin's Republican governor, Julius P. Heil, for "not sending any State aid" to the north of the state. Though many of his parishioners complained "bitterly," Gordon's response was blunt: "That's what you get for voting for a damn Republican."[40]

Gordon remained involved in farm unionizing until the 1940s, speaking at union events and reporting on them in the local press.[41] He fully backed Secretary of Agriculture Henry Wallace, and became friendly with the Wallace family.[42] Had Gordon lived to witness Wallace's bid for president with the Progressive Party in 1948, he may have been one of 2.4 percent of the electorate that voted for him. Other national figures Gordon met and befriended in the 1940s included Congress of Industrial Organizations founder, John L. Lewis, and New York governor Albert Smith.[43] In 1938, Gordon's involvement in Democratic politics prompted him to invite President Roosevelt to a planned Jubilee celebration in St. Paul to mark his twenty-five years in the priesthood.[44] The Jubilee took place in January 1939 and was attended by two hundred parishioners. Pope Pius XI sent "blessings and congratulations."[45] When he returned to Wisconsin, Gordon's mother, Ategekwe, died not long after, in March 1940. She had lived past eighty.[46] She and her husband had moved back to Gordon in 1939. After his wife's death, William Gordon, age ninety, moved in with his son James.[47]

Given Gordon's support of the Roosevelt administration and Democratic politics, he must have been pleased by the major changes that swept through the BIA in the 1930s. In 1933, the long struggle for Indian rights fought by Gordon and others was finally advanced by Roosevelt's appointment of John Collier to the post of commissioner of Indian Affairs. 1934 saw the passage of the Wheeler-Howard Indian Reorganization Act (IRA), or Indian New Deal, which encouraged more autonomy for tribal governments with increased negotiating power. The IRA, partly spurred by the Meriam Report, reinstated two million acres to Native peoples and offered low interest government loans to those on reservations.[48] Many boarding schools were transformed into day schools or shuttered for good.[49] Tribes were also given control over their trust funds, while New Deal programs helped improve reservation infrastructure.[50] Gordon, like many of the other Native activists he worked and fought with, had played a small but important part in the collective effort that informed these improvements in government policy.

In 1942, eighteen years after his arrival in Centuria, Gordon shared his thoughts with a local paper on the state of Indian affairs, expressing genuine optimism. "For many years," he explained, "Indians were . . . robbed . . . of all ideas of responsibility. Their morale was about shattered. Their health was in bad shape and the race seemed doomed to early extinction." But to him there had been positive changes. "Now we have new hopes," Gordon insisted. "And if the present Indian administration will continue its efforts with proper support of the states, like Wisconsin with its 10,000 Indians, there is a future for my race."[51] There was some justification for Gordon's optimism. Along with the benefits that came with the IRA, by 1930 the United States' Indian population had begun growing at twice the rate of the general population, destroying long-held myths concerning their being a dying people.[52]

In 1942 and 1943, Gordon became a worker for the Roosevelt administration and its New Deal programs, serving on the Consultant War Manpower Commission and the National Youth Authority's Wisconsin State advisory committee.[53] When the United States entered World War II in December 1941, he offered his services as an Army chaplain but did not receive an appointment due to his age.[54] Still wanting to be involved in the war effort, Gordon prepared broadcasts for the Office of Strategic Services (the forerunner of the Central Intelligence Agency) in Italian and German for KSTP radio in St. Paul. He also met with four hundred German prisoners of war when they were interned in Wisconsin. Gordon impressed them greatly with his command of German. He also took time to socialize, leading them in songs and preforming religious services for those prisoners who were Catholics. In May 1942, Gordon had the pleasure of returning to Odanah, on the Bad River Reservation, where he grew up. The occasion was the dedication of his alma mater, St. Mary's School, which had been completely rebuilt to accommodate its 184 students. Gordon delivered the ceremony's opening address.[55]

By the 1940s, Gordon had fully shed his status as a pariah in Washington. On May 11, 1942, Wisconsin representative Bernard J. Gehrmann presented a resolution by Gordon praising the National Youth Authority's training program. Gehrmann, in turn, took the opportunity to praise Father Gordon: "Mr. Speaker, Father Philip Gordon, perhaps the best-known Catholic priest in Wisconsin, lives in my district and has a parish in Centuria, Polk County. Father Gordon is famous all over the country, not only because he is an Indian priest, but mainly because of his great humanitarian nature and love for his fellow man be they white, Indian or Negro, be they rich or poor. Because of his understanding of human nature and his willingness to do things for his fellow man, he is sought out to serve on and usually head every public function near his home." Gehrmann then lauded Gordon's service on the advisory committee and introduced his recommendation that the program be continued.[56] A year later, Gordon addressed the chamber himself. On June 11, 1943, he became the first indigenous person to give an opening prayer before Congress. Donning his headdress, he offered a prayer that included Anishinaabe-mowin, "Bless, O Great Spirit, the Kitchi Manito of our forefathers, our Great White Father, our President and our Commander in Chief. Bless the Members of this Congress. Bless us all, dear Lord."[57]

Less than a week after Gordon's appearance in Washington—the culmination of his career—his father, William Gordon, died at age ninety-three. Philip was in Philadelphia and could not be reached when the local Superior paper printed the news.[58] No personal statements on his father's death appear to exist. As he himself aged, Gordon only collected more honors. In 1944, he received the Indian Achievement Award given by the Indian Council Fire in Chicago. Funnily enough, the ceremony was held at the city's YMCA. According to the press, Gordon displayed "wisdom and wit" in his informal talk at the event. The reporter noted that he "has been deeply interested in the problems of the Indian in America and has been a great fighter for justice and tolerance for all people, including those of his own race."[59] Though Gordon had lost the edginess of this former militancy—working with the U.S. government instead of against it—this was an accurate characterization of his life in Native activism.

CHAPTER 11

Paul Villaume, a Journey, and Philip Gordon's Final Years

W hile fighting for his social and political causes in later years, Philip Gordon maintained a personal life. At its center was a much younger man named Paul Villaume. Gordon met Villaume and his family at Calderwood Springs Resort at Bone Lake in 1925, while the Villaumes were summering there. Paul's older brother, Louis, was a member of Gordon's Boy Scout troop. The Villaume family cultivated a friendly relationship with Gordon and he confirmed each of their children at St. Patrick's Church. William Gordon was Paul's sponsor. After his confirmation, Paul, then thirteen years old, began making trips with Gordon to Lac Court Oreilles. There he was inducted into the tribe and given the name Kawahdin, or North Wind, also translated humorously as Hot Air. Paul's family called Gordon "the Chief," and Paul had his own room at Gordon's residence when his family visited the lakes.

In 1934, soon after Gordon had recovered from surgery, he and Paul took a three-month-long cruise around the Mediterranean, sharing a stateroom. Gordon was around forty-nine, Paul Villaume eighteen. Villaume's mother wrote him concerning the trip: "My dear boy: When you receive this letter, you will have started one of life's great journeys. You are a very lucky boy to have a friend like Father Gordon. It means much in life to know such a person. We are all happy to number him among our friends and it is our wish that you do all in your power to make Father Gordon's trip a perfect one." Villaume's primary responsibility was seeing to Gordon's headdress and harmonica. Together, they visited numerous sites along the Mediterranean, such as Casablanca, Gibraltar, Tunis, the

French Riviera, Malta, Sicily, and Naples. They then moved on to the Middle East, seeing Lebanon, Tel Aviv, and Cairo. The return trip took them through many European capitals, ending in Rome. On Easter Sunday, Villaume and Gordon visited the Vatican. Gordon's headdress made a tremendous impression on the crowd, which thronged to him.

After returning to Wisconsin, Gordon and Villaume continued to spend time together. They were separated when World War II began because Paul worked for the Red Cross in Chicago, and fuel rationing made travel difficult. (However, the two were together in Chicago when Gordon received the news of his mother's death.) During this time apart, Gordon wrote Villaume regular letters, usually about mundane matters such as daily routines and politics. Sometimes, each would write of how they missed each other's company. On May 16, 1942, Gordon wrote, "Paul, I was a little heart-sick when you wrote of so many things of the days gone by." Nearing age sixty, Gordon had perhaps begun to feel lonely. In his letters, he expressed hope that the war would soon end. "I bet you, Paul, we will do a lot of running around once the show is over," he happily predicted. "Just think of getting new cars, all the gas we need, and all the tires we can use! Then cash in on our bonds." In 1944, Gordon began writing his autobiography. He did not enjoy the work and thought it too monumental a task.

When the war concluded, Gordon and Villaume resumed their friendship, with Villaume spending much time at Long Lake. From that period on Gordon's health began to falter. He was hospitalized from November 1946 to January 1947. Worried that his death was imminent, he composed a letter of thanks to everyone he had known. "My debt to each and all can never be repaid," he wrote. "Left in our weak power is but to promise each a memento in my yet-to-be-read Holy Masses (may there be many) ere the twilight comes—prelude to the great adventure—and the evening comes, and the busy world is hushed, and the fever of life is over, and our work is done! Then in His mercy may He give us safe lodging and a holy rest, and peace at last!" Thinking that his friend would soon die, Villaume promised Gordon that if he had a son he would name him Philip. In 1947, Villaume took an extended trip to Europe. When he returned, Gordon had been in and out of St. John's Hospital in St. Paul and was being cared for by nuns at his residence. He appeared with a group of Ojibwe who had resolved to sue the United States government for claims due them for expropriated lands in July 1948. By that time, he was using a wheelchair. It was his last public act in the name of Native rights and his people.

In May 1948, Gordon and Villaume again spent time together at Long Lake. Gordon returned to St. John's Hospital weeks after. Villaume visited him on September 30 and remained until midnight. The following morning, he received news by telephone that Gordon was dying. He rushed to the hospital just in time to join a group of nuns in a final prayer. Philip recognized Paul's voice, then passed away. The date was October 1, 1948.[1] Following a funeral mass in the Centuria pastorate, Philip was buried in his family's plot in Gordon, Wisconsin.[2]

While contemporary sensibilities might excite the suspicion that the love between Gordon and Villaume was romantic in nature, it is difficult to leap to this conclusion considering how the relationship appeared to those who lived at the time. The sensitivities that now prevail had no relevance then, and there exists no evidence that points to such a supposition.

Conclusion

On October 2, 1948, the *New York Times* published the news of Father Philip Bergin Gordon's death. The obituary mentioned his twenty-plus years in Centuria, how during his time with the Bureau of Catholic Indian Missions he had "prompted a Government investigation by his reports of irregularities and discrimination at United States Indian schools," and why Gordon had received his famous nickname. "He was known as 'Wisconsin's Fighting Priest,'" the *Times* explained, "because of his campaigns for bettering the conditions of the Indians."[1] It remains unfortunate that someone who fought so strenuously for Native rights suffered so many defeats and did not make the progress he wished.

All considered, some scholars and readers may find this biography's subject unsympathetic. In his younger years, Gordon's character could be immensely difficult. His arrogance, quite clearly, often interfered with his personal and professional relationships. As one of the original radicals who pushed for BIA abolition, Gordon contributed greatly to the destructive factionalism within the Society of American Indians, which eventually caused the organization's demise. Some will also look askance at Gordon's efforts to shift Native belief systems and lifeways toward Catholicism and participation in U.S. society, not to mention his open disapproval of what he derogatorily termed "paganism" among the Ojibwe and other Indian nations.[2] Then there is Gordon's failure to discern the ongoing tragedy at Haskell Institute, blind as he was to anything amiss other than the Protestant machinations he perceived. While today such aspects of his activism are indefensible, Gordon was guided by sincere beliefs, convinced that religious and cultural assimilation were necessary for the salvation and survival of Indians within the United States. But rather than reject his roots, he saw indigenous ancestry as a source of strength and pride. Certain that once liberated from the bonds of the Bureau of Indian Affairs Native peoples would flourish, he fought to protect not only the Ojibwe as individuals but their lands and aspects of their heritage—for instance the dances he promoted and defended before white audiences. As a publishing pioneer, with *War-Whoop* and *Anishinabe Enamiad*, Gordon exposed government-imposed bondage and promoted ideals such as democracy and self-determination. For all the above reasons, "Wisconsin's Fighting Priest" will perhaps have a mixed legacy in scholarly literature.

Aside from devotion to spreading Catholicism, at the center of Gordon's life was his quest to dismantle the BIA reservation system forced upon Indians and his dogged efforts to counter the mismanagement, corruption, demoralization, and pain left in the bureau's wake. These objectives were products of his faith and his belief in human rights and fairness regardless of race, creed, or color. Choosing to pursue justice is a difficult road for any person to travel. Gordon's fight for the Ojibwe, which included publicizing their penury and fiercely lobbying every official channel for assistance and relief, was a daunting challenge, internally and externally. His work on the reservations and the need he witnessed brought him to tears. His opposition to the BIA and the Chippewa Flowage Project put him at odds with powerful interests that would stop at little to realize their ends. These were involvements that risked censure, and Gordon—after just several years of intense agitation—paid a high price for his outspokenness. In losing his Catholic mission in Reserve, Gordon lost his life's mission to minster to his own people. But still he fought, and still he looked into the sky for justice, as an Ojibwe, activist, and priest. Though the latter involved proselytizing for a "white" religion among an indigenous people in no need of spiritual guidance, this aspect of Gordon's activism should not overshadow his life story.

Had Gordon lived to the age of his father or grandfather, both of whom enjoyed excellent health until their nineties, it is likely that he would have attracted scholarly attention long before the publication of this meagre biography. Gordon, still alert in his eighties, would have also lived to see the Red Power, or American Indian Movement, blossom in the late 1960s and 1970s. In 1971, as part of this struggle for American Indian civil rights, the Lac Courte Oreilles Ojibwe occupied the dam built under the Chippewa Flowage Project in the 1920s and sought compensation for damages incurred since the site's theft.[3] Gordon would have surely joined his tribesmen, resolute as ever to pursue justice. The following year, 1972, the American Indian Movement's Trail of Broken Treaties march occurred, culminating in a three-day occupation of the Bureau of Indian Affairs' headquarters in Washington, DC. Among the demands made by the march's leaders were treaty review (with compensation for violations) and land restoration; monies for health care, education, and development; freedom to organize without federal interference; the right to preserve cultural traditions; and Father Philip Bergin Gordon's long-held desire: BIA abolition.[4] One can easily imagine him wearing his headdress in advanced old age, perhaps walking with the aid of a cane or being pushed in a wheelchair, on his way to Washington, still ready and willing to fight.

Notes

Introduction

1. "Rev. Philip Gordon," *New York Times*, October 2, 1948, 15.

2. Charles H. Burke to Everett Sanders, July 18, 1918, Papers of the Society of American Indians.

3. See Paula Delfeld, *The Indian Priest: Father Philip B. Gordon, 1885–1948* (Chicago: Franciscan Herald Press, 1977), 17; Mary Macaria, "Antoine Gordon, Grandfather of Father Philip Gordon," Franciscan Sisters of Perpetual Adoration Archives. Philip Gordon's birthyear is a matter of dispute in several of the sources used in this biography. Delfeld records the year as 1885, as does "Outline for Biography of a Chippewa Indian Who Became a Catholic Priest, Rev. Philip Gordon, LL.D. 'Tibishkogijik,'" Wisconsin Historical Society, Madison (see page 11). The birthyear of 1886 appears on Gordon's gravestone. See "Philip Bergin Gordon," https://www.findagrave.com/memorial/50549453/philip-bergin -gordon (accessed January 15, 2019). The same birth year, 1886, is also given in "Information Pertaining to Reverend [Philip] Gordon, LL.D., Chippewa Indian Priest," Franciscan Sisters of Perpetual Adoration Archives. However, it is clear from Gordon's early correspondence that he believed himself to have been born in 1885. An enclosure to one of his letters, dating from 1901, states that he is sixteen-and-a-half years old, meaning that he was born in 1885. See Philip Gordon to whom it may concern, May 8, 1901, Franciscan Sisters of Perpetual Adoration Archives. Why the date on his gravestone is apparently incorrect remains a mystery. There is also some mystery surrounding the translation of Gordon's Ojibwe name, Tibishkogijik (modern spelling, Dibishkoo-giizhig). Delfeld's *The Indian Priest* gives the translation Looking into the Sky and is the sole source to do so. (Another translation of Gordon's name, Sign in the Sky, is given in "Father Gordon Visits Buffalo," *American Indian Magazine*

4.1 (January–March 1916): 349–51. The article is a reprint from the *Buffalo Echo*.) Since Delfeld interviewed Gordon's surviving family and those who knew him, it is likely that they felt Looking into the Sky to be accurate—as it is likely that Gordon used the translation himself. University of Wisconsin Press has attempted to verify the translation. Two experts on Anishinaabemowin pointed out that Like the Sky or Like the Day would be literal translations, though Looking into the Sky might have been the meaning implied by the namer. They also stressed that Ojibwe names do not always translate well into English, and that there are many nuances in Anishinaabemowin that do not immediately reveal themselves in print. Email correspondence between Gwen Walker and Tadeusz Lewandowski, December 2018–January 2019. And finally, the name Tibishkogijik is sometimes hyphenated as Ti-Bish-Ko-Gi-Jik. I have used the spelling without hyphens on the advice of the aforementioned experts.

4. See "Father Gordon, Indian Priest, Plans Jubilee: Centuria Pastor Sends Invitation to President Roosevelt," *Telegram*, 1938, Franciscan Sisters of Perpetual Adoration Archives; "Outline for Biography," 24, 28.

5. The Bureau of Indian Affairs (originally the Office of Indian Affairs, or Indian Office) has been the official name of this government organ since 1947. Nonetheless, it was often referred to as the "bureau" prior to the name change. Bureau of Indian Affairs and Indian Bureau are employed here because of the ubiquity of the titles during the historical period with which this book deals. See C. L. Henson, "From War to Self Determination: A History of the Bureau of Indian Affairs," http://www.americansc.org.uk/Online/indians.htm (accessed January 3, 2018).

6. David Wallace Adams, *Education for Extinction: American Indians and the Boarding School Experience, 1875–1928* (Wichita: University Press of Kansas, 1995), 8–10; Peter J. Rahill, "The Catholic Indian Missions and Grant's Peace Policy, 1870–1884" (PhD diss., Catholic University of America, Washington, DC, 1953), 27.

7. Jacqueline Fear-Segal, "Nineteenth-Century Indian Education: Universalism versus Evolutionism," *Journal of American Studies* 33.2 (August 1999): 323–41.

8. Frederick E. Hoxie, *A Final Promise: The Campaign to Assimilate the Indians, 1880–1920* (Lincoln: University of Nebraska Press, 1984), 75–76.

9. See any number of accounts of the boarding-school experiment: Adams, *Education for Extinction*; Brenda J. Child, *Boarding School Seasons: American Indian Families, 1900–1940* (Lincoln: University of Nebraska Press, 1998); K. Tsianina Lomawaima, Brenda J. Child, and Margaret L. Archuleta, eds., *Away from Home: American Indian Boarding School Experiences, 1879–2000* (Phoenix:

Heard Museum, 2000); Clifford E. Trafzer and Jean A. Keller, eds., *Boarding School Blues: Revisiting American Indian Educational Experiences* (Lincoln: Bison Books, 2006); and most recently, Arnold Krupat, *Changed Forever: American Indian Boarding-School Literature* (Albany: State University of New York Press, 2018).

10. Leon Speroff, *Carlos Montezuma, MD, a Yavapai American Hero: The Life and Times of an American Indian, 1866–1923* (Portland, OR: Arnica, 2005), 69.

11. See Mark Thiel, "The Bureau of Catholic Indian Missions: 140 Years of Action," PowerPoint prepared for the Tekakwitha Conference, Fargo, North Dakota, July 24, 2014, https://www.marquette.edu/library/archives/Mss/BCIM/documents/BCIM-SC1-PictureHistory.pdf (accessed January 15, 2019).

12. Kevin Abing, introduction to "Directors of the Bureau of Catholic Indian Missions," 1994, http://www.marquette.edu/library/archives/Mss/BCIM/BCIM-SC1-directors.pdf (accessed April 4, 2018).

13. Thiel, "The Bureau of Catholic Indian Missions."

14. Delfeld, *The Indian Priest*, 10, 19; "Was Big Event in Our Village: Celebration Biggest Ever Seen Here," *Star* (Odanah) January 9, 1914, Franciscan Sisters of Perpetual Adoration Archives.

15. Marion A. Habig, *Heralds of the King: The Franciscans of the St. Louis-Chicago Province, 1858–1958* (Chicago: Franciscan Herald Press, 1958), 506.

16. Thiel, "The Bureau of Catholic Indian Missions."

17. One can find scattered references to Gordon in, for instance, Brenda J. Child, *Holding Our World Together: Ojibwe Women and the Survival of Community* (New York: Viking, 2012), 90; Hazel W. Hertzberg, *The Search for an American Indian Identity: Modern Pan Indian Movements* (Syracuse: Syracuse University Press, 1971), 140, 142, 147, 153–54, 170–71, 176, 182, 184, 187–88, 193, 198, 202, 204, 228; Speroff, *Carlos Montezuma*, 239, 360, 367, 382. Searches on the JSTOR (Journal Storage) and Project Muse databases turn up no articles dealing exclusively with Gordon in any academic journals on American Indian studies, including the relatively recent double issue of *Studies in American Indian Literatures* 25.2 and *American Indian Quarterly* 37.3 (Summer 2013). Titled *The Society of American Indians and Its Legacies: A Special Combined Issue of SAIL and AIQ*, the articles therein feature Red Progressives in the Society of American Indians and other themes relevant to the organization. Gordon is given only a few brief mentions in the issue, in P. Jane Hafen, "'Help Indians Help Themselves': Gertrude Bonnin, the SAI, and the NCAI," *Studies in American Indian Literatures* 25.2 and *American Indian Quarterly* 37.3 (Summer 2013): 210; and Thomas Constantine Maroukis, "The Peyote Controversy and the

Demise of the Society of American Indians," *Studies in American Indian Literatures* 25.2 and *American Indian Quarterly* 37.3 (Summer 2013): 167, 178. Yet figures of arguably lesser importance to the SAI—Laura Cornelius Kellogg, Marie Baldwin, and Henry Roe Cloud—are given longer treatments in full articles. See Kristina Ackley, "Laura Cornelius Kellogg, Lolomi, and Modern Oneida Placemaking," *Studies in American Indian Literatures* 25.2 and *American Indian Quarterly* 37.3 (Summer 2013): 117–38; Cathleen D. Cahill, "Marie Louise Bottineau Baldwin: Indigenizing the Federal Indian Service," *Studies in American Indian Literatures* 25.2 and *American Indian Quarterly* 37.3 (Summer 2013): 65–86; Renya K. Ramirez, "Ho-Chunk Warrior, Intellectual, and Activist: Henry Roe Cloud Fights for the Apaches," *Studies in American Indian Literatures* 25.2 and *American Indian Quarterly* 37.3 (Summer 2013): 291–309; and Cristina Stanciu, "An Indian Woman of Many Hats: Laura Cornelius Kellogg's Embattled Search for an Indigenous Voice," *Studies in American Indian Literatures* 25.2 and *American Indian Quarterly* 37.3 (Summer 2013): 87–115.

18. Lucy Maddox, *Citizen Indians: Native American Intellectuals, Race, and Reform* (Ithaca: Cornell University Press, 2005), 10–11.

19. Frederick E. Hoxie, *Talking Back to Civilization: Indian Voices from the Progressive Era* (New York: Bedford / St. Martin's Press, 2001), 11.

20. A few representative works on the Red Progressives cited in this biography include: Hertzberg, *The Search for an American Indian Identity*; Hoxie, *Talking Back to Civilization*; Maddox, *Citizen Indians*. See also the combined double issue of *Studies in American Indian Literatures* 25.2 and *American Indian Quarterly* 37.3 (Summer 2013).

21. For biographical treatments of Eastman, Parker, Montezuma, Roe Cloud, and Bonnin, see, respectively: Raymond Wilson, *Ohiyesa: Charles Eastman, Santee Sioux* (Urbana: University of Illinois Press, 1983); Joy Porter, *To Be Indian: The Life of Iroquois-Seneca Arthur Caswell Parker* (Norman: University of Oklahoma Press, 2001); Peter Iverson, *Carlos Montezuma and the Changing World of American Indians* (Albuquerque: University of New Mexico Press, 1982); Speroff, *Carlos Montezuma*; Joel Pfister, *The Yale Indian: The Education of Henry Roe Cloud* (Durham: Duke University Press, 2009); David W. Messer, *Henry Roe Cloud: A Biography* (New York: Hamilton Books, 2009); and Tadeusz Lewandowski, *Red Bird, Red Power: The Life and Legacy of Zitkala-Ša* (Norman: University of Oklahoma Press, 2016). Gordon's life, it must be noted, has been recorded in Paula Delfeld's book *The Indian Priest: Father Philip B. Gordon, 1885–1948*, published in Chicago by the Franciscan Herald Press in 1977. Though she did extensive research on her subject by interviewing numerous relatives and people who knew Gordon, Delfeld's biography cannot be considered scholarly

or definitive. *The Indian Priest* is a somewhat hagiographic effort punctuated by nostalgic stories, lacking any attempt to contextualize Gordon's life within Progressive-era Indian activism or within the field of Indigenous Studies. Due to the research behind it, however, Delfeld's book boasts great value as a source, primarily because she had access to some of Gordon's personal writings and other papers now unavailable. (For her list of sources see pages 149–51.) Even so, Delfeld contains nothing from the vitally important archives on which this biography relies: the Bureau of the Catholic Indian Missions Records, Raynor Memorial Libraries, Marquette University Archives, Milwaukee, Wisconsin; Franciscan Sisters of Perpetual Adoration Archives, La Crosse, Wisconsin; Carlos Montezuma Papers, Wisconsin Historical Society, Madison; Papers of the Society of American Indians, edited by John Larner, Cornell University Library, Ithaca, New York; Franciscan Provence of the Sacred Heart Archives, St. Louis, Missouri; Provence of the Sacred Heart Franciscan Records, Raynor Memorial Libraries, Marquette University Archives, Milwaukee, Wisconsin; and the United States Works Progress Association Chippewa Indian Historical Project Records, 1936–40, 1942, Wisconsin Historical Society, Madison. When Delfeld is cited in this biography it is mainly as a repository of quotes from primary sources and factual information unavailable elsewhere. This is particularly true of the last two chapters. To give some background: Paula A. Hoffman Delfeld was born in 1907 and was a life-long Wisconsin resident and Catholic. She studied in Fond du Lac and at the Rhinelander School of the Arts, later becoming a member of the Wisconsin Regional Writers' Society, Wisconsin Genealogical Society, and the National Writers' Club, among many others. Her primary vocation was that of photojournalist. She wrote numerous books, including her own autobiography. She died at Fond du Lac, age ninety-eight, in 2005. See "Paula A. Hoffman Delfeld," https://www.findagrave.com/memorial/66649224/paula-a .-delfeld (accessed August 16, 2018).

22. *War-Whoop*, January 1916, Franciscan Sisters of Perpetual Adoration Archives; Speroff, *Carlos Montezuma*, 383–95.

23. Porter briefly acknowledges such in her biography of Arthur C. Parker, *To Be Indian*. She writes that the "creeping sectarianism" in the SAI, "introduced with the prominence of Father Philip Gordon of Washington, served to heighten dissent" (see 126). This mention in scholarly literature is one the few to recognize Gordon's significance within the Society.

24. See Robert Allen Warrior, *Tribal Secrets: Recovering American Intellectual Traditions* (Minneapolis: University of Minnesota Press, 1995), 7–8. Warrior is critical of what he perceives as the "Christian and secular assimilationist" Red Progressives, who are part of an "integrationist legacy of post-Wounded Knee

existence." "The purpose of these authors," he continues, "was to gain sympathy from white audiences for the difficult, but to the authors necessary, process
of becoming American citizens."

25. See Maddox, *Indian Citizens*, 11–16, for a discussion of the goals and
stances of the SAI intellectuals. See also Philip J. Deloria, "Four Thousand
Invitations," *Studies in American Indian Literatures* 25.2 and *American Indian
Quarterly* 37.3 (Summer 2013): 25–43. Deloria argues that despite many of its
members being largely assimilated, the Society of America Indians "worked
actively to preserve elements of Native cultures and societies from destruction."
Therefore, "ranting about the supposedly assimilated Indians of the turn of the
twentieth century seem[s] a little quaint."

26. See, for instance, Philip Gordon, "Editorial," *A-ni-shi-na-be E-na-mi-ad*
1.2 (May 1918): 1, Franciscan Province of the Sacred Heart Archives.

27. Rafael Maris, "When Will an Indian Priest Serve a Mission Again?"
Catholic Herald Citizen, March 28, 1969; "Diocese's History Has Just One
Indian Priest," *Catholic Herald Citizen*, March 29, 1969, Franciscan Sisters of
Perpetual Adoration Archives.

Chapter 1. The Ojibwe and the Gordon Family

1. "Ojibwa Migrations," October 20, 2012, http://nativeamericannetroots
.net/diary/1392 (accessed November 12, 2018); Barry M. Pritzker, *A Native American Encyclopedia: History, Culture, People* (Oxford: Oxford University Press,
2000), 342–43; Charlie Otto Rasmussen, *Where the River Is Wide: Pahquahwong
and the Chippewa Flowage* (Odanah, WI: Great Lakes Indian Fish & Wildlife
Commission Press, 1998), 12–13; Anton Treuer, *The Assassination of Hole in
the Day* (St. Paul: Borealis Books, 2011), 13; Michael Witgen, *An Infinity of
Nations: How the Native New World Shaped Early North America* (Philadelphia:
University of Pennsylvania Press, 2012), 13–14, 44. Today, the Ojibwe populations in the United States and Canada number around three hundred thousand, the majority living in Canada. See "American Indian and Alaska Native
Populations," *Centers for Disease Control and Prevention*, https://web.archive
.org/web/20121231140455/http://www.cdc.gov:80/minorityhealth/populations/
REMP/aian.html (accessed August 1, 2018).

2. Child, *Holding Our World Together*, 8, 20–21, 25, 48, 92–93; Treuer, *The
Assassination of Hole in the Day*, 15–23, 29; John Phillip Well-Off-Man, "The
History of Chief Rocky Boy and His Band and the Founding of Rocky Boy
Reservation" (MA thesis, University of Montana, 2007); Witgen, *An Infinity of
Nations*, 19.

3. See Edward Benton-Banai, *The Mishomis Book: The Voice of the Ojibway* (Minneapolis: University of Minnesota Press, 2010), 2–8, 29–34, 68–73. There are several spellings of Kitchi Manito (some newer), and there are many variants of the name Nanabozho. Benton-Banai uses the spelling Gi'tchie Man-i-to and the Nanabozho variant Waynaboozhoo. It must also be noted that Ojibwe spiritual beliefs are far too complex to offer here with any adequacy in a mere précis. For more information, see Ruth Landes, *Ojibwa Religion and the Midéwiwin* (Madison: University of Wisconsin Press, 1968); Theresa S. Smith, *The Island of the Anishnaabeg: Thunders and Water Monsters and the Traditional Ojibwe Life World* (Moscow: University of Idaho Press, 1995); and Christopher Vecsey, *Traditional Ojibwa Religion and Its Historical Changes* (Philadelphia: American Philosophical Society, 1983).

4. French Jesuits appeared around the first half of the seventeenth century in areas such as present-day Sault Sainte Marie, Michigan. One missionary was Claude Allouez, who founded (then abandoned) a mission at La Pointe, located on Lake Superior's Madeline Island, in the 1660s. Though Catholic missionaries like Allouez saw Europeans as civilized and Natives as savages without knowledge of Christ and God, Allouez found similarities in Catholic and Ojibwe beliefs that he highlighted, hoping to make the Catholic message palatable to its hearers. See Rahill, "The Catholic Indian Missions," 87; Witgen, *An Infinity of Nations*, 44, 77–81. Witgen explains that both Jesuits and the Ojibwe believed that the world was permeated by spiritual power, and when Allouez spoke of the resurrection of Christ it rang true among the Ojibwe, who believed that when relatives were taken by death, their roles and identities could be taken on by the living. Children who had died could also be replaced by adoption, creating a restoration, or resurrection of sorts. French Jesuits had some previous success with this method among Native peoples in the East, even converting one Mohawk woman, Kateri Tekakwitha, who was later canonized as a Catholic Saint. See Rachael Donadio, "Pope Canonizes 7 Saints, Including 2 Women with New York Ties," *New York Times*, October 21, 2012. For a firsthand account of Kateri Tekakwitha's life, see Pierre Cholonec, *Kateri Tekakwitha: The Iroquois Saint*, trans. William Ingraham and Ellen H. Walworth (Merchantville, NJ: Arx, 2012). Regardless, Allouez and later missionaries had little success in converting the Ojibwe. Most of the clans would resist Christianity until the mid-nineteenth century, when they had become confined to reservations. See Vecsey, *Traditional Ojibwa Religion*, 45–46.

5. Pritzker, *A Native American Encyclopedia*, 342–43; Treuer, *The Assassination of Hole in the Day*, 36–37, 39.

6. See James A. Clifton, "Wisconsin Death March: Explaining the Extremes in Old Northwest Indian Removal," *Transactions of the Wisconsin Academy of Sciences, Arts and Letters* 75 (1987): 1–40.

7. Delfeld, *The Indian Priest*, 13.

8. Child, *Holding Our World Together*, 57; William W. Warren, *History of the Ojibway People* (St. Paul: Minnesota Historical Society Press, 1984), 9; Michael A. McDonnell, *Masters of Empire: Great Lakes Indians and the Making of America* (New York: Hill and Wang, 2015), 323.

9. Delfeld, *The Indian Priest*, 13.

10. Macaria, "Antoine Gordon, Grandfather of Father Philip Gordon."

11. Ross Enochs, "Native Americans on the Path to the Catholic Church: Cultural Crisis and Missionary Adaptation," *U.S. Catholic Historian* 27.1 (Winter 2009): 72; "Multinational Treaties at Prairie du Chien," http://treatiesmatter.org/treaties/land/1825-1830-Multinational (accessed November 12, 2018); Treuer, *The Assassination of Hole in the Day*, 14, 23, 35–37, 41–42, 44–49, 57. One of the first Catholic missionaries to establish himself among the Ojibwe was Father Francis Pierz, at Crow Wing, located in present-day Minnesota near Hole in the Day the Elder's stronghold, Gull Lake. See Stephen Bunson and Margaret Bunson, *Faith in the Wilderness: The Story of the Catholic Indian Missions* (Huntington, IN: Our Sunday Visitor Press, 2000), 196. Hole in the Day the Younger flirted with converting to Christianity but never did. See Treuer, *The Assassination of Hole in the Day*, 7, 111, 167, 181.

12. Macaria, "Antoine Gordon, Grandfather of Father Philip Gordon."

13. McDonnell, *Masters of Empire*, 321; Rahill, "The Catholic Indian Missions," 87.

14. Child, *Holding Our World Together*, 58.

15. Macaria, "Antoine Gordon, Grandfather of Father Philip Gordon."

16. Child, *Holding Our World Together*, 48.

17. Macaria, "Antoine Gordon, Grandfather of Father Philip Gordon." Gordon supplied this family history during his time at St. Thomas College upon the request of Sister Mary Macaria, who was preparing a volume entitled *Noble Lives of a Noble Race* (1943) with her pupils from St. Mary's School. The text is apparently a newspaper obituary from the *Superior Evening Telegram*. Gordon was unable to furnish information himself due to the degree of attention his studies required.

18. Macaria, "Antoine Gordon, Grandfather of Father Philip Gordon."

19. Unfortunately, no mention of any personal qualities of or anecdotes about Jean-Batiste Gaudin or Owanishan are found in "Antoine Gordon, Grandfather of Father Philip Gordon," "The Gordon Family," or Delfeld's *The*

Indian Priest. One can only conjecture about their views on Antoine's devotion to Catholicism.

20. Macaria, "Antoine Gordon, Grandfather of Father Philip Gordon." Delfeld notes that Antoine Gordon's education might have been supplemented by contact with Franciscans. See Delfeld, *The Indian Priest*, 16.

21. "The Gordon Family."

22. Macaria, "Antoine Gordon, Grandfather of Father Philip Gordon."

23. Delfeld, *The Indian Priest*, 14.

24. Warren, *History of the Ojibway People*, 9, 323.

25. See Marie D. Livingston, "An Indian Humorist," Franciscan Sisters of Perpetual Adoration Archives. The short text is quoted here:

> Some years ago, the Reverend Philip Gordon's grandfather owned a commercial store. He catered to his own people and had many charging accounts. He was known to be a witty old man throughout the Indian settlement; that he was always joking, first upon one thing, then upon another. One day he was exceptionally humorous. One of his Indian patrons went to the store for supplies. During his purchase, they were exchanging jokes. The customer became serious and asked the old man the date of the month. In asking the question in the Chippewa tongue, the question is similar to saying, "What price do you want for the sun?" Old man Gordon chuckled a bit and answered, "Well, I don't know how much I would charge if I had the sun for sale." The customer grunted and answered, "Yes, if you had the sun for sale no doubt you would charge plenty for it." Old man Gordon chuckled some more in merriment and replied, "Yes, if I did have the sun for sale, you no doubt would want to run your face for it." Eh'gi da wi boa'musina ah maw inuc. (To charge the sale of the sun to his credit.)

26. Delfeld, *The Indian Priest*, 147. See Genealogical Table.

27. After Daniel's death, Isabelle married a Frenchman, Le Noir, and bore three children. Le Noir later went insane and drowned himself in Chequamegon Bay. Isabelle then married a full-blooded Ojibwe named Osawaamikons (Yellow Little Beaver), brother of Chief Naganub. The couple had three children, two of whom died prematurely. One drowned in a shipwreck on Lake Superior, the other perished in a railroad accident. Osawaamikons was later murdered, forcing Isabelle to seek the care of her son, Charles, her fifth child by Daniel Dingley. Isabelle died in Superior around 1870 and was buried in a Catholic cemetery. The marriage between Antoine Gordon and Sarah Dingley likely took place at La Pointe or the mouth of Yellow River. Church records show that the marriage was "revalidated" at Reserve, Wisconsin, in 1893. Isabelle's father

may have been a clerk for the Northwest Fur Company, which established itself in Wisconsin around 1804. The Ojibwe gave him the name Mushkodence, meaning the Prairie. He had three other children; two of his sons are thought to have died in the Civil War. The birthdates of the persons discussed in chapter 1 are particularly hard to determine with complete accuracy due to conflicting information in source materials. See Delfeld, *The Indian Priest*, 147; "The Gordon Family."

28. Ronald N. Satz, *Chippewa Treaty Rights: The Reserved Rights of Wisconsin's Chippewa Indians in Historical Perspective* (Madison: Wisconsin Academy of Sciences, Arts and Letters, 1991), 9.

29. Treuer, *The Assassination of Hole in the Day*, 42.

30. Child, *Holding Our World Together*, 49.

31. Treuer, *The Assassination of Hole in the Day*, 63–66, 74–76.

32. Satz, *Chippewa Treaty Rights*, 15

33. Robert C. Nesbit, *Wisconsin: A History* (Madison: University of Wisconsin Press, 2004), 151.

34. Treuer, *The Assassination of Hole in the Day*, 88.

35. Erica Janik, *A Short History of Wisconsin* (Madison: Wisconsin Historical Society Press, 2010), 36.

36. On his way home from a diplomatic mission to the Ho-Chunk Indians concerning further treaty negotiations with the U.S. government, Hole in the Day drank too much whisky, fell from his horse-drawn cart, and was run over by one of its wheels. He died hours later. Though Hole in the Day the Younger was only nineteen, he announced his intentions to be the leader of all Ojibwe at a treaty negotiation with U.S. government representatives at Fond du Lac in 1847. Relying on his bravado and charisma, Hole in the Day the Younger dominated the proceedings largely unchallenged by the other chiefs present. Only the Milles Lacs Ojibwe formally refused to acknowledge his claim. Over the coming years, Hole in the Day played a major role in negotiations with the U.S. government, which treated him as the main leader. See Mark Diedrich, "Chief Hole in the Day and the 1862 Chippewa Disturbance: A Reappraisal," *Minnesota History Magazine* (Spring 1987): 195–96; Treuer, *The Assassination of Hole in the Day*, 80–81, 88–91.

37. See "Antoine Gordon, Grandfather of Father Philip Gordon"; "The Gordon Family"; Delfeld, *The Indian Priest*, 14–16. "The Gordon Family" gives a brief account of the five children born to Anton and Sarah: Edward (who fought in the Civil War and died in 1920), Lizzie (who married Hugo Neuma and died in Mora, Minnesota, in 1932), Agnes (who married a non-Catholic), Susan (who married John Bergin and lived and died in Gordon, Wisconsin),

and finally William Gordon, who was born on September 25, 1850. Philip Gordon's middle name apparently was taken from his aunt Susan's husband, John Bergin.

38. "Bayfield's Early Days," *Bayfield County Press*, April 6, 1906, https:// chequamegonhistory.wordpress.com/2016/12/22/bayfields-early-days/ (accessed February 28, 2018); "William Gordon, Father of Rev. Philip Gordon," Franciscan Sisters of Perpetual Adoration Archives.

39. See "The Gordon Family."

40. Treuer, *The Assassination of Hole in the Day*, 111.

41. Satz, *Chippewa Treaty Rights*, 69.

42. Edmund Jefferson Danziger, *Indians and Bureaucrats: Administering the Reservation Policy during the Civil War* (Urbana: University of Illinois Press, 1974), 139.

43. Mark Diedrich, *The Chiefs Hole in the Day of the Mississippi Chippewa* (Minneapolis: Coyote Books, 1986), 27.

44. Treuer, *The Assassination of Hole in the Day*, 112–13.

45. Anton Treuer, *Ojibwe in Minnesota* (St. Paul: Minnesota Historical Society Press, 2010), 24–25.

46. Danziger, *Indians and Bureaucrats*, 193.

47. The balance of the annuity payment due—unbeknownst to Hole in the Day the Younger—had been siphoned off by corrupt Indian Bureau officials responsible for disbursement. See Diedrich, "Chief Hole in the Day," 193–201.

48. Paul H. Carlson, *The Plains Indians* (College Station: Texas A&M University Press, 1998), 149–50.

49. Diedrich, "Chief Hole in the Day," 200–203.

50. Macaria, "Antoine Gordon, Grandfather of Father Philip Gordon." See also Delfeld, *The Indian Priest*, 21.

51. Diedrich, "Chief Hole in the Day," 193–203. For the Dakota, the Sioux Outbreak of 1862 did not end well. The U.S. Army ultimately executed thirty-eight Dakota combatants in the largest mass hanging in American history. Afterwards, Lincoln confiscated all Dakota Territory in Minnesota, forcing the rest of the tribe to flee either to the west or north to Canada. See Pritzker, *A Native American Encyclopedia*, 317.

52. The assassination of Hole in the Day the Younger made national news, though the motive for the killing was initially unclear. It was only learned decades later that the assassins from Leech Lake were hired by two businessmen, Clement H. Beaulieu and Charles Ruffee. Both feared that Hole in the Day was planning to ban them from operating on White Earth. See Treuer, *The Assassination of Hole in the Day*, 166–81.

53. "William Gordon, Father of Rev. Philip Gordon."

54. Delfeld, *The Indian Priest*, 16–17; Macaria, "Antoine Gordon, Grandfather of Father Philip Gordon."

55. Macaria, "Antoine Gordon, Grandfather of Father Philip Gordon." William's brother, Edward, worked as a mail carrier on the southern route to Rush City, Minnesota.

56. Delfeld, *The Indian Priest*, 17, 27, 47, 147. An alternative translation of Ategekwe is recorded as Woman Who Loves Gambling. There is limited information on Philip Gordon's many siblings, save the following: James Gordon became a respected public figure in Gordon, as did his brother Joseph. One son, George, went on to practice dentistry in San Francisco, while another, Robert, practiced medicine in New York. See "William Gordon, Father of Rev. Philip Gordon." James, George, and Robert also studied at the Normal School in Superior. See Gordon to Sister Catherine, March 14, 1909, Franciscan Sisters of Perpetual Adoration Archives. The letter to Sister Catherine reads: "Did you hear that James, George and Robert, my brothers, are attending the High School at Superior? This augurs well for their future careers. All three are 'alumni' of St. Mary's in what I think might be called the true spirit. With no intention of boasting and not wishing to have them held up as such, I do not think, Sister, one would wish to see a more conscientious set of boys when it is a question of going to Mass on Sundays or making the monthly Communion. This is truly wonderful by comparison of what might be the case, and actually is in some places."

Chapter 2. From Boyhood to the Priesthood

1. Gerald Vizenor, *The People Named the Chippewa: Narrative Histories* (Minneapolis: University of Minnesota Press, 1984), 98–99; Walker Demarquis Wyman, *The Chippewa: A History of the Great Lakes Woodland Tribe over Three Centuries* (River Falls: University of Wisconsin–River Falls Press, 1993), 101–2, 106, 117.

2. Louis H. Roddis, "The Last Indian Uprising in the United States," *Minnesota History Bulletin* 3.5 (1920): 273–90.

3. Wyman, *The Chippewa*, 101, 140–41.

4. Satz, *Chippewa Treaty Rights*, 125.

5. D. K. Meisenheimer Jr., "Regionalist Bodies / Embodied Regions: Sarah Orne Jewett and Zitkala-Ša," in *Breaking Boundaries: New Perspectives on Women's Regional Writing*, ed. Sherrie A. Inness and Diana Royer (Iowa City: University of Iowa Press, 1997), 114–15.

6. Vecsey, *Traditional Ojibwa Religion*, 29; Wyman, *The Chippewa*, 106–7.

7. Rahill, "The Catholic Indian Missions," 87.

8. Enochs, "Native Americans," 80, 82.

9. Smith, *The Island of the Anishnaabeg*, 36.

10. Child, *Holding Our World Together*, 91–92.

11. Vecsey, *Traditional Ojibwa Religion*, 71.

12. Child, *Holding Our World Together*, 10, 15.

13. Vizenor, *The People Named the Chippewa*, 49.

14. Delfeld, *The Indian Priest*, 10, 19; "Was Big Event in Our Village."

15. "Rev. Odoric Ignaz Derenthal, O. S. F.," *Shawano County Biographies* (Chicago: J. H. Beers, 1895), 348–49.

16. Delfeld, *The Indian Priest*, 17–27; "Indian Priest Ordained: Father Gordon, the First Indian Priest Ordained in America," Franciscan Sisters of Perpetual Adoration Archives; "Was Big Event in Our Village"; Wyman, *The Chippewa*, 140.

17. Delfeld, *The Indian Priest*, 35; "Will Enter Priesthood: Philip Gordon, A Resident of This Village Is Shortly to Become a Priest," *Star* (Odanah), Franciscan Sisters of Perpetual Adoration Archives. The names of the nuns appear in Gordon's later letters. See Gordon to Brother James (Gordon), May 8, 1901; Gordon to Sister Catherine, March 14, 1909.

18. "St. Mary's Industrial School, Odanah, Wisconsin," *Indian Sentinel* (1905–6): 10.

19. Delfeld, *The Indian Priest*, 35; "Indian Priest Ordained."

20. "The Rev. Philip Gordon," Franciscan Sisters of Perpetual Adoration Archives; "St. Mary's Industrial School," 10.

21. Delfeld, *The Indian Priest*, 35–40; Gordon to whom it may concern, May 8, 1901; Mary Macaria, "Reverend Philip Gordon, LL.D.," United States Works Progress Association Chippewa Indian Historical Project Records, 1936–40, 1942. The State Normal School at Superior, or Superior Normal School, later became the University of Wisconsin–Superior. See "Mission and History," https://www.uwsuper.edu/about/mission-history.cfm (accessed March 6, 2018).

22. Father Fardy would later become vicar general of the Diocese of Superior. He probably lived on or near the grounds of the Sacred Heart Church in Superior. See Gordon to Esteemed Sister (likely Sister Catherine), December 3, 1900, Franciscan Sisters of Perpetual Adoration Archives (The letter mentions: "Father Fardy's residence is about one half a mile from the Normal"); "Indian Priest Ordained"; "Bishop Schinner (1905–1913)," *History of Diocese of Superior*, http://archive.is/fSeHU#selection-1095.1-1095.28 (accessed March 6, 2018).

23. Delfeld, *The Indian Priest*, 38.

24. Gordon to Esteemed Sister (likely Sister Catherine), December 3, 1900, Franciscan Sisters of Perpetual Adoration Archives.

25. Gordon to Esteemed Sister Catherine, April 22, 1901, Franciscan Sisters of Perpetual Adoration Archives. The word "corrected" is not a quote from the letter.

26. Gordon to Brother James (Gordon), May 8, 1901, Franciscan Sisters of Perpetual Adoration Archives. The letter included the following enclosure: "To whom it may concern:—This is to certify that I, Philip B. Gordon have attended the Odanah Day School of Odanah Wis. for a period of three years and have been ably rewarded by being able to enter the State Normal School without preparatory studies, all due to what I think the concise explanations given by the teachers on points difficult to understand. I feel highly honored in being able to recommend the Odanah Day School. Philip Gordon Age 16½ years May 8, 1901." Gordon to whom it may concern, May 8, 1901.

27. Delfeld, *The Indian Priest*, 40; "Mission and History," *Northland College*, https://www.northland.edu/about/mission/ (accessed March 7, 2018); "Will Enter Priesthood."

28. Delfeld, *The Indian Priest*, 40–41; J. Rainer to Gordon, March 22, 1903, quoted in "Outline for Biography," 17; "Will Enter Priesthood." Gordon kept a copy of Rainer's letter for his records, having underlined the phrase: "doubts have been expressed concerning your vocation for the priesthood."

29. Merrill E. Jachow, *Private Liberal Arts Colleges in Minnesota: Their History and Contributions* (St. Paul: Minnesota Historical Society Press, 1973), 39–40; Terrence J. Murphy, *A Catholic University: Vision and Opportunities* (Collegeville, MN: Liturgical Press, 2001), 7.

30. Delfeld, *The Indian Priest*, 44–46.

31. "College of St. Thomas Report of Mr. Gordon from November 1, 1904, to December 23, 1904," Franciscan Sisters of Perpetual Adoration Archives. The copy was sent to Sister Catherine at St. Mary's Boarding School in Odanah, signed by the college president, H. Moynihan.

32. "St. Mary's Industrial School," 10.

33. Delfeld, *The Indian Priest*, 45.

34. Macaria, "Antoine Gordon, Grandfather of Father Philip Gordon."

35. Delfeld, *The Indian Priest*, 41, 46; "The Society and the State," *Wisconsin Magazine of History* 3.3 (March 1920): 379. Here Gordon speaks about indigenous traditions, saying "they must be preserved in books, not in men."

36. Gordon to Sister Catherine, March 14, 1909.

37. Thiel, "The Bureau of Catholic Indian Missions."

38. Gordon to Sister Catherine, March 14, 1909.

39. Delfeld, *The Indian Priest*, 43, 46, 52.

40. See Gordon to Odoric Derenthal, April 20, 1914, Province of the Sacred Heart Franciscan Records. Gordon writes: "My salary assured, naturally I am ready to do my best for the salvation of souls. This looks as if I was after the money. Well, let those that think so remain in their unworthy estimate of one who has spent over $5000 to educate himself for a life of sacrifice." Gordon's windfall probably came in 1909.

41. *Indian Sentinel* (1910): 48; "Indian Student for the Priesthood," *Indian Sentinel* (1912): 19. The first article from 1910 (untitled) contains the quote.

42. Delfeld, *The Indian Priest*, 55; "Full Blooded Indian Priest," *Red Man* (September 1915): 35–36. The last article is reprinted from the *New York Sun*.

43. "Will Enter Priesthood."

44. "First to Be Indian Priest: Philip B. Gordon First of His Race to Be Ordained in the United States," *Carlisle Indian School Newspaper*, December 26, 1913. The article, partially a reprint from the Odanah *Star* and bearing the same title, noted, "Father Gordon visited Carlisle a year ago on returning from his studies in Europe. We were especially impressed by his earnestness, which foretells of a useful life in helpful service to his people. With the great inducements of the present day for material gain, our administration is doubly stirred when we see a young man cast aside such opportunities in order to grasp the richer treasures of spiritual development and Christian service, and we commend this young man for his wise choice."

45. "First Indian to Be Priest," Franciscan Sisters of Perpetual Adoration Archives. The term "pro-cathedral" means a cathedral constructed for temporary use.

46. "Bishop Koudelka, 1913–1921," *History of Diocese of Superior*, http://www.catholic-hierarchy.org/bishop/bkoudelka.html (accessed March 11, 2018). Koudelka's main concern as bishop was supporting Wisconsin landowners in "colonization work"—that is, settling whites on fertile farm land for them to develop. His other main project was St. Joseph Children's Home, an orphanage in Superior. Koudelka spent many of his own funds on the construction of the orphanage, which housed two hundred children. It opened in 1917.

47. "A Second Indian Priest," *Indian Sentinel* (1914): 7. Albert Negahnquet worked mainly as a chaplain at the St. Louis School of the Osage Nation in Oklahoma. See Thiel, "The Bureau of Catholic Indian Missions."

48. "Indian Priest Ordained"; "St. Mary's Industrial School," 9.

49. Delfeld, *The Indian Priest*, 56; "Will Enter Priesthood."

50. "Electric Lights Possible: It Is Said That We May Have Our Village Lighted," *Star* (Odanah), ca. December 1913, Franciscan Sisters of Perpetual Adoration Archives.

51. "Catholic Church Now Remodeled," *Star* (Odanah), ca. December 1913, Franciscan Sisters of Perpetual Adoration Archives.

52. "Was Big Event in Our Village."

53. Untitled clipping, *Star* (Odanah), ca. January 1914, Franciscan Sisters of Perpetual Adoration Archives.

Chapter 3. The Society and the Missionary

1. The Society of American Indians was originally called the American Indian Association. Its cofounder, Fayette Avery McKenzie, was born in Pennsylvania in 1872. After an early life of study, he earned a doctorate from the University of Pennsylvania in 1906. He first encountered the BIA bureaucracy while working at the government-run Wind River Indian School in Wyoming. McKenzie's thesis, "The American Indian in Relation to the White Population in the United States," promoted the notion that "culture and civilization" could be instilled in American Indians within just a few generations, contingent on a program that eliminated "Indian retardation" and encouraged white contact, citizenship, and economic self-sufficiency. He published the dissertation as a book in 1908, hoping to spread his ideas. In his courses at Ohio State, McKenzie often featured indigenous guest lecturers such as Montezuma, so his students could witness living proof of his theories. McKenzie would go on to become president of Fisk University in Nashville, Tennessee, where he was instrumental in transforming the institution into the premier black college in the United States. See Christopher L. Nicholson, "To Advance a Race: A Historical Analysis of the Personal Belief, Industrial Philanthropy and Black Liberal Arts Higher Education in Fayette McKenzie's Presidency at Fisk University, 1915–1925" (PhD diss., Loyola University, Chicago, 2011), 299–318; Hertzberg, *The Search for an American Indian Identity*, 32–37.

2. Hertzberg, *The Search for an American Indian Identity*, 32–38, 79; Speroff, *Carlos Montezuma*, 333–34.

3. Hertzberg, *The Search for an American Indian Identity*, 43–44; Ruth Spack, "Dis/engagement: Zitkala-Ša's Letters to Carlos Montezuma, 1901–2," *MELUS: The Journal of the Society for the Study of the Multi-ethnic Literature of the United States* 26.1 (2001): 177–78, 185; Speroff, *Carlos Montezuma*, 1–2, 24–30, 47–63.

4. See, for instance, O. B. Super, "Indian Education at Carlisle," *New England Magazine* 18.2 (April 1895): 229.

5. Pfister, *The Yale Indian*, 131.

6. Speroff, *Carlos Montezuma*, 335–38. Despite the presence of Baldwin and Bonnin, the SAI was largely a male affair. The society counted only 66 women

among its 219 active members in 1912. See Deborah Sue Welch, "Zitkala-Ša: An American Indian Leader, 1876–1938" (PhD diss., University of Wyoming, 1985), 104.

7. Michael C. Coleman, "Motivations of Indian Children at Missionary and U.S. Government Schools," *Montana: The Magazine of Western History* 40 (Winter 1990): 30; Hertzberg, *The Search for an American Indian Identity*, 39–40.

8. Jerome A. Greene, *American Carnage: Wounded Knee, 1890* (Norman: University of Oklahoma Press, 2014), 288, 302–3.

9. Hertzberg, *The Search for an American Indian Identity*, 39–41; David Reed Miller, "Charles Alexander Eastman, The 'Winner': From Deep Woods to Civilization," in *American Indian Intellectuals*, ed. Margot Liberty (St. Paul: West, 1978), 61–70.

10. Katherine Ellinghaus, "Assimilation by Marriage: White Women and Native American Men at the Hampton Institute, 1878–1923," *Virginia Magazine of History and Biography* 108.3 (2000): 291–92; Hertzberg, *The Search for an American Indian Identity*, 46; Speroff, *Carlos Montezuma*, 336.

11. Hertzberg, *The Search for an American Indian Identity*, 37.

12. "The Objects of the Society," Papers of the Society of American Indians.

13. John Larner, "Society of American Indians," in *Native America in the Twentieth Century: An Encyclopedia*, ed. Mary B. Davis (New York: Garland, 1994), 603–4; *Platform of the Third Annual Conference of the Society of American Indians*, Papers of the Society of American Indians; Speroff, *Carlos Montezuma*, 336–43.

14. Richard Henry Pratt, "The Solution to the Indian Problem," *Quarterly Journal of the Society of American Indians* 1.1 (January–April 1913): 197–204.

15. Adams, *Education for Extinction*, 320–23. After his removal, Pratt began to lecture widely. Carlisle subsequently underwent major changes under Commissioner of Indians Affairs Francis Luepp. These reforms included the establishment of the Native Arts Department and a revamping of Indian history in a more positive cast. See also Hertzberg, *The Search for an American Indian Identity*, 17–18.

16. To sketch some of Ketcham's early history: Born William Henry Ketcham in 1868, in Sumner, Iowa, he had the distinction, unlike other directors of the BCIM, of not being born into a Catholic family. His ancestors, in fact, could be traced back to the Puritans of Plymouth Colony. Ketcham spent his childhood in Texas, becoming fascinated with Catholicism as a teenager. So great was his commitment that his conversion inspired the rest of his family to join the church, as well. In 1884, Ketcham enrolled in St. Charles' College in

Louisiana. He spent his summers doing missionary work. After attending an Ohio seminary in 1888 and continuing his missions among Indians in the Oklahoma Territory, Ketcham was ordained in 1892. By 1897, he was headquartered at Antlers, Choctaw Nation. See Kevin Abing, "Directors of the Bureau of Catholic Indian Missions: Monsignor William Henry Ketcham, 1901–1921," https://www.marquette.edu/library/archives/Mss/BCIM/BCIM-SC1-directors3 .pdf (accessed April 2, 2018).

17. William H. Ketcham, "Address by Father William H. Ketcham of Washington, D.C.," *Quarterly Journal of the Society of American Indians* 1.1 (January–April 1913): 193–94.

18. Hertzberg, *The Search for an American Indian Identity*, 79.

19. Porter, *To Be Indian*, 17–20, 23, 43, 60.

20. Arthur C. Parker to Gordon, December 18, 1913, Papers of the Society of American Indians.

21. Untitled clipping, *Star* (Odanah), ca. January 1914, Franciscan Sisters of Perpetual Adoration Archives.

22. Wyman, *The Chippewa*, 140–41.

23. Child, *Holding Our World Together*, 131.

24. Gordon to Derenthal, March 30, 1914, Province of the Sacred Heart Franciscan Records.

25. Gordon to Derenthal, April 7, 1914, Province of the Sacred Heart Franciscan Records.

26. Gordon to Derenthal, April 20, 1914, Province of the Sacred Heart Franciscan Records.

27. Gordon to Derenthal, April 24, 1914, Province of the Sacred Heart Franciscan Records.

28. Gordon to Bernadine Veis, June 20, 1914, Province of the Sacred Heart Franciscan Records.

29. Gordon to Derenthal, August 7, 1914, Province of the Sacred Heart Franciscan Records.

30. Gordon to Derenthal, August 12, 1914, Province of the Sacred Heart Franciscan Records.

31. See Gordon to Derenthal, January 3, 1915, Province of the Sacred Heart Franciscan Records. The friendly letter, which discusses church business and the state of the Ojibwe, displays no lingering conflict between the two men. It closes: "Happy New Year! Best wishes and kindest regards. Auf Wiedersehen, Philip B. Gordon."

32. Gordon to C. F. Schmit, October 12, 1914, quoted in Delfeld, *The Indian Priest*, 56–57.

33. See Gordon to Derenthal, January 3, 1915, Province of the Sacred Heart Franciscan Records; Macaria, "Reverend Philip Gordon, LL.D." In the January letter to Odoric, Gordon writes: "Two letters addressed to my old address at Reserve which were forwarded by you to Superior have just reached me. I meant to write to you in regard to any papers or mail that might reach Reserve for me. You may keep all the papers but the letters you might re-direct to the Apostolic Mission House, Washington, D.C. I suppose your friends at Hayward told you of my whereabouts long before this. I have been at the Mission House since I left Hayward and I like the course here mighty well." It is possible—but not certain—that Ketcham was influential in Gordon's decision to study in Washington, having suggested that he prepare for broader missionary work throughout the country. See "Full Blooded Indian Priest," *Red Man*, 36.

34. Delfeld, *The Indian Priest*, 57.

35. See Gordon to Cato Sells, October 7, 1915, Bureau of the Catholic Indian Missions Records.

36. *Baltimore Sun*, 1914, quoted in "Outline for Biography," 31.

37. See Gordon to Sister Catherine, March 14, 1909.

38. William H. Ketcham to Joseph Koudelka, March 6, 1915, quoted in Delfeld, *The Indian Priest*, 59.

39. Ketcham to Koudelka, March 25, 1915, quoted in Delfeld, *The Indian Priest*, 60.

40. Hertzberg, *The Search for an American Indian Identity*, 126–28.

41. Gordon to Parker, December 9, 1914, Papers of the Society of American Indians.

42. Parker to Gordon, May 18, 1915, Papers of the Society of American Indians.

43. Hoxie, *A Final Promise*, 108.

44. Hertzberg, *The Search for an American Indian Identity*, 128.

45. Arthur C. Parker, "Board of Indian Commissioners," *Quarterly Journal of the Society of American Indians* 2.4 (January–March 1914): 2–3.

46. Born in North Dakota, Baldwin spent her childhood in Minneapolis. Her wealthy father, Jean Baptiste Bottineau, was a lawyer heavily involved in representing his band in treaty disputes. Upon being barred from reservation lands by the BIA power structure, Bottineau relocated to Washington, DC, with Marie. (Marie had recently left or divorced a Minneapolis businessman, Fred S. Baldwin.) In Washington, Baldwin aided her father in his testimony before Congress and earned a degree from Washington College of Law. See Cahill, "Marie Louise Bottineau Baldwin," 69, 73. Before white contact, the Turtle Mountain Band Ojibwe resided in Michigan's Upper Peninsula near

Ontario. Their reservation was created in 1882 in North Dakota after negotiations with the U.S. government. For an overview of their history, see Stanley N. Murry, "The Turtle Mountain Chippewa, 1882–1905," *North Dakota History* 51.1 (1984): 14–37.

47. Gordon to Parker, January 8, 1915, Papers of the Society of American Indians.

48. Parker to Gordon, January 16, 1915, Papers of the Society of American Indians.

49. Parker to Gordon, May 18, 1915.

50. Ketcham to Koudelka, May 1, 1917, quoted in Delfeld, *The Indian Priest*, 60.

Chapter 4. A Conference and a Scandal at Haskell

1. Child, *Boarding School Seasons*, 7; Theresa Milk, *Haskell Institute: 19th Century Stories of Sacrifice and Survival* (Lawrence: Mammoth, 2007), 7, 15–19, 21.

2. Adams, *Education for Extinction*, 273–74.

3. Child, *Boarding School Seasons*, 27, 30, 33.

4. Milk, *Haskell Institute*, 76–77, 127–67.

5. Hoxie, *A Final Promise*, 108.

6. Child, *Boarding School Seasons*, 93.

7. "Rev. Philip Gordon Assigned New Work," *Indian Leader*, ca. Summer of 1915, Franciscan Sisters of Perpetual Adoration Archives. The *Indian Leader* erroneously reported that Gordon's "parents were pagans until their adult years, when they became Christians."

8. Gordon to Parker, August 27, 1915, Papers of the Society of American Indians.

9. Parker to Gordon, August 31, 1915, Papers of the Society of American Indians.

10. Gordon to Parker, September 5, 1915, Papers of the Society of American Indians. In this letter, Gordon supplies a list of hotels and reports that Haskell superintendent Wise has agreed to give government accommodations to thirty SAI delegates. Gordon was about to start touring Kansas reservations in a few days. Parker declared the hotel list "doubly helpful" because had not been able to get one from the Lawrence "Merchants Association." See Parker to Gordon, September 13, 1915, Papers of the Society of American Indians.

11. Hertzberg, *The Search for an American Indian Identity*, 135–38; Larner, "Society of American Indians," 604.

12. Parker personally invited Wilson, who in refusing asked Parker to "convey . . . my warm greetings to the conference and an expression of my very great interest in everything that affects the welfare and advancement of the American Indians." See Woodrow Wilson to Parker, September 24, 1915, Papers of the Society of American Indians. Father Ketcham also received Parker's personal invitation. See Parker to Ketcham, August 25, 1915, Papers of the Society of American Indians.

13. Pratt spoke on the theme, "Responsibility for the Red Man." See Parker to Richard Henry Pratt, April 23, 1915, Papers of the Society of American Indians.

14. *The Society of American Indians Fifth Annual Platform, Adopted at Lawrence, Kansas, Oct. 2nd, 1915*, Papers of the Society of American Indians.

15. Speroff, *Carlos Montezuma*, 346.

16. Carlos Montezuma, "Let My People Go," *Quarterly Journal of the Society of American Indians* 4.1 (January–March 1916): 33. Montezuma had visited Haskell once before, in January 1900. On a trip to California with the Carlisle football team to play University of California at Berkeley, he stopped at Haskell and several other southwestern boarding schools. Montezuma later wrote to Pratt: "Though Haskell has many advantages it does not come up to Carlisle. None of the schools have 'the outing system' nor do they seem to take any interest in that direction. All they seem to think of is to get as many pupils as possible to maintain their schools. That is a poor policy. When you are dealing with future men and women, get them out among the people and not confine them in convent-like methods (Indian schools)." Quoted in Speroff, *Carlos Montezuma*, 258–59.

17. Hertzberg, *The Search for an American Indian Identity*, 140, 144, 148.

18. Gordon's precise statements at the conference are not on record. See Gordon to Charles S. Lusk, October 4, 1915, Bureau of Catholic Indian Missions Records. In the letter, Gordon warns Lusk that he made some controversial comments about BIA abolition in Lawrence. Regarding Sloan's nomination, see Parker to Gordon, November 19, 1915, Papers of the Society of American Indians. See also Philip Gordon, "Opposition to the Indian Bureau," *American Indian Magazine* 3.4 (Fall 1916): 259–60. Here, Gordon speaks of the "nasty" remarks he made at the Lawrence conference.

19. Hertzberg, *The Search for an American Indian Identity*, 137.

20. See Arthur C. Parker, "The Editor's Viewpoint: The Functions of the Society of American Indians," *Quarterly Journal of the Society of American Indians* 4.1 (January–March 1916): 8–14.

21. Parker to Gertrude Bonnin, November 5, 1915, Papers of the Society of American Indians.

22. Lewandowski, *Red Bird, Red Power*, 11–13.

23. See Gordon to Ketcham, October 15, 1915, Bureau of Catholic Indian Missions Records. Gordon writes: "A Mrs. Bonnin from the Ute Indians in Utah told me a pitiable tale of neglect of those Indians. They have about forty Catholics at their home and the priest has come four times in the last twelve years! Some of these forty are Whites. The priest lives at Frutta, Colorado, but the Indians are in Utah. She wants you to look up the matter. The other churches are inactive, she says. In all, there are 1500 Indians. Of course, they are miserably poor." Ketcham was already very aware of the conditions at Uintah. Bonnin had been corresponding with him concerning just this matter since 1910. See Lewandowski, *Red Bird, Red Power*, 70–78.

24. See the photograph "Catholic Sioux Congress attendees, 1915," in the Bureau of Catholic Indians Records at Marquette University. Gordon was photographed with William Ketcham. Gordon attended again in 1916. See the photograph "Clergy and laity at Catholic Sioux Congress, 1916," in the Bureau of Catholic Indians Records at Marquette University. The legendary Oglala holy man Nicholas Black Elk also appears in the picture.

25. See "The Sioux Congress," *Indian Sentinel* 1.2 (1916–19): 27, 30. Gordon was attending these conferences until at least 1923, when he appeared in South Dakota with fellow Indian priest Albert Negahnquet to lead prayers. See William Huffer, "Catholic Sioux Congress of South Dakota: Indian Hospitality and Faith," *Indian Sentinel* 3.4 (1923): 147–48.

26. Gordon to Charles S. Lusk, October 4, 1915, Bureau of Catholic Indian Missions Records.

27. See Joseph G. Mannard, "American Anti-Catholicism and Its Literature," *Ex Libris* 4.1 (1981): 1–9.

28. Gordon to Sells, October 7, 1915, Bureau of Catholic Indian Missions Records. Sells telegrammed Gordon on October 8, promising to look into the issues he raised regarding a complete list of Catholic students at Haskell—one day too late, however, to stop Gordon from pursuing the matter further. Sells's telegram read: "In answer to your telegram of September 28 with reference to obtaining an accurate list of Catholic pupils at Haskell Institute, you are advised that I am looking into the matter complained of and will advise you further." See also Gordon to Lusk, October 8, 1915, Bureau of Catholic Indian Missions Records.

29. Gordon to Lusk, October 7, 1915, Bureau of Catholic Indian Missions Records.

30. Gordon to Sells, October 11, 1915, Bureau of Catholic Indian Missions Records.

31. Gordon to Lusk, October 11, 1915, Bureau of Catholic Indian Missions Records.

32. Gordon to Ketcham, October 12, 1915, Bureau of Catholic Indian Missions Records.

33. Gordon to Ketcham, October 15, 1915, Bureau of Catholic Indian Missions Records. Gordon wrote Ketcham just before embarking on a trip to Oklahoma under the auspices of the Bureau of Catholic Indian Missions. He later reported to Odoric: "I have been very busy giving missions and making investigations in Oklahoma. Some of our Indian missions are going downhill instead of up." See Gordon to Odoric, December 24, 1915, Province of the Sacred Heart Franciscan Records.

34. Gordon to Dear Catholic Parent, November 1915, Bureau of Catholic Indian Missions Records.

35. Gordon to Dear Sisters, November 1915, Franciscan Sisters of Perpetual Adoration Archives.

36. Gordon to Mary Macaria, February 8, 1916, Franciscan Sisters of Perpetual Adoration Archives.

37. Gordon to Dear Sisters, November 1915.

38. Howard M. Bahr, ed., *The Navajo as Seen by the Franciscans, 1898–1921: A Sourcebook* (Lanham, MD.: Scarecrow Press, 2004), 122.

39. "Editorials," *Indian Sentinel* (1916): 26. The *Indian Sentinel* also noted that readers could write Gordon at Haskell to learn more about the conditions Catholic students were forced to endure. See "Are Catholic Indian Schools Necessary?" *Indian Sentinel* (1916): 48.

40. "Rigid Investigation at Haskell Institute: Member of Indian Bureau and His Chief Inspectors Arrive in Lawrence This Week," *Catholic Register*, February 17, 1916.

41. "Bigoted Misrule at Haskell Proved: YMCA Secretary Is Ordered Off the Reservation by Interior Secretary Lane," *Catholic Register*, February 24, 1916.

42. "Rigid Investigation at Haskell Institute."

43. "Bigoted Misrule at Haskell Proved."

44. H. B. Peairs, formerly supervisor of Indian Schools in Washington, DC, replaced Wise in March 1917. See George K. Earnst to Gordon, March 29, 1917, Papers of the Society of American Indians. In this letter, Earnst, writing from the Catholic Rectory in Lawrence, Kansas, condemns the appointment of Peairs to Gordon: "He is all aflame for the welfare of the Indians—in reality a pietistic uplifter for the coin. His Methodist smirking hypocrisy is larded all over that letter. You are simply Mr. Gordon, he is the Moses of the Indians. . . . The best argument for the discontinuance of Haskell is such an ignoramus as

Peairs." Gordon disagreed, writing Peairs to congratulate him on becoming superintendent of Haskell School. "I feel sure," Gordon confided, "that your steady character and your well-known executive ability is going to make Haskell one of our best Indian schools. . . . You may rely upon me for such aid as I am able to render you. You may feel sure of my help wherever the good of my race is concerned." See Gordon to H. B. Peairs, March 13, 1917, Papers of the Society of American Indians.

45. Vizenor, *The People Named the Chippewa*, 102.

46. Treuer, *The Assassination of Hole in the Day*, 12.

47. Carlos Montezuma, for instance, had a cousin named Charles Dickens. See Speroff, *Carlos Montezuma*, 285–86.

48. Child, *Boarding School Seasons*, 12, 15, 66–67, 93–94; Milk, *Haskell Institute*, 127–67.

49. See Gertrude Bonnin's semi-autobiographical writings in the *Atlantic Monthly* under the name Zitkala-Ša: "Impressions of an Indian Childhood," *Atlantic Monthly* 85 (January 1900): 37–47; "The School Days of an Indian Girl," *Atlantic Monthly* 85 (February 1900): 185–94; "An Indian Teacher among Indians," *Atlantic Monthly* 85 (March 1900): 381–86; Laura Cornelius Kellogg, "Some Facts and Figures on Indian Education," *Quarterly Journal of the Society of American Indians* 1 (1913): 36–46; Henry Roe Cloud, "Education of the American Indian," *Quarterly Journal of the Society of American Indians* 2 (1914): 203–9. It bears mentioning that Arthur C. Parker, like Gordon, was unsympathetic to the suffering of Indian students at boarding schools. In August 1913, Parker was contacted by a Kickapoo Indian named Joe Pete, or Scho-tha, who had written to him in his capacity as SAI secretary-treasurer. Scho-tha complained that Haskell would not relinquish his son for the purposes of a short vacation back home. Scho-tha claimed that his agency superintendent, Edwin Minor, had "deceived" him and that he had gone to Haskell personally several times to appeal to Superintendent Wise, but his request would not be granted. Parker corresponded with Wise on the matter, and ultimately suggested that it was "better for the boy" to remain at Haskell. See Parker to John R. Wise, August 24, 1913, Society of American Indians Papers.

50. Gordon to Macaria, February 8, 1916.

51. See Gordon to Parker, November 3, 1915, Papers of the Society of American Indians.

Chapter 5. Carlos Montezuma, *War-Whoop*, and the Bureau

1. Gordon to Parker, November 3, 1915.

2. Parker to Gordon, November 19, 1915.

3. Gordon to Parker, January 11, 1916, Papers of the Society of American Indians.

4. "The War-Whoop," *War-Whoop*, January 1916, Franciscan Sisters of Perpetual Adoration Archives.

5. "Public Meeting" flyer, Papers of the Society of American Indians. According to the flyer, the "Public Meeting" was held on Tuesday evening, February 15, 1916, at 8:30 p.m.

6. "Apache Condemns Federal Indian Bureau," *Catholic Register*, February 17, 1916, Franciscan Sisters of Perpetual Adoration Archives.

7. Speroff, *Carlos Montezuma*, 382.

8. *War-Whoop*, February 1916, Franciscan Sisters of Perpetual Adoration Archives. Gordon wrote: "Unless there is voluntary protest on the part of the donors, the several contributions received at Lawrence, Kansas, for present and future copies of *War-Whoop* will be placed at the disposal of Dr. Montezuma together with the names of interested parties."

9. Speroff, *Carlos Montezuma*, 382, 508.

10. Parker to Gordon, March 10, 1916, Papers of the Society of American Indians.

11. "Conference Helped by Cedar Rapids Friends," *American Indian Magazine* 3.4 (Fall 1916): 221.

12. Hertzberg, *The Search for an American Indian Identity*, 146.

13. Sherman Coolidge, "Opening Address of the President," *American Indian Magazine* 3.4 (Fall 1916): 227–28.

14. "The Cedar Rapids Platform," *American Indian Magazine* 3.4 (Fall 1916): 223–24.

15. Vittorio Lanternari, *The Religions of the Oppressed: A Study of Modern Messianic Cults*, trans. Lisa Sergio (New York: Mentor Books, 1963), 65–67. Peyote is a small cactus that grows primarily in present-day Mexico. Its round top is edible and contains alkaloids such as mescaline, anhaline, and lophophorine. These elements cause the physiological effects of hallucination and sometimes nausea. Peyote is not classified as an addictive narcotic.

16. Weston LaBarre, *The Peyote Cult* (Norman: University of Oklahoma Press, 1989), 43–56.

17. Lanternari, *The Religions of the Oppressed*, 67, 97–100.

18. Hertzberg, *The Search for an American Indian Identity*, 145–46, 280–81, 311.

19. See Maroukis, "The Peyote Controversy," 167. Maroukis claims that Gordon was antipeyote but offers no supporting sources or evidence. Nonetheless, he is likely correct.

20. Richard Henry Pratt, "Remarks and Motion of Gen. Henry Pratt regarding Peyote," *American Indian Magazine* 3.4 (Fall 1916): 237–38.

21. Lewandowski, *Red Bird, Red Power*, 12–13, 92, 133, 136.

22. Delos Lone Wolf, "How to Solve the Problem," *American Indian Magazine* 3.4 (Fall 1916): 257–59.

23. Hertzberg, *The Search for an American Indian Identity*, 149.

24. "The Cedar Rapids Platform," 223–24.

25. Ira Isham, "The Case of the Lac Court Oreilles Reservation Chippewa," *American Indian Magazine* 3.4 (Fall 1916): 250.

26. Satz, *Chippewa Treaty Rights*, 83.

27. Child, *Holding Our World Together*, 84. Chief Cut-ear was killed in 1894.

28. Satz, *Chippewa Treaty Rights*, 125.

29. Prosper Guibord, "Certain Lumber Conditions at the Lac Court Oreilles Reservation," *American Indian Magazine* 3.4 (Fall 1916): 250–51.

30. "Open Debate on the Loyalty of Indian Employees in the Indian Service," *American Indian Magazine* 3.4 (Fall 1916): 252–56.

31. Gordon, "Opposition to the Indian Bureau," 259–60.

32. Carlos Montezuma, "Address before the Sixth Conference," *American Indian Magazine* 3.4 (Fall 1916): 160–62.

33. Hertzberg, *The Search for an American Indian Identity*, 147, 153.

34. Bonnin to Carlos Montezuma, December 10, 1916, Carlos Montezuma Papers.

35. Speroff, *Carlos Montezuma*, 361–62.

36. Gordon to Parker, November 22, 1916, Papers of the Society of American Indians.

Chapter 6. War in Europe, Battles at Home

1. Gordon to Parker, January 8, 1915.

2. David M. Kennedy, *Over Here: The First World War and American Society* (Oxford: Oxford University Press, 1980), 3–11.

3. Howard Zinn, *A People's History of the United States* (New York: Harper Collins, 1993), 134.

4. Kennedy, *Over Here*, 145–49.

5. Paul Boyer et al., *The Enduring Vision: A History of the American People, from 1865* (Boston: Houghton Mifflin, 2000), 663–67.

6. Ronald Schaffer, *America in the Great War: The Rise of the War Welfare State* (New York: Oxford University Press, 1991), 25–26.

7. Gilbert C. Fite and Harriet C. Peterson, *Opponents of War, 1917–1918* (Santa Barbara: Greenwood Press, 1986), 204.

8. Kennedy, *Over Here*, 80.

9. Speroff, *Carlos Montezuma*, 461.

10. William Rawlings, *The Second Coming of the Invisible Empire: The Ku Klux Klan of the 1920s* (Macon: Mercer University Press, 2016), 77–78.

11. Boyer et al., *The Enduring Vision*, 663–67.

12. Kennedy, *Over Here*, 39–40, 88–89, 91.

13. Thomas A. Britten, *American Indians in World War I* (Albuquerque: University of New Mexico Press, 1997), 62–63; Speroff, *Carlos Montezuma*, 413–14.

14. See Britten, *American Indians in World War I*, 43–44.

15. Hertzberg, *The Search for an American Indian Identity*, 170.

16. Bonnin to Parker, August 6, 1917, Papers of the Society of American Indians.

17. Hertzberg, *The Search for an American Indian Identity*, 170.

18. Britten, *American Indians in World War I*, 177–78.

19. Hertzberg, *The Search for an American Indian Identity*, 171–72; Parker to Bonnin, July 5, 1917, Papers of the Society of American Indians; Speroff, *Carlos Montezuma*, 362. Parker knew of Gordon's activities and was in touch with him that winter. Gordon had sent him a copy of *Pioneer Priests of North America*, by Father Thomas J. Campbell, and Parker thanked him. Parker gave a critique of the book worth noting:

> I am afraid that history will be prone to record that the Society of Jesus brought destruction upon itself by thinking too much of the Order and *also* the Deity. But, dear Father, I do not discount the wonderful heroism of the pioneer priests and missionaries. I think however that instead of ascribing all their woes and sufferings to the devil-infested Indians they should count as contributing their own tactical blunders. More than this the Indians saw that the Jesuits were the tools of French politicians or that when they were not this they were worldly ambitious to rule a domain of their own here in North America, like that in Paraguay. Father Campbell ought not to forget that the French also tortured and burned the Indians and that more than this the Indians have a side of the story not mentioned in any way in this book.

See Parker to Gordon, January 12, 1917, Papers of the Society of American Indians.

20. See Earnst to Gordon, March 29, 1917, Papers of the Society of American Indians; Gordon to Ketcham, December 4 and 8, 1916, Bureau of Catholic Indian Missions Records; Gordon to Parker, ca. Spring of 1917, Papers of the Society of American Indians.

21. Pratt to Gordon, January 12, 1917, Papers of the Society of American Indians.

22. Gordon to Pratt, January 16, 1917, Papers of the Society of American Indians.

23. Parker to Gordon, March 23, 1917, Papers of the Society of American Indians. When Gordon received this letter, he was staying at the White Earth Reservation in Minnesota. Parker also complained that Marie Baldwin was slow with her work and "due bills" had not gone out. Bonnin would soon come into conflict with Baldwin over the similar matter of her commitment.

24. Hertzberg, *The Search for an American Indian Identity*, 171–72; Parker to Bonnin, July 5, 1917; Speroff, *Carlos Montezuma*, 362.

25. Bonnin to My dear fellow-member, September 27, 1917, Papers of the Society of American Indians.

26. Gordon to Parker, ca. Spring of 1917.

27. Parker to Gordon, April 26, 1917, Papers of the Society of American Indians.

28. Hertzberg, *The Search for an American Indian Identity*, 171.

29. Bonnin to Parker, June 28, 1916, Papers of the Society of American Indians.

30. Hertzberg, *The Search for an American Indian Identity*, 171.

31. Lewandowski, *Red Bird, Red Power*, 121–23.

32. Speroff, *Carlos Montezuma*, 363.

33. Frederick E. Hoxie, *This Indian Country: American Indian Political Activists and the Place They Made* (New York: Penguin Press, 2012), 263, 265; Speroff, *Carlos Montezuma*, 420–25.

34. Delfeld, *The Indian Priest*, 65.

35. See Hertzberg, *The Search for an American Indian Identity*, 170, 333.

36. Gordon to Marie Baldwin, May 2, 1917, Papers of the Society of American Indians. The full quote reads: "I suppose Washington is in a hubbub about the war and I think there is good reason to be. Everything over here is being organized on a war basis. The women are doing much in their own way in an effective way."

37. Earnst to Gordon, March 29, 1917.

38. "The Society and the State," 379. The article, if it ever appeared, could not be found.

39. Wyman, *The Chippewa*, 144–45.

40. "Bishop Koudelka, 1913–1921," *History of Diocese of Superior.*

41. Nesbit, *Wisconsin*, 444, 448.

42. Janik, *A Short History of Wisconsin*, 117–19.

43. Nesbit, *Wisconsin*, 448.

44. Janik, *A Short History of Wisconsin*, 108.

45. Gordon to Ketcham, December 8, 1916.

46. Gordon to Ketcham, December 4, 1916.

47. See Abing, introduction to "Directors of the Bureau of Catholic Indian Missions." Gordon once complained to a friend, Inno McGill, in Haymarket, Virginia: "If poor Father Ketcham would devote more of his precious time to work for all the tribes instead of specializing in the Choctaws (where the success of church work is far below the ordinary) I imagine we would be better praised. Then too, Father Ketcham is paid to work for all Indians and not for Oklahoma Indians alone." See Gordon to Inno McGill, April 7, 1917, Papers of the Society of American Indians.

48. Gordon to Ketcham, December 8, 1916.

49. Ketcham to Theophile Meerschaert, May 2, 1917, Papers of the Society of American Indians.

50. "Outline for Biography," 23.

51. Ketcham to Koudelka, May 1, 1917, quoted in Delfeld, *The Indian Priest*, 61.

52. See Gordon to Ketcham, April 26, 1917, Papers of the Society of American Indians. The letter mentions that Gordon was informed of the discontinuance of his term with the BCIM on April 14, 1917.

53. Ketcham to Koudelka, May 1, 1917, quoted in Delfeld, *The Indian Priest*, 60–61.

54. "Editorials," *Indian Sentinel* 1.5 (1916–19): 18.

55. Gordon to Ketcham, April 26, 1917.

56. Ketcham to Meerschaert, May 2, 1917. An interesting letter from Gordon to Baldwin exists, also dated May 2, 1917, and sent from Brantford, Ontario, Canada. In it, Gordon describes an odd incident concerning an Indian imposter active on Ojibwe lands:

> In the Indian Office here I met about a week ago a Mr. Abraham who is the Agricultural Agent of the Department for teaching the Indians farming. And it is what he told me that makes me write you a longer letter than usual. He said to me I want ask him at once that I had never heard of such a person. So he began to tell me about this particular "Indian." Before he had spoken a dozen sentences I broke in with "You are not talking about an Indian; you are talking about a colored person." He merely said, "He says that he is of Indian descent," and that he came originally from Ohio. This "Afro-American-Indian," if I am not mistaken, is going about on all the reservations organizing what he styles lodges of

a protective Council for the protection of the Indians in their rights and persons, with membership dues of $2.50 per year. He claims that he can recover valuable Mohawk claims against the Government of the United States, having great influence with Congress and officials of the Administration in Washington. The claims give him a chance to delude the Mohawks living on this reservation and on the reservations in lower Canada. And so he has made a great deal of disturbance by having his followers depose the chiefs who do not at once take up his cause. I have learned that he is a forceful speaker and a man of much magnetism; he has much printed literature, but I have not read any of it to know exactly the extent of his claims. But as an example of his fraudulent practices I will take the name by which he is known, "Chief Ogemah Niagara, Thunder Water." You will at once recognize the second part of this title as the Chippewa "ogima," meaning a chief; the next, Niagara, is an Anglicized form of an old Huron and Iroquoian name for the site of Youngtown, Niagara County, N.Y., just above Fort Niagara. The white people are responsible for applying this name to the Falls of this name, for the Iroquois never so applied it. After thus misusing it the whites had to furnish it with a meaning suitable to such application, namely, "Thunder of the Waters" or "Thundering Water." This is then the source of the rascal's name, "Thunder Water," when used in connection with the word Niagara. The meaning of the word Niagara is "Bisected Bottom-land." A very tame meaning and one quite unsuitable for the name of an adventurer, you can see. So you see that just in the mixing up of Chippewa and Iroquois terms he has shown the cloven hoofs of an imposter. This will give you a clue to his character, for I told Mr. Abraham to write you about him, for I know that your connection with the Department and with the Society of American Indians would enable you to learn the true character of this new imposter. While believing in him some of the Indians here expressed to me their own suspicious that he has negro blood in his veins. Some even went so far as to say that he had frizzy hair around the edges of the hair of his head. I am trying to find out all I can about him as he has visited the New York reservations, I understand. I think he has been making Toronto his headquarters for a while at least. I hope you can find out more of his fraudulent work.

See Gordon to Baldwin, May 2, 1917, Papers of the Society of American Indians.

57. Ketcham to John Farley, May 6, 1917, Papers of the Society of American Indians. Ketcham also sent an enclosure titled "Notes on Father Gordon's Letter." Here, Ketcham counters Gordon's claims that he was "instrumental" in

getting Ketcham his doctorate from Fordham, and that Ketcham had "diverted" money to the Oklahoma Choctaws, who numbered twenty thousand. Along these lines Ketcham writes: "Had I done *nothing* for the Oklahoma Indians I would have been called a traitor to my bishop and my diocese. Since I have tried to do *something* for these Indians I must need have an eye on the diocese itself. God help us! I have heard this hateful insinuation for the last twenty years but have supposed it was a joke,—really it appears to have been circulated maliciously. . . . Whoever *informed* Father Gordon, may know the relations between my Bishop and myself better than I do, but I trust he was misinformed. However, I can see that activities such as Father Gordon's letter reveals are not calculated to foster the best of relations between the victimized priest and his Bishop." And finally, "Father Gordon has never had an unkind word, either spoken or written, from me."

58. Gordon to Chrysostom Verwyst, ca. Summer–Fall of 1917, quoted in Delfeld, *The Indian Priest*, 62.

59. Ketcham died on October 14, 1921. In his fifty-three years, he had made significant contributions to the welfare of American Indians. In 1917, he launched a campaign in Oklahoma to eliminate tuberculosis and trachoma. During World War I, he worked with the Knights of Columbus to ensure Indians on the home front were not neglected by the BIA. Ketcham also lobbied the U.S. military to provide appropriate conditions for Indian soldiers, inspecting Army camps throughout the country. In recognition of these activities and his life-long dedication, Pope Benedict XV made Ketcham a domestic prelate on April 5, 1919. See Abing, introduction to "Directors of the Bureau of Catholic Indian Missions."

Chapter 7. A New Appointment at Reserve

1. Macaria, "Reverend Philip Gordon, LL.D."

2. See Gordon to Koudelka, October 17, 1917, Papers of the Society of American Indians. Gordon mentions traveling to Kansas City, Baltimore, Chicago, Washington, DC, Philadelphia, and New York.

3. Gordon to Verwyst, ca. Summer–Fall of 1917, quoted in Delfeld, *The Indian Priest*, 61.

4. Born in Holland in 1841, Verwyst immigrated to the United States with his family at age six or seven. Raised in southern Wisconsin, he attended the Milwaukee Seminary and later took charge of Lake Superior County's Indian missions, headquartered in Bayfield. An accomplished man, Verwyst authored a book on Ojibwe grammar, a translation of the Bible, and the first Ojibwe prayer book, *The Path Leading to Heaven*. Father Verwyst died in 1925. His

obituary appeared in the *Indian Sentinel*, written by Odoric Derenthal. See Odoric Derenthal, "Reverend Chrysostom Verwyst, O.F.M.: Veteran Wisconsin Missionary," *Indian Sentinel* 5.4 (1925): 176–77; Lawrence T. Martin, "The Franciscan Mission to the Wisconsin Chippewa: The Evidence of Sermons," in *Papers of the Twenty-Seventh Algonquin Conference*, ed. David Pentland (Winnipeg: University of Manitoba Press, 1996), 196.

5. Gordon to Verwyst, ca. Summer–Fall of 1917, quoted in Delfeld, *The Indian Priest*, 62.

6. Gordon to Koudelka, October 17, 1917.

7. Koudelka to Gordon, December 6, 1917, Papers of the Society of American Indians.

8. See Giovanni (John) Bonzano to Koudelka, December 15, 1917, quoted in Delfeld, *The Indian Priest*, 63–64.

9. Bonzano to Koudelka, December 15, 1917, quoted in Delfeld, *The Indian Priest*, 63–64.

10. Delfeld, *The Indian Priest*, 68.

11. Quoted in Delfeld, *The Indian Priest*, 69.

12. See the January 1922 pamphlet Gordon distributed after the church's destruction. It features a photograph of the church and gives facts on its activities. The pamphlet can be found in the Carlos Montezuma Papers, Wisconsin Historical Society, Madison.

13. See Gordon to Koudelka, January 4, 1918, Province of the Sacred Heart Franciscan Records. The letter, written from Reserve, discusses an imminent visit to Odanah and insurance policies for Reserve and Mud Lake.

14. See E. B. Merritt to Henry McQuigg, January 28, 1918, Province of the Sacred Heart Franciscan Records.

15. See McQuigg to Gordon, February 9, 1918, Province of the Sacred Heart Franciscan Records.

16. See Gordon to Derenthal, February 25, 1918, Province of the Sacred Heart Franciscan Records. Gordon's letter contains an odd and rather cold comment about an Ojibwe woman who had recently passed away: "The Niganagijik girl died in Flambeau. I paid her one visit but she was obdurate. Thus she died."

17. See Gordon to Derenthal, March 2, 1918, Province of the Sacred Heart Franciscan Records.

18. See Gordon to Derenthal, March 9, 1918, Province of the Sacred Heart Franciscan Records.

19. See Gordon to Derenthal, March 12, 1918, Province of the Sacred Heart Franciscan Records.

20. Gordon to Derenthal, March 18, 1918, Province of the Sacred Heart Franciscan Records. Although Gordon titled his periodical *Anishinabe Enamiad*, today the preferred spelling of Anishinabe uses a double "a," reading: Anishinaabe.

21. See Alexander F. Chamberlain, "Translation: A Study in the Transference of Folk-Thought," *Journal of American Folklore* 14.54 (July–September 1901): 169. Enamiad translated literally would be "one who prays." The words "pagan" and "heathen" would be translated as Enamiassig, or "one who does not pray."

22. Philip Gordon, *A-ni-shi-na-be E-na-mi-ad* 1.2 (May 1918): 1–8, Franciscan Province of the Sacred Heart Archives. Sister Catherine from Odanah helped fund *Anishinabe Enamiad*. An undated letter from her to Gordon reads: "Enclosed find a little gift to help along the 'Anishinabe Enamiad.' Hope you will do great work among the poor Indians. Wishing you Godspeed in all your undertakings, I am, Sincerely yours in Jesus and the Sacred Heart." See Sister Catherine to Gordon, ca. May 1918, Franciscan Sisters of Perpetual Adoration Archives. Unfortunately, it proved impossible to acquire any issue of *Anishinabe Enamiad* save the May number quoted here. Copies of the April issue do not exist in either of the two archives that hold *Anishinabe Enamiad* (Franciscan Province of the Sacred Heart Archives in St. Louis, Missouri, and Province of the Sacred Heart Franciscan Records), nor do any other traces of the magazine.

23. Janik, *A Short History of Wisconsin*, 92.

24. Wyman, *The Chippewa*, 148.

25. Gordon, *A-ni-shi-na-be E-na-mi-ad* 1.2 (May 1918): 1–8. The phrase "Poor Lo" is taken from Alexander Pope's "Essay on Man," line 99. It reads: "Lo, the poor Indian!" S. Alice Callahan (Creek) used the phrase "Poor Lo" in her novel, *Wynema: A Child of the Forest* (1891). See S. Alice Callahan, *Wynema: A Child of the Forest* (1891), ed. A. LaVonne Brown Ruoff (Lincoln: University of Nebraska Press, 1997), 52, 110.

26. Gordon to Derenthal, May 8, 1918, Province of the Sacred Heart Franciscan Records.

27. See Gordon to Derenthal, December 5, 1918, Province of the Sacred Heart Franciscan Records. Of the eight sisters Gordon wrote Odoric: "I have received some complaints about the inefficiency of our holy Sisters here as teachers. What has been your experience with them along that line? Generally speaking, do you think the mission would be better for all with the Sisters or without them? Your ten years here with these women must have taught you something in regard to their status as religious, as teachers, as mission helpers and as catechiate."

28. Gordon to Derenthal, May 8, 1918. Regarding Odoric's injunction not to speak of his rumored imprisonment, Gordon writes: "Father Optatus in Odanah was obliged to mention it in the Church. However, I will follow your advice and not talk of it."

29. Gordon to Derenthal, May 23, 1918, Province of the Sacred Heart Franciscan Records. The Protestant preacher Mr. Murry had been an irritant for some time. That Spring, Gordon had discovered he was circulating "anti-Catholic" literature around Lac du Flambeau. In a letter on the matter, Gordon assured Odoric the situation was under control: "I secured many copies of all kinds of pamphlets against Confession, the Pope, etc., etc. The Reverend Mr. Murry in the meantime made all kinds of excuses to a Committee of Catholic men that visited him. He said he really did not know that he was giving out bad stuff about the Catholics and he said he would stop right away." See Gordon to Derenthal, December 20, 1918, Province of the Sacred Heart Franciscan Records.

30. Benedict and Margaret Gauthier to Derenthal, May 30, 1918, Province of the Sacred Heart Franciscan Records. The sentiments in the letter are addressed jointly to Gordon and Odoric. A fuller quote reads: "I always wonder why couldn't you and Father Gordon have both taken care of us poor miserable Indians you should not have left us all of a sudden as you did we just can't get [illegible] we think of you so much it always seems as though we will see you coming back to us again all though you deserve the change and pray that it will do you so much good that sometimes you will be able to come back and see your poor Flambeau People." Benedict and Margaret Gauthier were an Ojibwe couple that owned the Gauthier Resort on Long Lake as Lac du Flambeau. They were among the first to capitalize on the reservation's tourist boom that occurred in the 1920s. See Child, *Holding Our World Together*, 86–87.

31. Montezuma to Gordon, June 11, 1918, Carlos Montezuma Papers.

32. Irvine Lenroot to Sells, June 5, 1918, quoted in "Outline for Biography," 31. See also Gordon to Derenthal, March 18, 1918. The letter mentions that Senator Lenroot was planning to attend a gathering organized by Gordon.

33. Lewandowski, *Red Bird, Red Power*, 130–31; Speroff, *Carlos Montezuma*, 242.

34. See Hertzberg, *The Search for an American Indian Identity*, 175; Speroff, *Carlos Montezuma*, 242.

35. Britten, *American Indians in World War I*, 176; Speroff, *Carlos Montezuma*, 264. After Montezuma gave his address, one SAI member, Mrs. Rhoads, outright condemned him. Montezuma told Pratt: "When I finished reading, Mrs. Rhoads gave it to me hot and heavy. She lashed into me for about an hour.

Once I saw myself behind the bars for twenty years. She claimed that my paper was seditious, and that I was doing injustice to the Government that has been so kind to the Indian race, and that I was poisoning the good work of the Indian department. My! She laid me out flatter than a pancake."

36. Gertrude Bonnin, "Platform and Resolutions," *American Indian Magazine* 5.3 (July–September 1918): 139.

37. See Bonnin to Parker, October 3, 1918; Parker to Bonnin, October 14, 1918, Papers of the Society of American Indians. Baldwin was unhappy at being deposed as treasurer. According to Bonnin, she took revenge by delaying information needed to perform the duties of office. Bonnin even wrote Gordon to complain that the "former Treasurer has not turned over to the new Treasurer the Society's books, documents, check books, rubber stamp; nor the balance of Society Funds deposited in the bank by her during her term of office." See Bonnin to Gordon, October 14, 1918, Carlos Montezuma Papers. After leaving the Society, Baldwin continued her work for the BIA. She retired in 1932 for health reasons. In 1949, she moved from Washington, DC, to Los Angeles, dying in 1952 at age eighty-eight. The cause of death was cerebral hemorrhage. See Cahill, "Marie Louise Bottineau Baldwin," 82.

38. Hertzberg, *The Search for an American Indian Identity*, 175–76. The Society had become utterly ineffective, even failing to keep Carlisle in operation after the U.S. Army designated the site for a military hospital.

39. Gordon to Derenthal, December 20, 1918.

Chapter 8. Struggles and Injustices

1. Philip Gordon, "Immediate Aid Is Urged for Many Destitute Indians," *Sawyer County Record*, March 11, 1919. Superintendent McQuigg's letter had been posted to Sells on January 13, 1919.

2. Gordon to Franklin Knight Lane, March 31, 1919, Papers of the Society of American Indians.

3. Lane to Gordon, April 8, 1919, Papers of the Society of American Indians.

4. Janik, *A Short History of Wisconsin*, 191.

5. Wyman, *The Chippewa*, 141–48.

6. Child, *Boarding School Seasons*, 94; Janik, *A Short History of Wisconsin*, 122; Wyman, *The Chippewa*, 141. In the state of Wisconsin, eight thousand of the over three hundred thousand citizens who contracted the Spanish flu died.

7. Gordon to Derenthal, ca. May 1919, Province of the Sacred Heart Franciscan Records. Indeed, Gordon continued to be a proverbial thorn in Odoric's side. In June, Gordon insisted on his help in "preparing a general report for the Apostolic delegate," requesting voluminous information on various funds and

their distribution and censuses of Indian converts. See Gordon to Derenthal, June 24, 1919, Province of the Sacred Heart Franciscan Records. Then in August, Gordon took offense when Odoric made an unannounced inspection of his Indian missions. "Dear Father Odoric," he wrote, "Kindly inform me for my records on whose authority you recently visited my Indian missions, also what your object was in not informing me of your actions. I saw you both before and after your trip to Flambeau Farm and you said nothing. As soon as I hear from you, I will take the matter up with His Lordship and your Provincial." See Gordon to Derenthal, August 13, 1919, Province of the Sacred Heart Franciscan Records.

8. Wilson, *Ohiyesa*, 161–62.

9. Gordon to Derenthal, May 19, 1919, Province of the Sacred Heart Franciscan Records.

10. Gordon to Derenthal, September 15, 1919, Province of the Sacred Heart Franciscan Records.

11. Hertzberg, *The Search for an American Indian Identity*, 182–83; Speroff, *Carlos Montezuma*, 365.

12. Gertrude Bonnin, "Editorial Comment," *American Indian Magazine* 7.2 (Summer 1919): 61.

13. Philip Gordon, "Address by Father Philip Gordon, Vice-President," *American Indian Magazine* 7.3 (Fall 1919): 153.

14. Hertzberg, *The Search for an American Indian Identity*, 182–83; Speroff, *Carlos Montezuma*, 265.

15. Bonnin, "Editorial Comment," 62.

16. Hertzberg, *The Search for an American Indian Identity*, 184–85; Speroff, *Carlos Montezuma*, 266. Sloan and his mentor, Hiram Chase, were instrumental in laying the groundwork for the Native American Church, founded in October of 1918 in Oklahoma with the goal of legally protecting peyote's use in religious ceremonies. The charter read: "This corporation is formed to foster and promote the religious belief of the several tribes of Indians in the state of Oklahoma, in the Christian religion with the practice of the peyote sacrament." See Hertzberg, *The Search for an American Indian Identity*, 149; Thomas Constantine Maroukis, *Peyote and the Yankton Sioux: The Life and Times of Sam Necklace* (Norman: University of Oklahoma Press, 2004), 131. Warrior writes that the Native American Church "managed to accomplish what the U.S. government was unwilling to allow politically and culturally: internal, self-determined adaptation to a new situation." See Warrior, *Tribal Secrets*, 12.

17. Charles Eastman, "Opening Address by Charles Eastman," *American Indian Magazine* 7.3 (Fall 1919): 146.

18. Gordon, "Address by Father Philip Gordon, Vice-President," 152–53. Gordon's concern about finding employment for those Native peoples in the Indian Service was highly pertinent. By 1899, American Indians comprised 45 percent of the workforce of the BIA. See Wilbert H. Ahern, "An Experiment Aborted: Returned Students in the Indian Service, 1881–1909," *Ethnohistory* 44.2 (Spring 1997): 264.

19. Gertrude Bonnin, "Address by Gertrude Bonnin, Secretary-Treasurer," *American Indian Magazine* 7.3 (Fall 1919): 154.

20. Thomas L. Sloan, "Thomas L, Sloan, Omaha Indian," *American Indian Magazine* 7.3 (Fall 1919): 162

21. Hertzberg, *The Search for an American Indian Identity*, 188.

22. Welch, "Zitkala-Ša," 162–65.

23. Still determined to effect change, Bonnin stayed on in Washington, DC, working with the Indian Welfare Committee of the General Federation of Women's Clubs. In 1926, she formed her own Native rights group, the National Council of American Indians. For the next decade Bonnin worked tirelessly, traversing the country inspecting reservation conditions and reporting to Congress. She died in 1938, in Virginia, convinced that all her activism had produced little beneficial effect for Native peoples. For a summary of Bonnin's life and a reprinting of her most important works, see: Cathy N. Davidson and Ada Norris, introduction to *American Indian Stories, Legends, and Other Writings* (New York: Penguin Books, 2003), xi–xxxv.

24. See Wilson, *Ohiyesa*, 162. With his days in the society ended, Eastman continued to write with his wife, Elaine Eastman, until they separated in 1921. In his later years, Eastman lived in a cabin on Lake Huron while spending winters with his son in Detroit. He died in 1939, his estranged wife in 1953. For a summary of Eastman's life and thought, see Miller, "Charles Alexander Eastman," 61–70.

25. Gordon to Derenthal, December 14, 1919, Province of the Sacred Heart Franciscan Records.

26. "The Society and the State," 379–80.

27. Gordon to Warren G. Harding, December 16, 1920, Carlos Montezuma Papers. To quote at greater length: "With no wish to impel you to action, we do all feel the great importance of the Indian question where the lives and fortunes of so many human beings are so vitally concerned asks consideration on weighty matters as public officials give to, for example, Department of Agriculture affairs, whose veterinary positions pay more than the regular Indian Service physician and surgeon receives! We therefore take the greatest pleasure not to mention boldness in placing ourselves at your every service in this matter."

28. See Asst. Secretary to Gordon, February 1, 1921, Carlos Montezuma Papers. Oddly, the assistant secretary writes that it would be a "physical impossibility" for Harding to meet with the SAI due to his plans to remain in Marion, Florida, until the inauguration. Gordon's letter must not have received more than a glance because Gordon had suggested the meeting take place in . . . Marion!

29. Hertzberg, *The Search for an American Indian Identity*, 193–94.

30. Montezuma to Marie Montezuma (Dovie), August 19, 1921, Carlos Montezuma Papers.

31. Philip Gordon, "Present Day Indians of Upper Wisconsin," *Bayfield Progress*, March 8, 1921.

Chapter 9. Bitter Ends

1. See "Indians Build Unique Church: New $27,000 Building at Reserve Nears Completion; Rev. Philip Gordon is Receiving Strong Support from Outside," *Rice Lake Times*, ca. 1923, Wisconsin Historical Society; "Church Destroyed by Lightning," *Indian Sentinel* 2.8 (1920–22): 383. This first source gives the date as August 9, 1921, while the *Indian Sentinel* records the date as August 10.

2. Gordon, January 1922 pamphlet.

3. "Church Destroyed by Lightning," 383.

4. Gordon, January 1922 pamphlet.

5. See "Father Gordon Quits Reserve: Noted Indian Priest Appointed Pastor of Centuria Church by Bishop Pinten," *Telegram*, ca. May 1924, Provence of the Sacred Heart Archives. Other earlier published sources state the amount Gordon raised for the church's construction was less than $35,000, $27,000 in one instance. See "Indians Build Unique Church."

6. See the January 1922 pamphlet Philip Gordon distributed after the church's destruction; "Father Gordon, Indian Priest, Plans Jubilee: Centuria Pastor Sends Invitation to President Roosevelt," *Telegram*, 1938, Franciscan Sisters of Perpetual Adoration Archives.

7. "Laying of Cornerstone at Reserve," *Indian Sentinel* 2.11 (1920–22): 502.

8. Delfeld, *The Indian Priest*, 71.

9. "Red Man Worships in Red Man's Own Way in New Dream Church," *Wisconsin State Journal*, November 23, 1923.

10. Delfeld, *The Indian Priest*, 70–72.

11. Rasmussen, *Where the River Is Wide*, 15, 19, 24, 28. Post was the name given to Pahquahwong as it developed as a center of commerce in the nineteenth century. It was short for "trading post."

12. Mark W. Oberly, "Tribal Sovereignty and Resources: The Lac Courte Oreilles Experience," in *Buried Roots and Indestructible Seeds: The Survival of American Indian Life in Story, History, and Spirit,* ed. Mark Allan Lindquist and Martin Zanger (Madison: University of Wisconsin Press, 1995), 128–41.

13. Delfeld, *The Indian Priest,* 72–73.

14. "Bishop Koudelka, 1913–1921," *History of Diocese of Superior.*

15. Delfeld, *The Indian Priest,* 73–74.

16. Oberly, "Tribal Sovereignty and Resources," 141–43; Rasmussen, *Where the River Is Wide,* 36–38, 50.

17. Hertzberg, *The Search for an American Indian Identity,* 200–201.

18. Graham D. Taylor, *The New Deal and American Indian Tribalism: The Administration of the Indian Reorganization Act, 1934–45* (Lincoln: University of Nebraska Press, 1980), 69.

19. See Gertrude Bonnin, Charles H. Fabens, and Matthew K. Sniffen, *Oklahoma's Poor Rich Indians: An Orgy of Graft and Exploitation of the Five Civilized Tribes—Legalized Robbery* (Philadelphia: Indian Rights Association, 1924); Angie Debo, *And Still the Waters Run: The Betrayal of the Five Civilized Tribes* (Princeton: Princeton University Press, 1972), 103–4.

20. Hertzberg, *The Search for an American Indian Identity,* 200–201.

21. "Indian Leader Sees Bloodshed: Fears Braves, 'Crushed by White Rule,' Will Fight for Vote," *Milwaukee Journal,* April 20, 1923.

22. "Wisconsin Indian Petitions Congress to Protect Rights: Claim Government Paternalism Is Stifling Progress of Red Race," *Milwaukee Sentinel,* April 16, 1923.

23. "Indian Leader Sees Bloodshed."

24. Speroff, *Carlos Montezuma,* 259–331, 367, 441–43.

25. Hertzberg, *The Search for an American Indian Identity,* 197–98. In 1925, Parker became the director of the Rochester Museum of Arts and Sciences in upstate New York. In the 1930s, he worked for the Work Progress Administration, directing an Indian Arts Project, and was eventually elected as the first president of the Society for American Archaeology. He died in 1955. See Porter, *To Be Indian,* 167–71, 200–201, 239.

26. Speroff, *Carlos Montezuma,* 367. See also Maroukis, "The Peyote Controversy," 159–80. Though the issue of peyote is not stressed in this biography because none of Gordon's comments on it have survived, Maroukis distinguishes the disagreement over the Peyote Religion as a main force behind the Society of American Indians' ultimate unraveling.

27. Hoxie, *This Indian Country,* 269.

28. Debo, *And Still the Waters Run*, 331–34; Hertzberg, *The Search for an American Indian Identity*, 203; Welch, "Zitkala-Ša," 190–93.

29. Porter, *To Be Indian*, 139–41.

30. Hertzberg, *The Search for an American Indian Identity*, 202–4; Speroff, *Carlos Montezuma*, 369–70.

31. Gordon described the incident as such: "In September 1923, some disaffected Indians, mostly non-Catholic, led by a renegade Indian who had served time in a State prison and aided and abetted by certain government agencies, . . . filed absurd and ridiculous charges affecting the conduct of the writer. The subsequent 'investigation' of the government officials disclosed nothing and the Bishop himself conducted and undertook as secret inquiry . . . the complainants publicly known to be irresponsible and even immoral. Two of the complainants have now admitted by affidavit that the matter was the characteristic American 'frame up.'" See Delfeld, *The Indian Priest*, 76. Gordon had by this point mended his relationship with the Bureau of Catholic Indian Missions and befriended its new director, Reverend William Hughes. That year, 1923, Gordon had given an address at the Catholic Sioux Congress at Standing Rock Reservation, South Dakota, wherein he prayed that "God may call other Indian boys to the holy priesthood." See "Mission Crusade Rally at Cincinnati," *Indian Sentinel* 2.11 (1920–22): 512. Catholic Bureau of Indian Missions director Reverend William Hughes and Gordon had attended a mission crusade rally in Cincinnati, Ohio, where a pageant was performed. Gordon brought four Ojibwe children with him to partake in the festivities. The article mentions that Gordon was, once again, representing the Catholic Bureau, though not as a missionary under their direction.

32. Delfeld, *The Indian Priest*, 74–75.

33. "Outline for Biography," 25.

34. Delfeld, *The Indian Priest*, 77.

35. Warren C. Moorehead to Gordon, March 12, 1924, Papers of the Society of American Indians.

36. Gordon to Moorehead, March 31, 1924, Papers of the Society of American Indians. Gordon was arguably correct in his assessment of the dim hopes for change in the wake of the Committee of One Hundred's report. Only sixty of the members appeared for the committee's meeting in December 1923. The results, as David Messer puts it, were "subject to debate." The Committee of One Hundred is, however, usually given credit for helping spur the later Meriam Report (1928), if little else. See Messer, *Henry Roe Cloud*, 99; Wilson, *Ohiyesa*, 172–73.

Chapter 10. Continuing the Fight from Centuria

1. Delfeld, *The Indian Priest*, 79–80; "Outline for Biography," 25. Gordon lived at Long Lake until his death, but from 1926 held mass in Centuria, sometimes at the town hall, sometimes in an old department store. In 1929, he began constructing a new church in Centuria. See Delfeld, *The Indian Priest*, 82, 87, 96.

2. "Father Gordon Quits Reserve."

3. Philip Gordon, editorial, *Inter-County Leader*, May 26, 1924, quoted in Delfeld, *The Indian Priest*, 79.

4. Hoxie, *This Indian Country*, 274.

5. Speroff, *Carlos Montezuma*, 85.

6. Though a thorough discussion of the meaning of Indian citizenship is outside the scope of this biography, there is much scholarly debate about whether the ICA was a step forward or backward for indigenous nations, on whom the mantle of citizenship was thrust. For a discussion of such tensions, see, for instance, Kevin Bruyneel, "Challenging American Boundaries: Indigenous People and the 'Gift' of U.S. Citizenship," *Studies in American Political Development* 18 (Spring 2004): 30–43. Had Gordon lived to see the efforts made by the U.S. government to terminate tribes in the 1950s, he may have questioned the efficacy of citizenship. This speculation is based on his support for Indian identity and his promoting the ideals of tribal self-determination and democracy in *War-Whoop* and *Anishinabe Enamiad*.

7. Linda Gordon, *The Second Coming of the KKK: The Ku Klux Klan of the 1920s and the American Political Tradition* (New York: Liveright, 2017), 26–27.

8. See Delfeld, *The Indian Priest*, 82–83.

9. Gordon, *The Second Coming of the KKK*, 1–3, 41.

10. Gordon H. Lee, "The Ku Klux Klan in the 1920s" (MA thesis, Wisconsin State University–La Crosse, August 1968), 8.

11. Gordon, *The Second Coming of the KKK*, 84.

12. Lee, "The Ku Klux Klan in the 1920s," 10, 15.

13. Norman Frederic Weaver, "The Knights of the Ku Klux Klan in Wisconsin, Indiana, Ohio, and Michigan" (PhD diss., University of Wisconsin–Madison, 1954), 128.

14. Gordon, *The Second Coming of the KKK*, 86, 95.

15. Lee, "The Ku Klux Klan in the 1920s," 10, 15, 17–22.

16. L. J. Quigley to Gordon, April 22, 1926, quoted in Delfeld, *The Indian Priest*, 89–90.

17. Delfeld, *The Indian Priest*, 90–91.

18. Gordon, *The Second Coming of the KKK*, 103.

19. Delfeld, *The Indian Priest*, 90–91.

20. Lee, "The Ku Klux Klan in the 1920s," 21–22.

21. Quoted in Delfeld, *The Indian Priest*, 92, 95. Gordon was later an opponent of the anti-Semitic radio personality Father Coughlin. He wrote concerning the Ku Klux Klan affair: "I often wonder if the set of men and women who do so much criticizing of any anti-Semitic utterances in these days and are willing to bar Father Coughlin from the air, because of alleged anti-Jewish sentiments felt the same when their Catholic fellow-citizens and Catholic neighbors were under fire from the likes of the creature known as 'Pat Malone.'" Quoted in Delfeld, *The Indian Priest*, 92.

22. Weaver, "The Knights of the Ku Klux Klan," 128–30.

23. Rawlings, *The Second Coming of the Invisible Empire*, 235–36.

24. Gordon to Pietro Fumasoni Biondi, ca. 1925, quoted in Delfeld, *The Indian Priest*, 102–3.

25. Delfeld, *The Indian Priest*, 103.

26. "American Indian Pilgrimages," *Indian Sentinel* 6.3 (1926): 112.

27. St. Paul *Daily News*, quoted in Delfeld, *The Indian Priest*, 104. The Society of American Indians, though it existed in name after 1923, was essentially defunct. See Hertzberg, *The Search for an American Indian Identity*, 199–200.

28. In 1927, Gordon wrote Gertrude Bonnin hoping to interest her in reviving the Society of American Indians. Father Gordon told her that the Society was operating "feebly if at all." Bonnin expressed the opinion that the SAI was "top-heavy, without any body," and encouraged Gordon to join her organization, the National Council of American Indians. See Hafen, "Help Indians Help Themselves," 210.

29. Gordon to Everett Sanders, July 14, 1928, Papers of the Society of American Indians.

30. Charles H. Burke to Sanders, July 18, 1918, Papers of the Society of American Indians.

31. Delfeld, *The Indian Priest*, 105, 117.

32. Speroff, *Carlos Montezuma*, 370.

33. Delfeld, *The Indian Priest*, 117.

34. "Indian Priest Speaks Here: Rev. Philip Gordon to Tell of Race's Progress at Annual Fete," Franciscan Sisters of Perpetual Adoration Archives; Hertzberg, *The Search for an American Indian Identity*, 228–29.

35. See "Outline for Biography," 32. In Ireland, Gordon was the guest of the noted politician Eamon DeValera, who had been inducted into the Ojibwe tribe by Gordon on a visit to Reserve in 1919.

36. Delfeld, *The Indian Priest*, 115.

37. See untitled newspaper clipping, ca. 1942, Franciscan Sisters of Perpetual Adoration Archives; Delfeld, *The Indian Priest*, 123.

38. Delfeld, *The Indian Priest*, 124.

39. "Outline for Biography," 27.

40. Delfeld, *The Indian Priest*, 107, 110–11, 134. The letter that damned Governor Heil was written to Paul Villaume.

41. Philip Gordon, "Father Gordon Reports on Meeting of Catholic Clergy and Bishop at Birchwood to Discuss Farmer Problems," *Inter-County Leader*, August 9, 1945, Franciscan Sisters of Perpetual Adoration Archives. The article details Gordon's participation in the Rural Leaders Seminar in Birchwood, Wisconsin, held by the National Catholic Rural Conference and a local parish, St. John the Apostle of Birchwood. Gordon was interviewed after nineteen years in Centuria and had this to say about his work with the farm unions: "Probably one of the most interesting periods in my life has been here in this rural parish for the past nineteen years. The opportunity has been afforded me of contacting the big farm organizations, in particular the Farmers Union. A series of big picnics under the sponsorship of the Parish has brought here many prominent Americans, as speakers. Among these have been Governors of States (Philip LaFollette and others), Congressmen, U.S. Senators and Presidential Candidates. Rather interesting, I think." See Macaria, "Reverend Philip Gordon, LL.D."

42. Delfeld, *The Indian Priest*, 113.

43. "Outline for Biography," 28, 36; "American Indian Priest Has No Indians in His Parish," ca. 1942, Franciscan Sisters of Perpetual Adoration Archives. To give more of an idea of Gordon's political sympathies, he was also a fan of Eleanor Roosevelt. One of his letters to Paul Villaume, ca. 1944, reads: "By the way, I hope that opportunist Wendell W[illkie] does not run again. He would not get to first base, I think, old Chief Blow Hard. I am almost in favor of another term for FDR. Let him die in office and Eleanor can take over, nes't pas? Infant terrible! Sepragemon! (My French spelling is awful.)" See Delfeld, *The Indian Priest*, 132.

44. "Father Gordon, Indian Priest, Plans Jubilee: Centuria Pastor Sends Invitation to President Roosevelt," Franciscan Sisters of Perpetual Adoration Archives. Gordon stated: "If the president accedes to the wishes of those that will invite him, of course, it will be a striking honor to yours truly, to the Indian race, and to the Catholic church."

45. "Father Gordon Honored, Pope Sends Message," *Telegram*, January 5, 1939, Franciscan Sisters of Perpetual Adoration Archives.

46. Delfeld, *The Indian Priest*, 147.

47. Obituary of William D. Gordon, "Pioneer Son of Gordon's Founder Dies There at 93," June 16, 1943, Franciscan Sisters of Perpetual Adoration Archives.

48. Porter, *To Be Indian*, 140–41; Taylor, *The New Deal and American Indian Tribalism*, 12–13. Gordon and Collier were apparently acquaintances but not in any way close. See Macaria, "Reverend Philip Gordon, LL.D."

49. Child, *Boarding School Seasons*, 40.

50. Wyman, *The Chippewa*, 159.

51. "American Indian Priest Has No Indians in His Parish." The article showed Gordon in his headdress next to a photograph of New York Governor Alfred Smith.

52. Wyman, *The Chippewa*, 159.

53. See Macaria, "Reverend Philip Gordon, LL.D."

54. Delfeld, *The Indian Priest*, 112, 131.

55. Mary Macaria, "New Odanah School Dedicated," *Indian Sentinel* 22.6 (1942): 85.

56. "Father Gordon Presents Resolution Praising NYA Training Program," May 11, 1942, excerpt from the *Congressional Record*, Franciscan Sisters of Perpetual Adoration Archives.

57. "Fr. Philip Gordon Is Tribesman," ca. June 1943, Franciscan Sisters of Perpetual Adoration Archives; *Congressional Record, Proceedings and Debates of the 78th Congress*, June 11, 1943, found in "Outline for Biography," 39. The prayer read in full:

Father Almighty, we lift our mind and hearts to Thee in sacred communion for these brief moments.

We praise and adore Thee. We thank thee for the evidences of Thy good will and love toward our people and our Nation.

The black chimneys of industry and the glittering temples of commerce that dot our vast lands all too well bespeak Thy favors afforded opportunity given to our Nation to advance the welfare of its peoples.

Let us, O good Lord, not forget that we need a faith in Thee reared like the bosom of the earth. Grant us, we beseech Thee, a firm belief in Thy power and majesty, Thy justice and charity.

Grant, we pray, that this legislative body be guided by true Christian principles, so that in the twilight of the lives of its individual Members well may be it said of them in the words of the ancient Lain hymn:

"Xexilla Regis prodeunt
Fulget Crucis mysterium."

Bless, O Great Spirit, the Kitchi Manito of our forefathers, our Great White Father, our President and our Commander in Chief. Bless the Members of this Congress. Bless us all, dear Lord.

We beg these favors of Thee in the name of the Father, the Son, and the holy Trinity—Father, Thee, and the Holy Ghost. Amen.

58. "Pioneer Son of Gordon's Founder Dies There at 93"; "Dies in Village Father Started: W. D. Gordon Mourned in Douglas County; Town Bears His Name," Franciscan Sisters of Perpetual Adoration Archives.

59. "Father Philip Gordon Wins Achievement Medal," ca. September 1944, Franciscan Sisters of Perpetual Adoration Archives. The day, September 22, was "observed as American Indian Day in Illinois." See "Indian Pastor to Be Awarded Council Medal," ca. September 1944, Franciscan Sisters of Perpetual Adoration Archives.

Chapter 11. Paul Villaume, a Journey, and Philip Gordon's Final Years

1. Delfeld's account and all the letters quoted can be found in *The Indian Priest*, 121–45. Delfeld interviewed Villaume in St. Paul, Minnesota, when he was in his fifties. See also "Nation's Only Indian Priest, Fr. Gordon, Dies in St. Paul," *Telegram*, October 2, 1948, Franciscan Sisters of Perpetual Adoration Archives. Villaume also wrote the foreword to Delfeld's book. It reads:

The Indian Priest is the life-story of a dear friend of mine, a wonderful priest, a holy man, a proud American Indian, and good citizen.

Father Gordon deserves what Paula Delfeld has so carefully researched and written. She writes gloriously of his pride in his Indian heritage. She tells of his priestly qualities. He loved God through his deep Catholicity; he loved the priesthood of the Catholic Church. Most importantly she tells the reader about a man who was loved by those who knew him well—as a priest, a scholar, a raconteur, a leader in the fight for man's dignity no matter what his origin.

He was a most important part of my life from 1925 to 1948, age 10 to age 33. In the book he comes to life in a very real sense.

In this short introduction I pay tribute to my dear friend and to the lovely lady who has done her difficult job so well. Father Gordon would have loved it. P.V.

See Paul Villaume, foreword to *The Indian Priest*, v.

2. "Information Pertaining to Reverend [Philip] Gordon, LL.D., Chippewa Indian Priest." The plot where the Gordons are buried is now part of the Gordon Memorial Cemetery. Both of Philip Gordon's parents are buried there, as are four of his siblings. Father Gordon's gravestone is modest. It lists the

date of ordination, while "Chippewa Indian Priest" is inscribed in its middle. See "Philip Bergin Gordon," https://www.findagrave.com/memorial/50549453/philip-bergin-gordon (accessed January 15, 2019).

Conclusion

1. "Rev. Philip Gordon," 15.

2. See Gordon, "Editorial," Franciscan Province of the Sacred Heart Archives.

3. See Oberly, "Tribal Sovereignty and Resources," 142–43. The Lac Courte Oreilles Ojibwe sued the Northern States Power Company, which had taken over the running of the Chippewa Flowage Project in the 1920s, for compensation for the full fifty years since the dam had been in operation. The lawsuit was settled in 1985, with the Ojibwe taking control of the dam and constructing their own energy plant. The Northern States Power Company also ceded 4,500 acres of land they owned to the Lac Courte Oreilles and paid a cash settlement that included legal fees.

4. See Troy R. Johnson, *Red Power: The Native American Civil Rights Movement* (New York: Chelsea House, 2007), 9–10, 53–55; Paul Chaat Smith and Robert Allen Warrior, *Like a Hurricane: The Indian American Movement from Alcatraz to Wounded Knee* (New York: New Press, 1996), 153–68.

Bibliography

Archives

Bureau of the Catholic Indian Missions Records. Raynor Memorial Libraries, Marquette University Archives. Milwaukee, Wisconsin.
Carlos Montezuma Papers. Wisconsin Historical Society. Madison, Wisconsin.
Franciscan Provence of the Sacred Heart Archives. St. Louis, Missouri.
Franciscan Sisters of Perpetual Adoration Archives. La Crosse, Wisconsin.
Papers of the Society of American Indians. Cornell University Library. Ithaca, New York.
Provence of the Sacred Heart Franciscan Records. Raynor Memorial Libraries, Marquette University Archives. Milwaukee, Wisconsin.
United States Works Progress Association Chippewa Indian Historical Project Records, 1936–40, 1942. Wisconsin Historical Society. Madison, Wisconsin.

Other Sources

Adams, David Wallace. *Education for Extinction: American Indians and the Boarding School Experience, 1875–1928*. Wichita: University Press of Kansas, 1995.
Ahern, Wilbert H. "An Experiment Aborted: Returned Students in the Indian Service, 1881–1909." *Ethnohistory* 44.2 (Spring 1997): 263–304.
"American Indian Pilgrimages." *Indian Sentinel* 6.3 (1926): 111–12.
"Are Catholic Indian Schools Necessary?" *Indian Sentinel* (1916): 48.
Bahr, Howard M., ed. *The Navajo as Seen by the Franciscans, 1898–1921: A Sourcebook*. Lanham, MD: Scarecrow Press, 2004.
Benton-Banai, Edward. *The Mishomis Book: The Voice of the Ojibway*. Minneapolis: University of Minnesota Press, 2010.
"Bigoted Misrule at Haskell Proved: YMCA Secretary Is Ordered Off the Reservation by Interior Secretary Lane." *Catholic Register*, February 24, 1916.

Bonnin, Gertrude. "Address by Gertrude Bonnin, Secretary-Treasurer." *American Indian Magazine* 7.3 (Fall 1919): 154–57.

———. "Editorial Comment." *American Indian Magazine* 7.2 (Summer 1919): 61–63.

———. "Platform and Resolutions." *American Indian Magazine* 5.3 (July–September 1918): 139–40.

Bonnin, Gertrude, Charles H. Fabens, and Matthew K. Sniffen. *Oklahoma's Poor Rich Indians: An Orgy of Graft and Exploitation of the Five Civilized Tribes—Legalized Robbery.* Philadelphia: Indian Rights Association, 1924.

Boyer, Paul S., Clifford E. Clark, Joseph F. Kett, Neal Salisbury, Harvard Sitkoff, and Nancy Woloch. *The Enduring Vision: A History of the American People, from 1865.* Boston: Houghton Mifflin, 2000.

Britten, Thomas A. *American Indians in World War I: At Home and at War.* Albuquerque: University of New Mexico Press, 1997.

Bunson, Stephen, and Margaret Bunson. *Faith in the Wilderness: The Story of the Catholic Indian Missions.* Huntington, IN: Our Sunday Visitor Press, 2000.

Cahill, Cathleen D. "Marie Louise Bottineau Baldwin: Indigenizing the Federal Indian Service." *Studies in American Indian Literatures* 25.2 and *American Indian Quarterly* 37.3 (Summer 2013): 63–86.

Callahan, S. Alice. *Wynema: A Child of the Forest.* Edited by A. LaVonne Brown Ruoff. Lincoln: University of Nebraska Press, 1997. (Originally published in 1891.)

Carlson, Paul H. *The Plains Indians.* College Station: Texas A&M University Press, 1998.

"The Cedar Rapids Platform." *American Indian Magazine* 3.4 (Fall 1916): 223–24.

Chamberlain, Alexander F. "Translation: A Study in the Transference of Folk-Thought." *Journal of American Folklore* 14.54 (July–September 1901): 165–71.

Child, Brenda J. *Boarding School Seasons: American Indian Families, 1900–1940.* Lincoln: University of Nebraska Press, 2000.

———. *Holding Our World Together: Ojibwe Women and the Survival of Community.* New York: Viking, 2012.

"Church Destroyed by Lightning." *Indian Sentinel* 2.8 (1920–22): 383.

Clifton, James A. "Wisconsin Death March: Explaining the Extremes in Old Northwest Indian Removal." *Transactions of the Wisconsin Academy of Sciences, Arts and Letters* 75 (1987): 1–40.

Coleman, Michael C. "Motivations of Indian Children at Missionary and U.S. Government Schools." *Montana: The Magazine of Western History* 40 (Winter 1990): 30–45.

"Conference Helped by Cedar Rapids Friends." *American Indian Magazine* 3.4 (Fall 1916): 221.

Coolidge, Sherman. "Opening Address of the President." *American Indian Magazine* 3.4 (Fall 1916): 227–29.

Danziger, Edmund Jefferson. *Indians and Bureaucrats: Administering the Reservation Policy during the Civil War.* Urbana: University of Illinois Press, 1974.

Davidson, Cathy N., and Ada Norris, eds. Introduction to *American Indian Stories, Legends, and Other Writings.* New York: Penguin Books, 2003.

Debo, Angie. *And Still the Waters Run: The Betrayal of the Five Civilized Tribes.* Princeton: Princeton University Press, 1972.

Delfeld, Paula. *The Indian Priest: Father Philip B. Gordon, 1885–1948.* Chicago: Franciscan Herald Press, 1977.

Deloria, Philip J. "Four Thousand Invitations." *Studies in American Indian Literatures* 25.2 and *American Indian Quarterly* 37.3 (Summer 2013): 25–43.

Donadio, Rachael. "Pope Canonizes 7 Saints, Including 2 Women with New York Ties." *New York Times*, October 21, 2012.

Derenthal, Odoric. "Reverend Chrysostom Verwyst, O.F.M.: Veteran Wisconsin Missionary." *Indian Sentinel* 5.4 (1925): 176–77.

Diedrich, Mark. "Chief Hole in the Day and the 1862 Chippewa Disturbance: A Reappraisal." *Minnesota History Magazine* (Spring 1987): 193–203.

———. *The Chiefs Hole in the Day of the Mississippi Chippewa.* Minneapolis: Coyote Books, 1986.

Eastman, Charles. "Opening Address by Charles Eastman." *American Indian Magazine* 7.3 (Fall 1919): 146.

"Editorials." *Indian Sentinel* 1.5 (1916–19): 18.

Ellinghaus, Katherine. "Assimilation by Marriage: White Women and Native American Men at the Hampton Institute, 1878–1923." *Virginia Magazine of History and Biography* 108.3 (2000): 279–303.

Enochs, Ross. "Native Americans on the Path to the Catholic Church: Cultural Crisis and Missionary Adaptation." *U.S. Catholic Historian* 27.1 (Winter 2009): 71–88.

"Father Gordon Visits Buffalo." *American Indian Magazine* 4.1 (January–March 1916): 349–51.

Fear-Segal, Jacqueline. "Nineteenth-Century Indian Education: Universalism versus Evolutionism." *Journal of American Studies* 33.2 (August 1999): 323–41.

Fite, Gilbert C., and Harriet C. Peterson. *Opponents of War, 1917–1918.* Santa Barbara: Greenwood Press, 1986.

"Full Blooded Indian Priest." *Red Man* (September 1915): 35–36.

Gordon, Linda. *The Second Coming of the KKK: The Ku Klux Klan of the 1920s and the American Political Tradition*. New York: Liveright, 2017.

Gordon, Philip. "Address by Father Philip Gordon, Vice-President." *American Indian Magazine* 7.3 (Fall 1919): 152–53.

———. "Father Gordon Reports on Meeting of Catholic Clergy and Bishop at Birchwood to Discuss Farmer Problems." *Inter-County Leader*, August 9, 1945.

———. "Immediate Aid Is Urged for Many Destitute Indians." *Sawyer County Record*, March 11, 1919.

———. "Opposition to the Indian Bureau." *American Indian Magazine* 3.4 (Fall 1916): 259–60.

———. "Present Day Indians of Upper Wisconsin." *Bayfield Progress*, March 8, 1921.

Greene, Jerome A. *American Carnage: Wounded Knee, 1890*. Norman: University of Oklahoma Press, 2014.

Guibord, Prosper. "Certain Lumber Conditions at the Lac Court Oreilles Reservation." *American Indian Magazine* 3.4 (Fall 1916): 250–51.

Habig, Marion A. *Heralds of the King: The Franciscans of the St. Louis-Chicago Province, 1858–1958*. Chicago: Franciscan Herald Press, 1958.

Hafen, P. Jane. "'Help Indians Help Themselves': Gertrude Bonnin, the SAI, and the NCAI." *Studies in American Indian Literatures* 25.2 and *American Indian Quarterly* 37.3 (Summer 2013): 199–218.

Hertzberg, Hazel W. *The Search for an American Indian Identity: Modern Pan-Indian Movements*. Syracuse: Syracuse University Press, 1971.

Hoxie, Frederick E. *A Final Promise: The Campaign to Assimilate the Indians, 1880–1920*. Lincoln: University of Nebraska Press, 1984.

———, ed. *Talking Back to Civilization: Indian Voices from the Progressive Era*. New York: Bedford / St. Martin's Press, 2001.

———. *This Indian Country: American Indian Political Activists and the Place They Made*. New York: Penguin Press, 2012.

Huffer, William. "Catholic Sioux Congress of South Dakota: Indian Hospitality and Faith." *Indian Sentinel* 3.4 (1923): 147–48.

"Indian Leader Sees Bloodshed: Fears Braves, 'Crushed by White Rule,' Will Fight for Vote." *Milwaukee Journal*, April 20, 1923.

"Indian Student for the Priesthood." *Indian Sentinel* (1912): 19.

Isham, Ira. "The Case of the Lac Court Oreilles Reservation Chippewa." *American Indian Magazine* 3.4 (Fall 1916): 250.

Jachow, Merrill E. *Private Liberal Arts Colleges in Minnesota: Their History and Contributions*. St. Paul: Minnesota Historical Society Press, 1973.

Janik, Erica. *A Short History of Wisconsin*. Madison: Wisconsin Historical Society Press, 2010.

Johnson, Troy R. *Red Power: The Native American Civil Rights Movement*. New York: Chelsea House, 2007.

Kennedy, David M. *Over Here: The First World War and American Society*. Oxford: Oxford University Press, 1980.

Ketcham, William H. "Address by Father William H. Ketcham of Washington, D.C." *Quarterly Journal of the Society of American Indians* 1.1 (January–April 1913): 193–94.

LaBarre, Weston. *The Peyote Cult*. 5th ed. Norman: University of Oklahoma Press, 1989. (Originally published in 1935.)

Landes, Ruth. *Ojibwa Religion and the Midéwiwin*. Madison: University of Wisconsin Press, 1968.

Lanternari, Vittorio. *The Religions of the Oppressed: A Study of Modern Messianic Cults*. Translated by Lisa Sergio. New York: Mentor Books, 1963.

Larner, John W. "Society of American Indians." In *Native America in the Twentieth Century: An Encyclopedia*, edited by Mary B. Davis, 603–4. New York: Garland, 1994.

"Laying of Cornerstone at Reserve." *Indian Sentinel* 2.11 (1920–22): 502.

Lee, Gordon H. "The Ku Klux Klan in the 1920s." MA thesis, Wisconsin State University–La Crosse, 1968.

Lewandowski, Tadeusz. *Red Bird, Red Power: The Life and Legacy of Zitkala-Ša*. Norman: University of Oklahoma Press, 2016.

Lone Wolf, Delos. "How to Solve the Problem." *American Indian Magazine* 3.4 (Fall 1916): 257–59.

Macaria, Mary. "New Odanah School Dedicated." *Indian Sentinel* 22.6 (1942): 85.

Maddox, Lucy. *Citizen Indians: Native American Intellectuals, Race, and Reform*. Ithaca: Cornell University Press, 2005.

Mannard, Joseph G. "American Anti-Catholicism and Its Literature." *Ex Libris* 4.1 (1981): 1–9.

Maroukis, Thomas Constantine. *Peyote and the Yankton Sioux: The Life and Times of Sam Necklace*. Norman: University of Oklahoma Press, 2004.

———. "The Peyote Controversy and the Demise of the Society of American Indians." *Studies in American Indian Literatures* 25.2 and *American Indian Quarterly* 37.3 (Summer 2013): 159–80.

Martin, Lawrence T. "The Franciscan Mission to the Wisconsin Chippewa: The Evidence of Sermons." In *Papers of the Twenty-Seventh Algonquin Conference*, edited by David Pentland, 195–204. Winnipeg: University of Manitoba Press, 1996.

McDonnell, Michael A. *Masters of Empire: Great Lakes Indians and the Making of America*. New York: Hill and Wang, 2015.

Meisenheimer, D. K., Jr. "Regionalist Bodies / Embodied Regions: Sarah Orne Jewett and Zitkala-Ša." In *Breaking Boundaries: New Perspectives on Women's Regional Writing*, edited by Sherrie A. Inness and Diana Royer, 109–23. Iowa City: University of Iowa Press, 1997.

Messer, David W. *Henry Roe Cloud: A Biography*. New York: Hamilton Books, 2009.

Milk, Theresa. *Haskell Institute: 19th Century Stories of Sacrifice and Survival*. Lawrence, KS: Mammoth, 2007.

Miller, David Reed. "Charles Alexander Eastman, the 'Winner': From Deep Woods to Civilization." In *American Indian Intellectuals*, edited by Margot Liberty, 61–70. St. Paul: West, 1978.

"Mission Crusade Rally at Cincinnati." *Indian Sentinel* 2.11 (1920–22): 512.

Montezuma, Carlos. "Address before the Sixth Conference." *American Indian Magazine* 3.4 (Fall 1916): 160–62.

———. "Let My People Go." *Quarterly Journal of the Society of American Indians* 4.1 (January–March 1916): 32–33.

Murphy, Terrence J. *A Catholic University: Vision and Opportunities*. Collegeville, MN: Liturgical Press, 2001.

Murry, Stanley N. "The Turtle Mountain Chippewa, 1882–1905." *North Dakota History* 51.1 (1984): 14–37.

Nesbit, Robert C. *Wisconsin: A History*. Madison: University of Wisconsin Press, 2004.

Nicholson, Christopher L. "To Advance a Race: A Historical Analysis of the Personal Belief, Industrial Philanthropy and Black Liberal Arts Higher Education in Fayette McKenzie's Presidency at Fisk University, 1915–1925." PhD diss., Loyola University, Chicago, 2011.

Oberly, Mark W. "Tribal Sovereignty and Resources: The Lac Courte Oreilles Experience." In *Buried Roots and Indestructible Seeds: The Survival of American Indian Life in Story, History, and Spirit*, edited by Mark Allan Lindquist and Martin Zanger, 127–53. Madison: University of Wisconsin Press, 1995.

"Open Debate on the Loyalty of Indian Employees in the Indian Service." *American Indian Magazine* 3.4 (Fall 1916): 252–56.

Parker, Arthur C. "Board of Indian Commissioners." *Quarterly Journal of the Society of American Indians* 2.4 (January–March 1914): 2–3.

———. "The Editor's Viewpoint: The Functions of the Society of American Indians." *Quarterly Journal of the Society of American Indians* 4.1 (January–March 1916): 8–14.

Pfister, Joel. *The Yale Indian: The Education of Henry Roe Cloud.* Durham: Duke University Press, 2009.

Porter, Joy. *To Be Indian: The Life of Iroquois-Seneca Arthur Caswell Parker.* Norman: University of Oklahoma Press, 2001.

Pratt, Richard Henry. "Remarks and Motion of Gen. Henry Pratt Regarding Peyote." *American Indian Magazine* 3.4 (Fall 1916): 237–38.

———. "The Solution to the Indian Problem." *Quarterly Journal of the Society of American Indians* 1.1 (January–April 1913): 197–204.

Pritzker, Barry M. *A Native American Encyclopedia: History, Culture, People.* Oxford: Oxford University Press, 2000.

Rahill, Peter J. "The Catholic Indian Missions and Grant's Peace Policy, 1870–1884." PhD diss., Catholic University of America, Washington, DC, 1953.

Rasmussen, Charlie Otto. *Where the River Is Wide: Pahquahwong and the Chippewa Flowage.* Odanah, WI: Great Lakes Indian Fish & Wildlife Commission Press, 1998.

Rawlings, William. *The Second Coming of the Invisible Empire: The Ku Klux Klan of the 1920s.* Macon, GA: Mercer University Press, 2016.

"Red Man Worships in Red Man's Own Way in New Dream Church." *Wisconsin State Journal,* November 23, 1923.

"Rev. Odoric Ignaz Derenthal, O. S. F." In *Shawano County Biographies,* 348–49. Chicago: J. H. Beers, 1895.

"Rev. Philip Gordon." *New York Times.* October 2, 1948, 15.

"Rigid Investigation at Haskell Institute: Member of Indian Bureau and His Chief Inspectors Arrive in Lawrence This Week." *Catholic Register,* February 17, 1916.

Roddis, Louis H. "The Last Indian Uprising in the United States." *Minnesota History Bulletin* 3.5 (1920): 273–90.

Satz, Ronald N. *Chippewa Treaty Rights: The Reserved Rights of Wisconsin's Chippewa Indians in Historical Perspective.* Madison: Wisconsin Academy of Sciences, Arts and Letters, 1991.

Schaffer, Ronald. *America in the Great War: The Rise of the War Welfare State.* New York: Oxford University Press, 1991.

"A Second Indian Priest." *Indian Sentinel* (1914): 7.

"The Sioux Congress." *Indian Sentinel* 1.2 (1916–19): 27–30.

Sloan, Thomas L. "Thomas L. Sloan, Omaha Indian." *American Indian Magazine* 7.3 (Fall 1919): 162.

Smith, Paul Chaat, and Robert Allen Warrior. *Like a Hurricane: The Indian American Movement from Alcatraz to Wounded Knee*. New York: New Press, 1996.

Smith, Theresa S. *The Island of the Anishnaabeg: Thunders and Water Monsters and the Traditional Ojibwe Life World*. Moscow: University of Idaho Press, 1995.

"The Society and the State." *Wisconsin Magazine of History* 3.3 (March 1920).

Spack, Ruth. "Dis/engagement: Zitkala-Ša's Letters to Carlos Montezuma, 1901–1902." *MELUS: The Journal of the Society for the Study of the Multi-ethnic Literature of the United States* 26.1 (2001): 173–204.

Speroff, Leon. *Carlos Montezuma, MD, a Yavapai American Hero: The Life and Times of an American Indian, 1866–1923*. Portland, OR: Arnica, 2005.

"St. Mary's Industrial School, Odanah, Wisconsin." *Indian Sentinel* (1905–6): 5–16.

Super, O. B. "Indian Education at Carlisle." *New England Magazine* 18.2 (April 1895): 224–40.

Taylor, Graham D. *The New Deal and American Indian Tribalism: The Administration of the Indian Reorganization Act, 1934–45*. Lincoln: University of Nebraska Press, 1980.

Treuer, Anton. *The Assassination of Hole in the Day*. St. Paul: Borealis Books, 2011.

———. *Ojibwe in Minnesota*. St. Paul: Minnesota Historical Society Press, 2010.

Vecsey, Christopher. *Traditional Ojibwa Religion and Its Historical Changes*. Philadelphia: American Philosophical Society, 1983.

Vizenor, Gerald. *The People Named the Chippewa: Narrative Histories*. Minneapolis: University of Minnesota Press, 1984.

Warren, William, W. *History of the Ojibway People*. St. Paul: Minnesota Historical Society Press, 1984.

Warrior, Robert Allen. *Tribal Secrets: Recovering American Intellectual Traditions*. Minneapolis: University of Minnesota Press, 1995.

Weaver, Norman Frederic. "The Knights of the Ku Klux Klan in Wisconsin, Indiana, Ohio, and Michigan." PhD diss., University of Wisconsin–Madison, 1954.

Welch, Deborah Sue. "Zitkala-Ša: An American Indian Leader, 1876–1938." PhD diss., University of Wyoming, 1985.

Wilson, Raymond. *Ohiyesa: Charles Eastman, Santee Sioux*. Urbana: University of Illinois Press, 1983.

"Wisconsin Indian Petitions Congress to Protect Rights: Claim Government Paternalism Is Stifling Progress of Red Race." *Milwaukee Sentinel*, April 16, 1923.

Witgen, Michael. *An Infinity of Nations: How the Native New World Shaped Early North America*. Philadelphia: University of Pennsylvania Press, 2012.

Wyman, Walker Demarquis. *The Chippewa: A History of the Great Lakes Woodland Tribe over Three Centuries*. River Falls: University of Wisconsin–River Falls Press, 1993.

Zinn, Howard. *A People's History of the United States*. New York: Harper Collins, 1993.

Index

Allouez, Claude (Catholic mission-
ary), 141n4
American College in Rome, 30
American Fur Company, 13, 15
American Indian Defense Associa-
tion (AIDA), 112
American Indian Magazine (AIM),
37, 62, 80, 97, 102, 106, 135
American Public Utilities, 109–10
Amik, Wisconsin, 17–20. *See also*
Gordon, Wisconsin
Anishinaabe. *See* Ojibwe
Anishinaabeg. *See* Ojibwe
Anishinabe Enamiad (Gordon's jour-
nal), 92–94, 96, 132, 167n20,
167n22, 175n6
Ashland, Wisconsin, 26–27
Ategekwe (Sarah Mekins; Gordon's
mother), 20, 24, 30, 109, 124, 129,
146n56

Bad River Reservation, Wisconsin, 6,
17, 24, 30, 38–39, 84, 101, 108, 126
Baldwin, Marie (Ojibwe, SAI member), 35, 138n17, 162n36; background of, 153n46; and Bonnin,
83, 97, 162n23, 169n37; death of,

169n37; and Gordon, 43, 163n56,
169n37; illustration of, 72; and
Parker, 162n23; and SAI, 47–48,
64–65, 83, 97, 150n6, 162n23,
169n37
Bayfield, Wisconsin, 6, 17–18, 20, 23
Bayley, James Roosevelt (archbishop
of Baltimore), 6
Beaulieu, Clement H. (Hole in the
Day assassination conspirator),
145n52
Beaulieu, Theodore D. (Ojibwe, SAI
member), 104
Biondi, Pietro Fumasoni (apostolic
delegate in Washington, DC),
121
Birch, Mr. (Baptist missionary,
Haskell employee), 50–53
Bishop, Thomas (SAI member), 106
Black Elk, Nicholas (Oglala Lakota
holy man), 156n24
Blaine, John J. (Wisconsin governor),
109, 119–20
Blanchet, Augustin Magloire Alexan-
der (bishop of Nesqually), 6
Blanchet, Francis (archbishop of
Oregon City), 6

Index

McQuigg, Henry (Lac Court Oreilles Reservation superintendent), 92, 98–100, 110, 169n1

Medegan, John (Gordon's Ojibwe friend and theological student), 27

Meerschaert, Theophile (bishop of Oklahoma City), 86–88

Mekins, Sarah (Gordon's mother). *See* Ategekwe

Menominee Reservation incident, 101–2

Meriam, Lewis (Meriam Report director), 123

Meriam Report, 125, 174n36

Merritt, E. B. (assistant commissioner of Indian Affairs), 41

Mesabi, Joe (Gordon's uncle), 23

Milles Lacs Ojibwe, 144n36

Milles Lacs Reservation, Wisconsin, 18

Minnesota, 10, 12–14, 16–19, 22, 27, 30–32, 81, 86, 100–101, 104, 114–15, 142n11, 144n37, 145n51, 146n55, 162n23, 179n1

missionaries, 6, 62, 161n19; Catholic, 6, 14, 141n4, 142n11; Protestant, 14, 97, 168n29

Montezuma, Carlos (Yavapai physician, SAI activist), 7, 118, 138n21, 150n1; background of, 34–35; and BIA, 35, 47, 59, 81, 96, 168n35; and BIO investigation; 83; and Bonnin, 48–49, 66, 102; death of, 112; and Eastman, 74, 101–3; and Gordon, 47–48, 58–59, 62, 65, 80–81, 95–97, 101–3, 105–7, 112–13, 116; illustrations of, 72, 74; and Menominee Reservation incident, 101–2; and Pratt, 35, 60, 81, 96,

155n16, 168n35; and SAI, 34, 47, 63–66, 83, 96–97, 103, 106, 113, 168n35; and *War-Whoop*, 59–60, 159n8; and *Wassaja*, 7, 60, 83, 102; wife of, 106, 112; and WWI, 80, 83; Yavapai name of, 34

Montezuma, Marie (Carlos Montezuma's wife), 106, 112

Moorehead, Warren C. (anthropologist), 115–16

Murray, Mr. (Protestant preacher), 97, 168n29

National Council of American Indians (NCAI), 171n23, 176n28

Native American Church, 170n16

Negahnquet, Albert (Potawatomi Catholic priest), 31, 149n47, 156n25

New Post, Wisconsin, 111

New York Times, 3, 131

North Dakota, 10, 12, 34, 153–54n46

North Wisconsin Academy, Wisconsin, 26

Odanah, Wisconsin, 6, 24–26, 28–30, 32–33, 37–40, 51, 55, 68, 93, 101, 126, 148n26, 148n31, 149n44, 166n13, 167n22, 168n28

Office of Indian Affairs. *See* Bureau of Indian Affairs

Office of the Catholic Indian Commissioner (OCIC), 6

Ojibwa. *See* Ojibwe

Ojibway. *See* Ojibwe

Ojibwe (Chippewa, Anishinaabe, Anishinaabeg, Ojibwa, Ojibway), and alcohol, 22, 38, 93; bands of, 10, 18; beliefs of, 10–12, 23; and boarding school, 21, 38, 54–55; and